Guide to Equipment Inventories

Standards, Strategies, and Best Practices

Guide to Equipment Inventories

Standards, Strategies, and Best Practices

Robert Keady

Developed with the cooperation and support of the
Construction Specifications Institute

WILEY

Cover Image: © Andrei Merkulov/iStockphoto
Cover Design: John Wiley and Sons, Inc.

This book is printed on acid-free paper.

Published by John Wiley & Sons, Inc., Hoboken, New Jersey
Published simultaneously in Canada

For general information about our other products and services, please contact our Customer Care Department within the United States at (800) 762-2974, outside the United States at (317) 572-3993 or fax (317) 572-4002.

Wiley publishes in a variety of print and electronic formats and by print-on-demand. Some material included with standard print versions of this book may not be included in e-books or in print-on-demand. If this book refers to media such as a CD or DVD that is not included in the version you purchased, you may download this material at http://booksupport.wiley.com. For more information about Wiley products, visit www.wiley.com.

ISBN 978-1-118-52385-8 (pbk); ISBN 978-1-118-55485-2 (ebk); ISBN 978-1-118-55529-3 (ebk); ISBN 978-1-118-55535-4 (ebk)

Printed in the United States of America

10 9 8 7 6 5 4 3 2 1

To my best friend and wonderful, funny, vivacious wife, Dania, who I still believe was temporarily insane when she agreed to marry me, and our amazing sons, Robert and Shawn, who remind me daily, as they climb the bookshelves, that boys are different from girls.

I would also like to dedicate this book to all of those government workers who believe in their government, who sit in small dingy cubicles in offices with no windows, using computers that are ten years old and dodging conflicting politics, while they work tirelessly to make their government a better, more efficient institution, and to save taxpayers money, one dollar at a time. They receive only negative media, and public opinion is always against them.

I believe in what you do and thank you. What you do every day, no matter how small, does make a difference.

Contents

Acknowledgments

There are so many people I would like to thank for their inspiration and help. This is my first book, and it still amazes me; I really want to thank Wiley Publishing for agreeing to partner with me on this endeavor. A special thanks to my first ever editor, Kathryn Bourgoine, senior editorial assistant Danielle Giordano, and senior production editor Doug Salvemini. They supported me every step of the way, made this book better with their suggestions, and answered my thousand questions. Let's face it; technical books like this are not exactly page turners. Also huge thanks to my mother, Patricia Dixon, an artist, who helped me with the illustrations and so many other things.

I especially would like to thank Roger Mason, my government supervisor, who allowed me, and the rest of his staff, to do what we do best, gave us the authority and responsibility to get done what had to get done, backed us no matter the politics, always tried to do what was right for the public, and trained us to do the same. He never quibbled over the little things. He embodied what a manager should be, and now that he is retired, drinking beer and playing golf, he is already missed.

When you look at the huge number of people involved in improving industry standards, you always end up finding the same core people at the heart of the effort to make the industry better. Surprisingly, it is actually a rather small group who all know each other. I am thankful they listened to my ideas, improved upon them, and encouraged them. Of that small group, I would specifically like to thank Peggy Yee for supporting my efforts, for helping me out, and for her continued efforts to make the government and industry standards better, even though she has no staff, minimum funding, and now no coordinating industry conferences. She listened to my ideas and helped support my concepts. Thank you, Calvin Kam, who was Peggy's predecessor and provided a lot of support for my ideas. A special thanks to Charles Matta for the foresight, fortitude, and guidance he provided to Peggy Yee and Calvin Kam. Much respect and gratitude are due to Greg Ceton from Construction Specification Institute, who I believe has the hardest job in the industry because he has to read, coordinate, and review industry standards. Greg then must coordinate volunteers, and still be enthusiastic about tirelessly trying to make industry standards better. I would also like to thank Bill Brodt for acting like my mentor, always answering my questions, introducing me to the people who knew the answers, keeping an open mind, and supporting my ideas in the industry. And in no specific order, I would like acknowledge and thank that small group of core people who are always trying to improve the industry: Dr. Charles Eastman, the godfather of BIM; Stephen Hagan, one of the godsons of BIM; Deke Smith, another godson of BIM; innovator Renee Tietjen, who is always trying to improve the government; Bill East, innovator and creator of COBie; and Kimon Onuma and Igor Starkov, who both have had a huge positive impact on the industry. If I missed your name, I apologize. After the publishing of this book, I know I am going to think, "How could I have forgotten them?!" Again, I apologize.

Finally, I would like to thank Dr. Kerry M. Joels, who encouraged me when I told him about my concept for this book and provided me with a lot of guidance on the ins and outs of authors and publishing. I still owe him a dinner.

CHAPTER 1

Introduction

Why are equipment inventories critical? The bottom line: They are the basic requirement for every aspect of facility management. Equipment inventories affect facility safety as well as how the facility is operated, maintained, and forecasted. They also have a direct impact on facility costs. If the equipment inventory is not accurate, the facility and the organization will not be as effective. One adage is you cannot manage what you do not know. If the equipment inventory is not accurate, it is costing the organization time, manpower, and money.[1]

This guide was written to give facility managers, owners, and the industry personnel the tools they need to understand, capture, and properly set up equipment inventories.

In 2004, the National Institute of Standards and Technology (NIST) estimated the cost of inadequate interoperability in the U.S. capital facilities industry to be approximately $15.8 billion per year.

A building's performance will decline because of its age, the use it receives, or functional adaptation to new uses, but its performance will decline at an optimized rate with proper maintenance. Without appropriate maintenance, or with the owner's decision to defer required maintenance, the building's usefulness will decrease at an accelerated rate.

The total cost of ownership is the total of all expenditures an owner will make over a building's service lifetime. Failure to recognize these costs and to provide adequate maintenance, repair, and renewal results in a shorter service life, more rapid deterioration, higher operating costs, and possible mission degradation over the life cycle of a building. With available data on facility subsystems, an estimate can be made regarding maintenance, repair, and renewal requirements during the remaining asset lifetime. Managing this data is of critical importance to effectively provide optimum services to the facility owner and users.[2]

To reiterate, that's a $15.8 billion annual loss because the industry is unable to transfer data and information in a usable format from design and construction to facility management. Most of that cost is absorbed by the owner of the facility. Equipment information in the form of equipment inventories is one of the major data losses resulting from this failure of interoperability of systems. Chapter 2, "Financial and Resource Impact of Equipment Inventories on Facilities," will cover a lot of the costs related to this poor or missing data. Figure 1.1, from the NIST report *Cost Analysis of Inadequate Interoperability in the U.S. Capital Facilities Industry*, gives a very good indication of what happens to facilities with poor equipment inventories. Without the equipment information, you cannot set up a normal maintenance program; therefore, you have premature aging of your facility, and that will be a significant cost to any organization.

What would happen if all of the related facility management organizations, industries, and owners in the nation sent personnel to a single location for a year, to define and agree upon the format for all the data related to the operation of a facility? They would define the format, decide how to transfer the data, agree upon a solution, and so forth. Pick an insane and absurd cost for this conference—counting salaries, hotels, and food. Say it costs $100 million to come up with an agreed-upon solution. The simple payback for that $100 million solution to the industry would be 2.3 days! Meanwhile, the industry loses $15.8 billion in 2002 dollars every year there isn't a solution. That is the thought process behind this book. In this book, I try to define all of the information that is related to equipment and inventories and explain how all that information is interrelated.

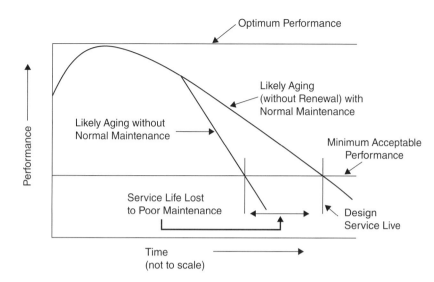

FIGURE 1.1 Maintenance Effect on Facility Performance (Source: *Cost Analysis of Inadequate Interoperability in the U.S. Capital Facilities Industry,* Michael P. Gallaher, Alan C. O'Connor, John L. Dettbarn, Jr., and Linda T. Gilday, NIST GCR 04-867, August 2004.)

A lot of data must be transferred and formatted between design and construction and facility management; this guide focuses on defining only the data set related to equipment.

Currently, the equipment inventory solutions found throughout the industry are typically company or organization specific; they do not follow industry standards, they are inconsistent in their application, and they are not even typically applied uniformly within those organizations that do have some sort of partial solution. Because of this, there is a vital need for industry standards. It is interesting to note that there are numerous energy manuals, facility operation manuals, and other books on equipment maintenance planning. All these books usually have two sentences in common, concerning equipment inventories: "You have to have an equipment inventory," and "Equipment inventories are important." Truth be told, equipment inventories are not "sexy." But equipment inventories and information are the core data, the foundation, for almost every task performed by facility management teams.

Imagine that your organization installed a state-of-the-art thermal storage system, upgraded all of the motors to high-efficiency motors with variable frequency drives, and installed solar heating units on the roof. The organization is utilizing high-end energy strategies. The company gets applauded in the news. This is cutting-edge technology. That same organization, however, does not capture the equipment inventory and therefore does not include the equipment in its maintenance contracts. The high-end energy equipment is not maintained, and within a few years all those predicted savings do not materialize. The ripple effect is that the executive board is very likely to stop supporting the installation of energy-saving equipment in future facilities, and that impacts the company's sustainability and possible future savings. Yes, this is exactly what happens every day throughout the industry. This is a key reason that some energy savings contracts have a bad reputation. It is hard to perform measurement and verification on equipment that does not exist in your maintenance databases.

Equipment inventories are not sexy, but they are critically important to organizations. This book provides the reasons they are important, an explanation of the different types of inventory systems, suggested data points important to equipment information, and methods of identifying and tagging equipment. The ultimate concept (Figure 1.2) of this guide is defining the core information needed for equipment, and defining the boxes—using industry standards where available—to place that equipment data into. These definitions would ensure that everyone in the industry is using the same terminology and concepts, allowing everyone to cross-communicate and integrate equipment information.

There are many ways to identify equipment information, and there is always room for improvement. Developing a list of these improvements and applying those to the next project can significantly improve the process, thus reducing costs and saving valuable resources. The important thing to remember is that, in this world of ever-increasing competition, where everyone is striving to increase efficiency while reducing the use of dwindling resources, any improvement to any process, no matter how small, improves this world for everyone.

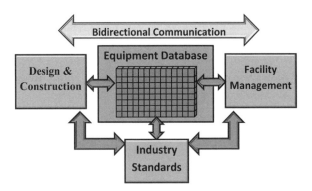

FIGURE 1.2 Equipment Guide Concepts

ENDNOTES

1. "Financial Impact and Analysis of Equipment Inventories," by Robert Keady, *Facility Engineering Journal*, Association of Facility Engineering, Nov–Dec, Jan–Feb, 2009–2010.

2. *Cost Analysis of Inadequate Interoperability in the U.S. Capital Facilities Industry*, Michael P. Gallaher, Alan C. O'Connor, John L. Dettbarn, Jr., and Linda T. Gilday, NIST GCR 04-867, August 2004. Pages 1–22.

CHAPTER 2

Financial and Resource Impact of Equipment Inventories on Facilities

I realize how difficult it is for facility managers to research and perform business cases to support their actions. This chapter is written to give facility managers the tools and information needed to answers questions from senior management—specifically, the question of why they should spend money to ensure that their organization has an accurate inventory. It does not matter what industry you are in—retail, medical, research, education, manufacturing, or government—if you own a facility, you need accurate equipment data. This chapter answers the question: How is equipment inventory critical to your organization?

In 2010, I wrote a two-part article about the importance and impact of equipment inventories on facilities: Parts 1 and 2 of "Financial Impact and Analysis of Equipment Inventories," by Robert Keady, in the November/December 2009 and January/February 2010 issues of the *Facilities Engineering Journal,* published by the Association for Facilities Engineering. In this chapter, I will go into more depth about the costs of inventories and their impact on your organization.

It is not uncommon for facility management (FM) and owners to have an incomplete concept of equipment inventories: their importance, how they are used, and how to maintain them. Even the best facility managers often differ about what an equipment inventory comprises and how to create, develop, establish, and maintain one.

Why are equipment inventories critical? The bottom line: They save the organization resources and money. Equipment information is a basic requirement for almost every aspect of facility management. They also have a direct impact on facility costs. If the equipment inventory is not accurate, the facility and the organization will not be as efficient. One adage is: "You cannot manage what you do not know." If the equipment inventory is not accurate, there is a lot you do not know, and it is costing the organization time, manpower, and money.

In Figure 2.1, I tried to graphically represent the complex relationships between equipment inventories and finances, and how those finances are directly or indirectly affected. I would point out that more relationships exist than are depicted in the figure. If I added all the possible relationships, the figure would get significantly more complex, and I am sure savvy facility managers could add additional complexity. Equipment inventories are the foundation of facility management. Without the foundation, the organization starts to crumble, and its costs start to increase.

Instead of fixing the very common problem of incomplete, inaccurate, and self-generated equipment inventories, organizations will compensate by

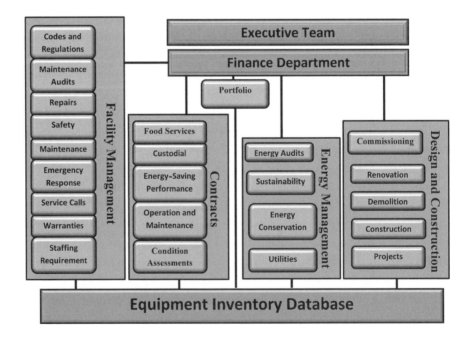

FIGURE 2.1 Equipment Impact on Organizations

spending millions of dollars and thousands of man-hours putting out fires. This seems counterproductive in a global competitive market where the focus is on waste reduction, increased efficiency, and increased oversight of spending. Organizations can no longer afford to consistently waste time, manpower, and funds on a "concept" that has a simple solution.

While it would seem obvious that a complete inventory would be the most beneficial to an organization, the reality is that most organizations do not understand the impact that equipment inventories have on their business. This accounts for the vast majority of poor to substandard inventories in the industry. One of the major causes is that most facility managers are under the false impression that a preventive maintenance inventory is more than sufficient to properly budget, operate, and maintain a facility. Another contributing factor is upper management's false impression that "inventory is a maintenance function" and therefore does not impact the corporation. Because of these impressions, the majority of chief financial officers (CFOs) and chief executive officers (CEOs) are not provided with the proper information to develop accurate budgets and make critical long-term strategic decisions related to their facilities.

It is important to understand that accurate equipment inventories affect many different aspects of building management, including: management of energy, projects, operations, maintenance, design and construction, and customer service. Therefore, the quality of the data affects the overall finances of an organization. For example: If an inventory is not accurate, an organization does not have the ability to reduce peak load during curtailment periods, and this increases the utility bill and costs. Another example: If an accurate equipment inventory is not maintained, the number of man-hours needed to maintain and operate the facility cannot be easily calculated. Therefore, personnel must be sent to the facility every time a project, contract, audit, or assessment of the facility is performed, to capture the equipment inventory in order to accurately calculate man-hours. This method can easily create inaccurate costs in contracts, audits, and projects, which in turn create contract modifications that further increase the waste of manpower, cause increases in staffing, and negatively impact finances. These simple examples of wasted manpower show that accurate equipment inventories are important to all levels of facility management, such as the facility manager, property manager, contract officer, portfolio manager, human resources manager, financial manager, and especially the chief executive officer.

To better understand the costs and resource drains that inaccurate inventories and data have on an organization, it is important to compare the cost relations between two types of inventories. I will use preventive maintenance inventories and component-level inventories for comparisons (See Chapter 3, "Equipment Inventory Types and Systems," for the definitions of the different types of equipment inventories). In business and contracts, it is vitally important to define the terms you are using. This is the only way to ensure that you are receiving the proper goods and services. Equipment inventories can be broken into partial, preventive maintenance, nonpreventive maintenance, component-level, and complete inventories. Nonpreventive, component-level, and complete inventories are new to the industry and have not been previously defined. A component-level inventory is basically a preventive maintenance and a nonpreventive maintenance inventory combined. There are other types of inventories important to facilities such as consumables, tools, and personnel, but this guide's focus is equipment or otherwise known as components.

The most direct means to show that an accurate equipment inventory is a cost-effective measure is to provide the cost savings to an organization through projected energy savings. I would like to point out that energy savings are only the tip of the iceberg; the real savings are in manpower and resources. While the resource savings are intuitive, it is a concept that is, at the present time, hard to quantify in the industry. To date, there has been no major study on the impact equipment has on facilities. Until now, a good case has not been made for such a study.

ENERGY SAVINGS

The Department of Energy's Federal Energy Management Program (FEMP) states that:

> Effective O&M (Operations and Maintenance) is one of the most cost-effective methods for ensuring reliability, safety, and energy efficiency. Inadequate maintenance of energy-using systems is a major cause of energy waste in both the Federal government and the private sector. Energy losses from steam, water and air leaks, un-insulated lines, maladjusted or inoperable controls, and other losses from poor maintenance are often considerable. Good maintenance practices can generate substantial energy savings and should be considered a resource. Moreover, improvements to facility maintenance programs can often be accomplished immediately and at a relatively low cost.
>
> It has been estimated that O&M programs targeting energy efficiency can save 5% to 20% on energy bills without a significant capital investment. From small to large sites, these savings can represent thousands to hundreds-of-thousands of dollars each year, and many can be achieved with minimal cash outlays. [1]

The foundation for an effective O&M strategy is to have an accurate equipment inventory (Figure 2.1). An O&M strategy cannot exist without it. An accurate equipment inventory provides the facility management team with the ability to identify all components that affect energy usage, require maintenance, and assist in safe operations. A preventive maintenance inventory does not identify all of the equipment that uses energy in a facility, only those pieces of equipment that require maintenance. A component-level inventory identifies all of the equipment in a facility, whether or not maintenance is performed on that equipment, and it should therefore identify all the equipment necessary for efficient operation of a facility.

To be able to evaluate the cost savings to a facility, the first thing that has to be established is the cost of having an outside contractor take an equipment inventory. After working with four major companies that specialize in taking equipment inventories, I developed a tiered baseline cost for capturing equipment inventories within existing buildings, based on the square footage of an office facility (Table 2.1). The costs would be different if the inventory was captured during design, construction, or during projects.

Based on Table 2.1, it would cost an estimated $0.50/gross square foot for an accurate component-level equipment inventory. For equipment inventory

TABLE 2.1 Equipment Inventory Office Building Costs and Tiers

	Office ($/GSF)		
Types of Manual Inventories (1)	**Min**	**Max**	**Tier**
Equipment List	$0.05	$0.10	1
Preventive Maintenance Inventory	$0.10	$0.15	2
Condition Monitoring of PM Inventory	$0.20	$0.25	3
Component-Level Identification BIM Model	$0.25	$0.30	4
Component-Level Inventory Walk-Through	$0.45	$0.50	5
Complete Inventory	N/A	N/A	6
Warehouse-Type Facility	N/A	N/A	−1 Tier

Tiers 1–3: Costs based on average cost in industry per gross square foot (GSF).

Tiers 4–6: Projected cost per gross square foot by industry, not to be used for contracts until base cost can be determined. Costs are conservative on the high end.

*Warehouses should define their required inventory tier (1–6) then drop down one tier for the cost: Therefore, if a warehouse wants a tier 6 inventory, the cost should be around those for tier 5.

"Office Building Equipment Inventory Costs versus Tiers, Financial Impacts and Analysis of Equipment Inventories," by Robert Keady, *Facility Engineering Journal*, Association of Facility Engineering, Nov–Dec, Jan–Feb, 2009–2010.

definitions, see Chapter 3. While that seems expensive, remember that the quality of the inventory is very important. It is also important to note that, since component-level and complete inventories are new to the industry, the overall costs should decrease as the industry becomes more proficient.

The next cost determination that has to be established is the average electrical energy cost per square foot of a facility. The Department of Energy published a report January 3, 2001, that estimated the electrical consumption per square foot of an office to be around 18.9 kWh (Table 2.2). It should be noted that these figures do not take into account the energy savings and advances in technology. It can be argued that without proper inventories that these energy savings and technologies are not properly utilized.

Given the cost per square foot to take an equipment inventory, the average energy consumption per square foot of electrical energy, and a projected savings of 5–25%, the cost per kilowatt hour and square footage of your facility can be used to calculate a simple payback (Table 2.3). At the time I wrote this,

TABLE 2.2   Electrical Consumption of Facilities by Function

SUMMARY COMPARISON TABLE			
	Total Energy Consumption per Square Foot (thousand Btu)	Electricity Consumption per Square Foot (kWh)	Natural Gas Consumption per Square Foot (cubic feet)
All Commercial Buildings	90.5	13.4	49.7
Building Activity			
Retail and Service	76.4	11.8	45.2
— Retail	61.7	11.6	27.4
— Strip Mall	62.8	13.4	27.4
— Enclosed Mall	51.5	12.3	9.1
— Other Retail	65.1	10.1	35.9
— Service	113.9	12.3	98.5
Office	97.2	18.9	35.7
Warehouse	38.3	6.4	22.4
Public Assembly	113.7	12.7	51.9
Education	79.3	8.4	41.1
Food Service	245.5	36	153.5
Religious Worship	37.4	3.4	28
Vacant	21.5	3.9	38.8

Electrical Consumption of Facilities by Function, Department of Energy Cost/Square Foot 2001, DOE, DOE Commercial Electrical Usage, Summary Comparison Table, September 11, 2000. www.eia.gov/emeu/consumptionbriefs/cbecs/pbawebsite/summarytable.htm.

TABLE 2.3   Simple Payback for Manual Equipment Inventory

Manual Equipment Inventory of Building						
Gross Square Feet (GSF)	Inventory Cost/GSF (1)	Total Inventory Cost	Annual Energy Cost (2)	Percent Savings	Estimated Energy Savings	Simple Payback Estimate (Years)
500,000	$0.50	$250,000.00	$1,134,000.00	3.00%	$34,020.00	7.35
				5.00%	$56,700.00	4.41
				15.00%	$170,100.00	1.47

(1) Table 2.1 Office Building Equipment Inventory Costs versus Tiers, Tier 5 high end cost.
(2) Table 2.2 Department of Energy Cost/Square Foot 2001, Office Building: 18.9 kWh/sq-ft (X) $0.12/kWh = $2.268/sq-ft XE "Figures:Simple Paynack"

the average cost of a kilowatt hour, including the supply and demand charges or capacity, was around $0.12/kWh.

Estimated Simple Payback
Given:
Energy cost for a 500,000-square-foot facility
Energy cost per square foot:

$$18.9 \text{ kWh/sq-ft } (\times) \$ 0.12/\text{kWh} = \$2.268/\text{sq-ft}$$

Estimated annual electrical energy cost:

$$500,000 \text{ sq-ft } (\times) \$2.268/\text{sq-ft} = \$1,134,000.0/\text{year}$$

The payback using a very conservative estimate of 3% savings will provide a payback in 7.35 years on the investment. Using a conservative 5% savings, the payback will be in 4.41 years. According to many energy experts, a more realistic estimate of 15% would be achieved; since such a significant portion of operations and maintenance, and energy projects themselves, are based on inventory, the equipment inventory would most likely pay back in 1.47 years.

I realize that in the federal government a seven-, four-, or two-year payback is considered an excellent investment, but most corporations will not fund a project without a return on investment of one year or less. Therefore, we will now concentrate on the major resource savings that accrue in addition to the energy payback. Please be aware that the payback calculated is for electrical only. When you start adding steam and gas to the equation, your payback becomes significantly better. The energy savings only take into account actual electrical energy savings based on efficient operations. There are numerous other potential energy savings when an organization has an accurate equipment inventory. For example, smart grid and building technology depend on having an accurate inventory. A major contributor to the failure of energy projects is improper measurement and verification. However, you cannot have proper measurement and verification if you cannot capture, trend, and measure the energy equipment installed. For example, your company installs a 90% efficient motor in the facility. Because the motor was not captured in the inventory, no maintenance is performed, and therefore over the life of the motor, it will significantly lose its efficiency as it degrades. Thus, you have lost all of the projected energy-savings, and you still have to pay for the motor. Not recouping projected energy-savings is a common problem in the industry, and improper equipment inventories are a major cause for these failures.

As a minimum, a preventive maintenance inventory is important for identifying equipment that requires maintenance. Maintaining equipment ensures that the equipment is operating properly and efficiently in order to prolong the life of the equipment. Preventive maintenance inventories are also important for properly scheduling and defining maintenance labor resources. For a more accurate measure of the cost and resources needed for the operation of a facility, it is crucial to know the average costs of repairs, service calls, emergency response, regulatory compliance, energy management, manpower, safety, and impact on executive decisions. Accurate costs can only be calculated if both preventive maintenance and nonpreventive maintenance inventories are captured. The following examples will explore the limitations of preventive maintenance inventories and provide senior management and facility managers with the tools to evaluate their level of exposure.

REPAIR AND SERVICE CALLS

When an organization only has an accurate preventive maintenance inventory, the organization can capture the repair and service calls only on equipment that is maintained. They are unable to tie those costs to nonpreventive maintenance equipment. Nonpreventive maintenance equipment can be and usually is captured in service calls, but because the equipment itself is not in the equipment database, the service call or repair cannot be tied to that specific equipment. For a medium-sized or large organization to budget for these costs, develop business decisions, identify overpayments, or troubleshoot its facility, it would have to manually sort any available existing service call or repair data. This task is manpower intensive in gathering, sorting, defining, and finding the text stored data and is usually not performed unless there is a catastrophic event related to that equipment. The expenditure of these resources could be avoided. For example: Imagine a scenario in which a 12-inch isolation valve exists on a cooling tower. The isolation valve does not require regular maintenance, and therefore it is not in the inventory; its operation would be verified when the maintenance on the cooling tower is performed. What if that same valve had been repaired or replaced four times within a two-year period? Because the valve is not in inventory, a repair or service call cannot be written and linked to the equipment, and therefore the history of the valve cannot be tracked. The valuable data are lost. Your organization cannot verify the services, and the data cannot be referenced in the future. No one can answer the following questions: Was the organization charged multiple times for a repair not performed? Why is the valve repetitively failing? Is a problem with the type or placement of the valve causing its failure? Were the subsequent repairs under warranty? Thousands of repairs like this occur every day, and no one is tracking the results.

EMERGENCY RESPONSE

Having only a preventive maintenance inventory reduces the readiness of an organization to respond to emergencies. For example, a facility experiences a domestic water line break on the fifth floor of its facility. The length of time it takes for responders to find the isolation valve for the leak increases significantly if the information is not readily available. A 1-inch isolation ball valve does not normally require preventive maintenance. There isn't very much to maintain. Because it is not maintained, the valve would not be tracked in a preventive maintenance inventory. Therefore, there would be no knowledge of its location. The main valve to the facility would have to be closed, which could cause the entire facility to be shut down. Shutting down a facility affects the productivity of the staff and inconveniences customers within the building; it is therefore very cost prohibitive. The end result of the wasted time it took to find the isolation valve is that the organization is faced with the possibility of having to renovate all four floors under the break, instead of dealing only with the costs of cleaning up one room. The ability to recover from this event and the speed of recovering—from this event, or a fire, an explosion, or some other emergency—depends on the ability to determine which systems and components have been affected by the event. This information is critical to mitigating their impact on the operations of the facility because it has an impact on the speed at which facility staff can bypass or isolate those affected systems to permit continued operations. The emergency response includes the ability to identify replacement components, the ability to accurately scope the work to repair teams or contractors, and the ability to accurately estimate the project costs for management. A facility with only a preventive maintenance inventory cannot respond as fast or as effectively.

REGULATORY COMPLIANCE

There are numerous federal, state, and local standards in effect, and they vary significantly from location to location. North Dakota is not as concerned with hurricanes as is Florida. Facility managers and owners are responsible for ensuring that their organization complies with numerous federal, state, and local codes and regulations. Since a significant number of building codes and regulations deal directly or indirectly with the types of equipment within a facility, an organization with only a preventive maintenance inventory increases its exposure to violating regulations on equipment that would be otherwise captured with a component-level inventory. The Environmental Protection Agency requires the continued monitoring of all underground storage tanks. Facilities that no longer use their tanks, and have not done so for some years, might not keep the component in their preventive maintenance inventory. This could lead to fines and oversight by outside regulators. There are numerous examples of corporations having released large amounts of oil into the environment simply because equipment was not maintained. The finding for most of these accidents is that the equipment was not in the inventory or on the preventive maintenance schedule, as it should have been. This is the difference in philosophy between having all your equipment inventory data or just having the data of equipment requiring maintenance. The cleanup and resultant fines alone would have paid for an accurate and high-quality component-level inventory many times over. Preventive maintenance inventories, because they focus on just equipment that has to be maintained, can easily miss the inventory of critical equipment. Component-level and complete inventories identify all of the equipment within a facility, eliminating the decision of whether or not equipment belongs in the inventory. A component-level or complete inventory assists the facility manager in ensuring that all equipment is properly identified for regulatory compliance. For example, small oil-filled transformers do not require maintenance. But if there are a significant number of oil-filled transformers on-site, such that the number of gallons of oil reaches a regulatory threshold, compliance with an environmental regulation is required. Therefore, the organization has to ask itself: How many gallons of oil are in the transformers on the site? Why doesn't the organization have that information readily available? How many man-hours will it take to gather that information for this one scenario?

ENERGY MANAGEMENT

As an energy manager, I am constantly surprised by how many energy projects do not supply accurate equipment inventories to facility managers, to ensure proper maintenance. A facility manager's ability to predict, reduce, and plan the energy usage for a facility is based directly on equipment inventories. For example: I install a state-of-the-art tracking photovoltaic array at my facility, but I do not add the motors into my inventory for maintenance. At some point, the arrays will fail to track, and I will start to lose my energy-savings. Or, suppose I install an award-winning green roof on my facility, but then do not add the type of plants (yes, plants are a planned maintenance task) and equipment needed to maintain the roof to my inventory. Soon I have a brown roof. Another normal industry occurrence for a large organization is to fail to perform maintenance on electric duct heaters or on motors under 1 horsepower. The reason for this decision is that this equipment is usually run-to-failure and has no actual maintenance. The cost for preventive maintenance would be more than the cost of replacement. Because of this decision, the equipment is not captured. The curtailment plan for the facility staff is now limited in its ability to reduce peak load during high-demand periods. This oversight has now cost the organization increasing electrical costs every year. A component-level or complete inventory would have captured all of the equipment within the facility, allowing proper operational planning. The ability of the facility to reduce peak usage, plan energy conservation methods, and predict future energy usage is directly impacted by the type of inventory, which, in turn, affects the financial costs to any organization.

MANPOWER

The selective exclusion of components from an inventory based on maintenance negatively affects any manpower resource that requires an accurate accounting of those assets. The lack of a comprehensive inventory impacts an organization's ability to successfully perform essential tasks in a timely and efficient manner. There are a number of manpower-resource-related tasks that become repetitive capital expenditures that could be avoided. When personnel have to travel to a site, schedule time to stop equipment to gather data, review blueprints, find the equipment on the site, record the information, find a place to store the information, develop a method to organize that data, and so on, the manpower involved cannot be recovered by the facility management team. For example, a team has a project to schedule the replacement of all high-energy lighting (T-12) with low-energy lighting. Someone will have to go to the facility and count all of the light fixtures, take down their make and model, and count the number of tubes per type of fixture. This could take a minimum of 8 hours for a small facility and days for a large facility. Compare that to an organization that has a component-level inventory and can pull up the information in less than 10 minutes. That is a 48:1 ratio of manpower usage for a small facility. Now expand the scale to every project that has to be developed for a facility. The larger the number of facilities an organization is required to maintain, the larger the repetitive losses. This is information that should have been in the equipment inventory already.

Most O&M contracts have a maintenance performance cost based on the type and number of equipment components in the facility. I have seen a large-facility O&M contract sent out to bid that was based on a small inventory. After the O&M contractor won the bid, it immediately found thousands of components that needed to be maintained that were not in the original contract. Besides the substantial unplanned change to the O&M costs, the contract had to be renegotiated because more equipment was determined to exist. Renegotiating a contract means a large cost in manpower. Personnel have to rewrite and negotiate those modifications. Unluckily, this is not an uncommon occurrence in the industry.

After an emergency or catastrophic event, there are a couple of things that need to be accomplished. For example, suppose there is a car fire in one of your parking garages. First, there should be a failure event analysis of the equipment to determine how it operated, whether it operates, and what the impact was on other related equipment. Also, the facility has to start planning to replace any affected equipment. Both of these processes typically involve gathering equipment information about previous equipment failures, repair history, maintenance history, make, model, serial numbers, counts, and so forth. Gathering this information will cost manpower, if the information has not been properly captured previously in a component-level inventory. Most facility managers probably do not know that there are typically two types of sprinkler heads in a parking garage. They do tend to find out quickly, though, when they replace sprinkler heads with the wrong type, and the fire marshal shuts down their garage.

When a building life-cycle cost analysis has to be done to determine the viability of work or projects, an equipment inventory has to be performed.

When a large organization is determining chargebacks, an accurate inventory has to be performed. When doing a major renovation, one of the first tasks an architect is going to perform is an equipment inventory, and I find it hard to believe it will be done for free. As you can see, a lot of tasks require accurate equipment inventories. Organizations with poor inventories absorb those manpower costs repeatedly. It is important to note that you not only have to capture an accurate inventory, you also have to maintain that inventory. As you can surmise, the manpower to maintain the inventory should be significantly less expensive than the repeated regathering of the data.

SAFETY

Safety is the one area of equipment inventories, aside from cost, that should have all corporations immediately addressing their inventories. Personnel are routinely placed in hazardous situations because they do not have accurate data and information related to the equipment they are servicing. For example, federal, state, and local regulations are very stringent about working on energized equipment. With the exception of organizations where this information is already deemed vital—such as the military, industrial corporations, or nuclear power plants—I have yet to find, in the hundreds of buildings I have reviewed or audited, an accurate electrical equipment inventory or breaker book. Therefore, when repairs are performed on the ballast of a 277-volt fluorescent light fixture, the maintenance repairer is usually required to turn off the power at the breaker for the ballast. Realistically, one of two things normally occurs: (1) two personnel "flip breakers," one at the ballast and one at the breaker panel(s), cycling the different breakers until they find the correct power, or (2) one person replaces the ballast "live" without turning off the power. The act of "flipping breakers" for all of the repairs over the course of a year is a significant outlay of manpower—not to mention that for some facilities this is not at all practical. The CEO tends to be upset when the lights in his conference room are turned off during a board meeting. If you extrapolate the data, the facilities probably spend hundreds of thousands of man-hours a year just "flipping breakers." The second action, working the component "live," exposes the organization to legal, safety, and regulatory ramifications. People die changing "live" ballasts. A component-level inventory that captures the electrical distribution system of a facility to include electrical breakers could dramatically mitigate, if not eliminate, these costs.

EXECUTIVE STRATEGIC PLANNING AND DECISIONS

The accuracy of your equipment inventory directly impacts the decisions and strategies made by your executive team. If you refer back to Figure 2.1, you can see how inventories impact a multitude of program areas, which in turn impact the decisions at progressively higher levels. For example, if an organization does not have an accurate account of repairs and service calls for preventive and nonpreventive equipment maintenance, the facility manager cannot accurately project related costs in the future months or years. If the facility manager cannot accurately project the costs, the executive team cannot strategically plan for future expenditures. A 12-inch valve is not cheap to replace in a system that has to be running for the facility to operate. Therefore, an organization will be required to develop contingency funds for events that adversely affect their strategic positioning. With a more accurate inventory, an organization can improve the accuracy of its financial budgets, forecasting, and costing information. Metrics used for equipment, operations, and maintenance decisions by the executive team will be improved. Accurate and complete equipment data provide the facility manager with the ability to develop projects for immediate implementation, for one year ahead, five years, and so on, and send them to the executive team for approval. This is a vast improvement over the standard "we have some money, tell us what projects need to get done" approach to facility strategic planning. The final point about the impact on the executive team is that a building is built and designed for a specific purpose. When it does not perform to meet that purpose, the related personnel and goals of that corporation are affected. A building that can be operated and maintained properly due to the existence of the inventory data offers significantly improved customer service.

One of the methods of developing an operations and maintenance projected cost is to use the average cost of O&M for all of the facilities in a portfolio per the overall square footage. For example, if my portfolio consists of two million square feet at a total O&M cost of $4 million, then my average cost is $2.00/square foot. The flaw with this method is that it is based on the actual O&M costs—the same O&M costs that were developed using poor or inaccurate equipment data. Recently, I was asked to estimate the O&M costs for a two-million-square-foot facility that had an equipment inventory of 1,200 pieces of equipment! Realistically, the facility should have over 20,000 pieces of equipment that require maintenance. The original O&M contract for that facility was missing large chunks of equipment and therefore did not represent what the actual O&M costs should be. The overall cost/square foot for any

CASE STUDY 1   Equipment Inventories

TABLE 2.4   Equipment Inventory Case Study 1

| Number of Buildings | Gross Square Footage | Equipment Inventory | | | | Type |
		Existing	Found	Delta	Per/GSF	
15 (Campus)	33,000,000	0	250,000	250,000	0.0011	Component-Level
1	3,100,000	1,300	22,000	20,700	0.0071	Preventive Maintenance
1	900,000	2,500	8,000	5,500	0.0089	Preventive Maintenance
1	400,000	3,718	3,913	195	0.0098	Preventive Maintenance
1	300,000	0	6,054	6,054	0.0202	Preventive Maintenance
78 (Campus)	600,000	0	2,800	2,800	0.0047	Preventive Maintenance
1	50,000	0	1,144	1,144	0.0229	Preventive Maintenance
					0.0107	Average

Information provided by Rhodus Sloan Industries: Equipment Inventory Case Study 1, Rhodus Sloan Industries, http://rhodussloan.com/.

Table 2.4 is provided by Rhodus Sloan (RS) Industries, which specializes in capturing equipment inventories in existing facilities. The table shows the disparity between existing inventories in use by the organization and what was actually found when an accurate inventory was taken in 2011 by a specialist. RS Industries uses component-level inventories based on formatting the data to its specific element and including the equipment assembly relationship. The company was not given initial equipment inventories, either because they did not exist or because the existing ones were suspect. Table 2.4 shows the extent of the problem for equipment inventories. Every single inventory performed by RS Industries found missing equipment, equipment that was not being maintained, or equipment that was not accounted for on an operations and maintenance contract. For example, the 3,100,000-gross-square-foot facility was being maintained using an equipment list consisting of 1,300 pieces of equipment. RS Industries found 22,000 pieces of equipment that required maintenance, a difference of 20,700!

portfolio with this type of large facility, without an accurate equipment inventory, would be drastically skewed. As a result, the facilities using this pricing standard would all suffer and would not be maintained to the level required to ensure their upkeep. These facilities will age prematurely.

FINAL ANALYSIS

Energy-savings, repair/service calls, emergency response, regulatory compliance, energy management, manpower savings, safety, and executive strategic planning and decisions are only some of the many reasons that an accurate component-level inventory is important for a facility. I am positive there are numerous other examples, such as security, environmental concerns, water or steam savings, and the like, that facility managers could include. The bottom line for any owner or organization is that an accurate, well-maintained, component-level inventory can reduce wasted manpower, energy usage, and costs.

An inaccurate equipment inventory has a significant negative financial impact on any organization. What most organizations do not realize is that they are already paying the cost for not ensuring that equipment inventories are accurate and up to date. This is especially distressing, considering that fixing the problem is not that difficult. The old idea that "inventory is a maintenance function" is an outdated and costly mistake.

How does your organization determine the level of exposure it faces? Request an equipment inventory from the facility manager. How long does it take to get the list of the equipment? The length of time it takes to get the results determines how accessible the equipment information is to the facility management team. This demonstrates their knowledge and familiarity with the inventory. The quality of the inventory is directly related to how well a facility is maintained. Does the inventory match up with the O&M contracts? Is the organization exposed to the problems defined in this guide?

ENDNOTES

1. Operations & Maintenance, Energy Efficiency and Renewable Energy, Federal Energy Management Program, Department of Energy: www1.eere .energy.gov/femp/operations_maintenance/.

CHAPTER 3

Equipment Inventory Types and Systems

EQUIPMENT INVENTORY TYPES

An equipment inventory is a detailed account of all of the equipment and related information within a facility that is required to be tracked or maintained. Because most facility managers have differing concepts of what equipment inventories consist of, it is important to define the different types of equipment inventories. The following definitions are a means to differentiate among the different types of equipment inventories:

Partial Inventory

A partial inventory is an equipment list that is not tied directly to any specific standard, maintenance schedule, or controlled process. Partial inventories can be similar to paper or digital equipment lists given to a facility after construction. That list of equipment sitting in a drawer somewhere would be considered a partial inventory.

Because these lists are typically on paper and not maintained, some common problems related to partial inventories are: the equipment listed may not be the equipment actually installed, the equipment counts may be inaccurate, and the list may omit important pieces of information, such as equipment attributes or physical locations.

Preventive Maintenance (PM) Inventory

A preventive maintenance (PM) inventory is an inventory of all the equipment, down to the component level, that remains with the facility during transfer of ownership; is tracked, serviced, or repaired; and requires preventive maintenance. The component level consists of quantifiable equipment that is maintained or tracked, but it does not include disposable or supply parts. For example, preventive maintenance component level would contain air handling units but not filters. Equipment that does not require maintenance, nonpreventive maintenance equipment, is not included in this inventory.

Preventive maintenance inventories are the most common type of inventory found in facility management. One of the most common problems related to preventive maintenance inventories is that the equipment inventory is typically based on one type of discipline, such as HVAC, mechanical, electrical, or fire safety. Therefore, equipment can be, and usually is, missed because only a specific type of inventory is being taken. For example, a contractor is tasked with taking a mechanical inventory of a facility. The contractor does not inventory a fuel oil tank level switch because he or she is under the impression that the fuel oil tank is part of the emergency generator system and therefore belongs to the electrical distribution system. The contractor hired to perform an inventory of the electrical system believes that the level switch and tank are part of the mechanical system. The level switch is therefore not added to the preventive maintenance schedule and is not maintained. When all of the equipment within a facility is not captured, there are serious gaps in the equipment inventory that can lead to significant errors in operation. Chapter 2, "Financial and Resource Impact of Equipment Inventories on Facilities," covers some of the major problems of having only a preventive maintenance inventory.

Nonpreventive Maintenance Inventory

Nonpreventive maintenance (NPM) inventories are inventories that normally consist of equipment, down to the component level, that remains with the facility during transfer of ownership; is tracked, serviced, or repaired; and does not require preventive maintenance. The component level consists of quantifiable equipment that is maintained or tracked, but it does not include disposable or supply parts. For example, component level would contain lighting fixtures but not light bulbs, electrical outlets, or mounting hardware. The preventive maintenance equipment is not included in this inventory.

The nonpreventive maintenance inventories have the same problems as the preventive maintenance inventories. Inventories are typically only based on one type of discipline, such as HVAC, mechanical, electrical, or fire safety. Of course, another major problem with this type of inventory is that the equipment that requires maintenance is not included.

Component-Level Inventory

A component-level inventory is an inventory that includes both the PM and NPM equipment down to the component, or product, level. A component-level inventory normally consists of equipment that remains with the facility during transfer of ownership, or is tracked, serviced, repaired, or maintained by the organization. Component-level inventories are as in-depth as possible for an existing building without actually performing destructive testing to determine what is behind the walls or underground. This type of inventory does not normally include disposable inventories such as supplies. For example: A component-level inventory would contain lighting fixtures but not light bulbs, electrical outlets, or mounting hardware. Disposable inventory or supplies would be captured in a completely separate set of tables than the equipment database described in this book. While they have some similar data as that of equipment, their setup would be different and therefore are not covered by this book.

With the exception of not having a list of disposable components, this type of equipment inventory solves the problems related to PM and NPM inventories. This is the most in-depth equipment inventory possible for an existing facility. Having all of the components in the inventory allows the facility management and owners to determine what equipment needs to be maintained without missing any important information. This type of inventory is the basis for improving the financial impact equipment has on a facility.

Complete Inventory

A complete inventory is an inventory that includes all equipment within the building envelope and site boundaries. Complete inventories capture the equipment that a component-level inventory is not able to capture and are normally obtainable only during new construction. Complete inventories are common in organizations such as nuclear power plants, oil rigs, manufacturing companies, and ships; they reflect the understanding within these organizations that equipment inventories are important to the success of overall operations.

Equipment Inventory Disciplines

There are multiple engineering and operation disciplines, such as electrical, mechanical, civil, environmental, historical, and so forth. Each of the different types of inventories can be further subdivided according to the engineering discipline or the requirements of the facility owner. For example: A facility could have a mechanical preventive maintenance inventory, a lighting nonpreventive maintenance inventory, a component-level fire safety inventory, and a partial inventory of doors. A good place to start is determining what type and related discipline of inventory your facility has. The goal for any premiere facility management team should be to have at least a component-level equipment inventory for all disciplines. Separating and identifying the different types of inventories by their disciplines can ensure that all of the different equipment is captured properly.

The following is a list of the disciplines or equipment that should be considered when developing an inventory:

- Electrical
- Mechanical
- Heating and ventilation
- Plumbing
- Architectural (roof, doors, windows, etc.)
- Civil (storm drains, retaining wall, etc.)
- Fire and life safety
- Environmental
- Vertical and horizontal transportation
- Instrument and control
- Historical preservation
- Food services
- Custodial
- Landscaping/horticulture
- Child care (bassinets, cribs, etc.)
- Medical (operations table, nurse call box, etc.)
- Scientific (microscope, exhaust fume hoods, etc.)
- Educational (group seating, educational casework, etc.)
- Religious (pews, pulpits, etc.)

THE IMPORTANCE OF DATA AND ITS FORMAT

This book propounds the use of relational or object-oriented databases to improve efficiency. A relational database is a database in which a collection of data is organized as a set of tables from which data can be accessed easily. The data and tables can then be related to each other in multiple ways. There are numerous books and articles that can be found on the web on databases such as relational, hierarchical, and network, so I will not go into detail on the different types. I would like to note that at this time the industry appears to be leaning towards Extensible Markup Language (XML) databases in which data are stored in XML format. XML databases are usually associated with standard relational or object-oriented databases.

Before discussing the different types of equipment inventory systems and methods, industry standards, or what equipment information is needed, it is important to discuss how data are formatted and stored in any database system. The misunderstanding and misconception of data format is such a huge problem in facility management that it is probably one of the largest contributors to errors in facility management programs, operations, software applications, and databases; all of which result in waste of costs and resources. The actual concept is very simple: format the data correctly and put the right data in the right box. The execution of the concept is another matter altogether. In database programming the process is called data normalization.

Table 3.1 is an example of the common misconceptions prevalent when developing equipment database systems. Facility managers and even computerized maintenance management systems (CMMS) programmers combine data to try to make each piece of data unique: FX-F1-001-C02-4TH Floor-Room 412-Wing A or MOT-43-AHU-12-40HP-480VAC-B1-MechRoom. The two pieces of equipment shown in this example are actually the combination of multiple pieces of information that should be subdivided and stored in the database in their own separate data fields (normalized). For example: in FX-F1-001, the FX is the acronym associated with the type of equipment (fire extinguisher), the F1 is the job plan title, and the 001 is the equipment sequence number. Each of these pieces of information should actually be stored in its own data field. The main cause behind storing data in the same manner that you use it is that users are typically the same people setting up the database and believe that the way they view the data is the same way they have to set up and store the data in the database. This is completely untrue. The database format and structure in no way has to look like what an end user (facility manager) or programmer wants to view. If you properly set up the data and place it in separate data fields, any program can take those different pieces of data and combine them to create whatever view the end user wants to see. For example: In Table 3.1, if the data were formatted and stored properly, they could be combined to create any equipment label reading MOT-43, MOT-43-AHU 12, MOT-43-B1-Mechanical Room, or any combination that the user wanted. It is

TABLE 3.1 Equipment Identification versus Data Parsing

Acronym	Equipment Type	Sequence Number	Equipment Identification	Specification Unit	Specification Valve	Job Task	Job Task	Job Task	Floor	Space	Architectural Zone
FX	Fire Extinguisher	001	FX-001	Retardant	CO_2	F1	F2	F3	4	412	Wing A

FX-F1-001-CO2-4TH-412-WING A

Acronym	Equipment Type	Sequence Number	Equipment Identification	Assembly	Specification Unit	Specification Valve	Specification Unit	Specification Valve	Floor	Space
MOT	3 Phase Motor	43	MOT-43	AHU-12	HP	40	VAC	480	B1	Mechanical Room

MOT-43-AHU-12-40HP-480VAC-B1-MechRoom

critical to understand that each piece of information has to be separated and placed in its own properly formatted data field in order to get the flexibility out of the database that an organization needs in order to be efficient and effective.

The next major misconception is that the user has to make the equipment data unique in order to differentiate the data in the database. A database does have to have a unique identifier to pin all of the related data fields for that record to—that's a fact. For example: All of the data related to MOT-43 in Table 3.1 have to have some way to tell the database that the 40 HP, B1, Mechanical Room, and the rest is information related to that specific motor. I discuss unique identifier (UUID, UID, and GUID) data fields in depth in Chapter 5. The misconception is the belief that the user or database programmer has to combine data fields to create this unique identifier. This notion is absolutely false, and most database programs even state that the user/programmers should not create their own unique identifier but allow the database program to create its own. Self-development of unique identifiers is a major cause of database problems in the industry. If you or your database programmers are self-developing database unique identifiers, there is a major and costly problem with your database. Unique identifiers and equipment tags should not be confused. A unique identifier is used within a database to attach all of the related data within a database record or table. For example, a UUID would be used to connect all of the data of a specific instance of equipment including the equipment tag information. While an equipment tag identifier is used to identify a specific piece of equipment within a specific facility. Using an equipment tag as a unique identifier would create numerous problems in a database, especially if a portfolio contained multiple facilities, multiple tasks per piece of equipment, or if equipment is moved from one facility to another.

Table 3.2 shows the unique identifier concept within a database. Notice that the primary key, or the unique identifier, is what all the information for each piece of equipment is connected to. For example: All data such as facility number, equipment acronym, equipment sequence, floor, room number, etc. for AHU-001 are attached within the database to the primary key AfYh01DE817JmW01. Primary keys are how databases group data. Notice

TABLE 3.2 Unique Identification and Primary Key Example Data Set

Equipment Database Record Example							
Type	Primary Key	Facility Number	Equipment Acronym	Equipment Sequence	Equipment Priority	Floor	Room Number
GUID	AfYh01DE817JmW01	ABC0000	AHU	1	2	8	8140
UID	AHU-0000002-UID	ABC0000	AHU	2	3	7	7120

that AfYh01DE817JmW01 is not understandable by the user, and it does not have to be. It is critical to understand that the unique identifier does not have to be understandable or even seen by the user. When you buy a television, do you understand the Universal Product Code (UPC) on the box? Typically you don't, but the scanner at the checkout knows all the information about that product. Once you start using unique identifiers, duplicate information is not a problem in the database. In Table 3.2, it should be noted that each record has AHU and ABC0000 in common, and because a UID is used, no conflicts are created in the database. The database understands that the information belongs to different records.

The last important concept about developing standards defining data and data formats for equipment is to keep it simple and not combine data into a single field that is not useful or that adversely impacts the flexibility of your database. Tables 3.3 and 3.4 show an example of a common mistake in equipment database development. A significant number of facility management organizations incorporate portions of their preventive maintenance program job task identifications into their equipment identifications. In Table 3.3, the preventive maintenance identification is added to the equipment identification. For example: 17A is added to the equipment identification AHU-17A-001. The problem is that it complicates queries performed on the database and creates a situation that impacts metrics developed from the database. Looking at the Database Equipment Records in Table 3.3 will show that the number of database entries (records) created is six. The six entries are created because multiple preventive maintenance (PM) tasks must be performed on each one

TABLE 3.3   Using PM Identifications for Equipment Identification Example 1

Equipment Identification Standard	PM Identification	Preventive Maintenance Guide Title	Database Equipment Records
AHU-17A	17A	Annual Air Handling Unit 0-2000 SCFM	AHU-17A-001
AHU-17B	17B	Annual Air Handling Unit 2000 - 8000 SCFM	AHU-17D-001
AHU-17C	17C	Annual Air Handling Unit 8000 - 12000 SCFM	AHU-17B-002
AHU-17D	17D	Quarterly Air Handling Unit 0-2000 SCFM	AHU-17E-002
AHU-17E	17E	Quarterly Air Handling Unit 2000 - 8000 SCFM	AHU-17B-003
AHU-17F	17F	Quarterly Air Handling Unit 8000 - 12000 SCFM	AHU-17E-003

TABLE 3.4 Normalized Equipment Cross-Referenced to Preventive Maintenance Example 1

GUID	Acronym	Sequence Number	Equipment Identification	Specification Unit	Specification Value	Job Task (1)	Job Task (N)
HytY7...	AHU	001	AHU-001	SCFM	1500	17A	17D
Ptyr9...	AHU	002	AHU-002	SCFM	7500	17B	17E
ZzTOp2...	AHU	003	AHU-003	SCFM	6000	17B	17E

of the same type of equipment. Including the PM identification in the equipment identification creates a situation in which there are now six separate entries, AHU-17A-001 to AHU-17E-003, related to only three actual pieces of equipment: AHU-001 to AHU-003 in the database. Therefore, you have now created duplicate database entries for a single piece of equipment. If the data were normalized instead, as shown in Table 3.4, there would be only three records. The relationship between the equipment and the preventive maintenance tasks is created within the database itself. Since the majority of database programs used today include data relationships, there is absolutely no reason to include the PM identification in the equipment identification. The correct preventive maintenance can even be automatically determined by the database itself if business rules are developed for the program that assign the proper preventive maintenance task to the equipment, based on its equipment type and specifications. Therefore, when the standard cubic feet per minute SCFM for that air handler is entered into the specification data field, the database can automatically determine all of the preventive maintenance required for that air handling unit.

Tables 3.5 and 3.6 are a second example of the combining of data. As the size and complexity of the database get larger, the problems get worse. Notice that in Table 3.5 there are now 12 data entries for equipment in the Database Equipment Records, while Table 3.6 shows that there are really only four pieces of equipment. There are two Database Equipment Records columns in Table 3.5. The two columns illustrate the problems with sequential numbering in a database using a combination of equipment identifications in one data field. Two different methods to sequentially number the equipment have been created by not normalizing the data correctly. The errors shown in Table 3.3 and Table 3.5 carry over to all of the metrics, contracts, resources, and executive decisions made using that organization's data set. Developing queries and metrics using normalized data, as shown in Tables 3.4 and 3.6, will be easier and more effective and accurate. For example, if I did an equipment inventory count for a facility with data formatted using Table 3.5, I would get the result

TABLE 3.5 Using PM Identifications for Equipment Identification Example 2

Equipment Identification Standard	PM Identification	Preventive Maintenance Guide Title	Database Equipment Records	Database Equipment Records
FX-F1	F1	CO2 Fire Extinguisher Annual	FX-F1-001	FX-F1-001
FX-F2	F2	CO2 Fire Extinguisher Quarterly	FX-F2-001	FX-F2-002
FX-F3	F3	CO2 Fire Extinguisher 5 Year Hydro	FX-F3-001	FX-F3-003
FX-F4	F4	PKP Fire Extinguisher Annual	FX-F1-002	FX-F1-004
FX-F5	F5	PKP Fire Extinguisher Quarterly	FX-F2-002	FX-F2-005
FX-F6	F6	PKP Fire Extinguisher 5 Year Hydro	FX-F3-002	FX-F3-006
FX-F7	F7	AFFF Fire Extinguisher Annual	FX-F4-003	FX-F4-007
FX-F8	F8	AFFF Fire Extinguisher Quarterly	FX-F5-003	FX-F5-008
FX-F9	F9	AFF Fire Extinguisher 5 Year Hydro	FX-F6-003	FX-F6-009
			FX-F7-004	FX-F7-010
			FX-F8-004	FX-F8-011
			FX-F9-004	FX-F9-013

that there are twelve fire extinguishers within the facility, as opposed to the accurate count of four fire extinguishers when data are formatted per Table 3.6.

The conclusion is that normalizing data and placing the right data in the right box is one of the most important things to consider when developing an equipment database. Data need not and should not be combined, and there is absolutely no reason to use the equipment identification as a unique identifier. It is also very important that facility management and owners understand and determine the design and database structure for your equipment database. Let's face it, database programmers can and will state that if you just tell them the information you want, they can develop the database and parse and slice the data any way you want. While this is true, the problem is that it actually

TABLE 3.6 Normalized Equipment Cross-Referenced to Preventive Maintenance Example 2

GUID	Acronym	Sequence Number	Equipment Identification	Specification Unit	Specification Value	Job Task	Job Task	Job Task
Ht4ty...	FX	001	FX-001	Retardant	CO2	F1	F2	F3
J9tye...	FX	002	FX-002	Retardant	CO2	F1	F2	F3
A6g7...	FX	003	FX-003	Retardant	PKP	F4	F5	F6
L3ty...	FX	004	FX-004	Retardant	AFFF	F7	F8	F9

costs your organization significant money and manpower for a programmer to create the extra macros and queries to get the information needed, if the data are formatted incorrectly. The database programmer is also not an expert in facility management and the data and metrics your organization needs; therefore, errors will be introduced into your database as you continually have to modify and adjust the information.

With the concept of developing a correct normalization of data for the equipment database in mind, it is now very important to discuss the different types of equipment inventory systems, methods, and database designs that can be adopted to create an efficient and accurate equipment data schema.

EQUIPMENT INVENTORY METHODS AND SYSTEMS

The equipment contained in an inventory list can be identified and labeled by various different methods. The equipment can be identified by preventive maintenance, by the type of equipment, by the function it performs, and so forth. For example, a pump can be identified as a chill water pump or a centrifugal pump, or it can be identified through a self-generated method, such as identifying a fire extinguisher as F1 (Table 3.5) per its preventive maintenance guide designation. The way an inventory list identifies its equipment is called an equipment identification system.

There are two basic ways to develop an equipment identification system. There are self-generated identification systems, and there are industry standard identification systems. Self-generated identification systems are the prevalent type of identification systems used in the industry.

Self-Generated Identification System

Self-generated identification systems, also known as legacy systems, are internal identification systems developed for a specific organization. Self-generated systems are normally proprietary and inconsistent with other identification systems in use within the industry. Therefore, transferring data from an architect to a self-generated system would require converting industry standards used by the architect to those used by the organization (cost). Typically, self-generated systems are inconsistent with other application systems in use within that same organization. For example, the way equipment is identified within one facility may be different from the way it is identified in another facility. Another example that points out this problem is that the way a corporation's facility management identifies equipment might not be the same as the method used by their portfolio management department. The problems created by different facilities within the same organization using the different identification systems should be obvious. Nevertheless, in industry, it is not at all uncommon for this to occur.

A self-generated identification system also requires frequent updates when new equipment comes on the market, or when changes are made to the identification system. For example, when a new type of pump comes on the market, the appropriate changes to the equipment identification system would have to be made. Those changes would have to be made at all of the facilities and to all the different identification systems and applications in use within that organization.

Figure 3.1 graphically demonstrates the complexity of self-generated systems versus the simplicity of using standards. The use of self-generated systems requires each application, program, or database within the organization to be integrated with each of the different applications, systems, departments, and databases in order to work effectively; that costs money and resources. Self-generated systems are very complex to use, integrate, and maintain. Industry standards use universal data formats that allow applications, systems, departments, and databases to seamlessly integrate, making the integration less complex and more streamlined since all applications and handoffs are using the same conventions. Because of their complexity, self-generated systems require

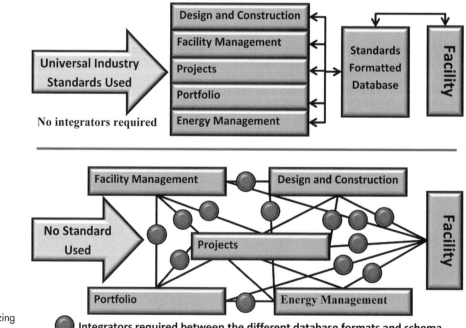

FIGURE 3.1   Standardizing Data

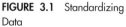 **Integrators required between the different database formats and schema**

more capital resources and additional labor hours to maintain their uniquely coded system and to properly implement that system. The result is additional costs not created by industry standard–based systems.

A self-generated inventory identification system can be generated from several facility-related sources. Preventive maintenance documents are a common source used in the development of these identification systems. For example: A motor has preventive maintenance performed upon it as described in the maintenance card MT-01. The motor is therefore identified within the inventory system with its sequential number (001 for this example) as MT01-001. Now if the organization changes the nomenclature of the maintenance card, all of the affected components previously identified as MT01-001 within the organization have to be reidentified. For example, if I change the maintenance card identifier to MOT01, do I now have to go back and relabel all of that equipment? If a second maintenance card exists, because of different maintenance requirements for the same motor—for example MT-02—there now exists the real possibility of having both MT01-001 and MT02-001 within the equipment database. I now have two different identifications in the database referring to the exact same piece of equipment. This is a common practice and problem found in facility management databases.

Self-generated systems, by definition, are not consistent or compliant with standards or systems used by other industries or organizations. Because self-generated systems are not based on industry standards, a communication gap often occurs between different disciplines, especially between the construction and the operations of facilities (Figure 3.2). Organizations that build, own, and operate facilities are consistently compensating for this gap in communications. Design and construction entities often have a unique equipment identifier (e.g., Apple) for a piece of equipment, which is typically based on an industry standard such as National CAD Standards™ (NCS), while a facilities operation entity can have a different equipment identifier (e.g., Orange) for the same piece of equipment. Cross-entity differences concerning the data for a piece of equipment can lead to confusion and misunderstanding and thereby

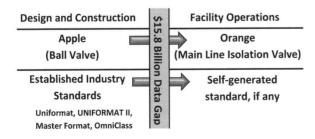

FIGURE 3.2 Data and Communication Gap between Construction and Operations

loss of data. When a new facility is brought online, the facility has to convert the data created by the construction entity, using industry standards, to the standard used by the facility manager or owner. The cost of the conversion is a recurring nonrefundable cost. What typically occurs when a brand-new facility is transferred to the facility management team is that the facility has to be reinventoried. Reinventorying a newly constructed facility seems silly, but it occurs all the time. The cost to reinventory a million-square-foot facility at a cost of $0.10/gross square foot (Table 2.1, Equipment Inventory Office Building Costs and Tiers) for a preventive maintenance inventory equates to a $100,000 additional cost associated with using a self-generated system. If the facility management used the same industry standards that the design and construction teams used, the data would transfer from the construction database to the facility management database accurately—and free. This is capital that could be used for other mission-specific aspects of the facility.

Self-generated systems also introduce training and human error costs to the organization. When new facility staff comes onboard, they have to be trained that 17A is an air handling unit (Table 3.3). Oh, and 17D is the same air handling unit, which should not be confused with 17B and 17E. . . . Confused yet? The ideal situation is for communicating entities to use the same industry standard for equipment identification.

The conclusion is that the cost and resources for maintaining and integrating data, and dealing with database errors, miscommunication, and training errors are just some of the major reasons that self-generated systems should not be used.

Industry Standard Identification System

Industry standard identification systems use agreed-upon standards and codes to implement a universal identification system for components to be inventoried. These standards provide a standard data format that reduces or bridges the gap between construction, facility management, and owners. For example, when a new facility is brought online, an equipment inventory can be transferred directly between entities, from design and construction to facility management, into an organization's database, rendering the database usable immediately at minimal additional cost. A similar cost savings can be realized during renovations because the data can be back fed to design and construction. The use of industry standards also ensures that various departments and branches within the organization are using the same language and that all data and metrics are consistent. Standards facilitate communication internally and externally with other corporations, organizations, and facilities. State and federal agencies using the same standards would effectively reduce their communication gap, especially in emergency situations.

Using standard identification systems facilitates the integration of facility management systems by not requiring the change of equipment identification codes between disciplines. If the architect used industry codes such as National CAD Standards for equipment and the same codes were adopted by facility management, then the equipment lists generated during the design and construction phases could be used to generate the initial inventory list for the facility. Using this convention minimizes the need for facility management to pay to reinventory the equipment. For example, if an architect/engineer installed an air handling unit and labeled that unit AHU-01 on the blueprints, and facility management used the same industry codes, then the air handling unit would be loaded into the facility management database as AHU-01. There would be no loss of information and no cost to convert that data to a different system. The only time the inventory list for a facility would need to be changed is when the facility adds or removes equipment. The requirement for an architectural firm to provide the list in a usable format can be written into the construction agreement if everyone agrees on the industry standard. Standards ensure that the right data format is used to enable the right information to be placed in the right box.

Comparing self-generated identification systems to those developed using industry standards shows that the better option of the two is to base an equipment identification system on an industry standard. Whenever an organization uses a self-generated system they incur costs from communication errors, redundancy, and noncompliance, and these costs are not recoverable. In the United States, good sources of information on the standards for facility management are the Federal Facility Council (FFC) and the National Institute of Building Sciences (NIBS). They will have the most up-to-date industry standards and recommendations. An analysis of the current industry standards is given in Chapter 4, "Industry Standards."

System- and Object-Based Identification System

When selecting an industry standard, it is important to be able to properly evaluate which standards to use. Therefore, you must understand the difference between a system-based design and an object-based design and understand how the identification of the actual equipment is designated within these types of systems.

System-Based Design

A system-based design is one in which the components within the identification system are identified according to the relationships the equipment has with the building or component systems. For example, a system-based approach would include a condensate return system pump, a condensate supply system pump, and a wastewater pump. The equipment nomenclature is identified by the system in which it is installed. A centrifugal pump, which is common to a lot of systems, would have to be replicated in all of the different systems within the identification system. You would have a domestic water centrifugal pump, a chill water centrifugal pump, a condenser supply centrifugal pump, a fire centrifugal pump, and so on. Notice that the type of equipment—centrifugal pump—is the same in all of these instances. You then have to repeat this process for all of the different types of pumps: axial flow pumps, reciprocating pumps, diaphragm pumps, and the like, in all of the systems. You are basically combining two different pieces of data: system and equipment. The data are not normalized. You can start to see the complexities of a system-based approach in the sheer size of all the duplication of equipment types in all of the different systems. Imagine the size of the database to handle just all of the different possible types of valves in all of the different systems! Because system-based component identification systems are inherently very large, they are costly to maintain in manpower and computing data space. This type of approach to identifying components is expensive and complicated to maintain.

Another disadvantage to a system-based approach occurs when a new type of equipment, such as a new type of pump, has to be added to all of the systems. If you miss entering the new type of equipment into one of the systems, you create errors in your equipment identification system. For example, I want to identify a diaphragm pump in the fire suppression system, but the system does not have a diaphragm pump listed under it. I have to identify the pump using another one in the list, add the pump to an update of the standard, and correct the error at a later date. This design of an identification system is very susceptible to human error. Another example: Is a sump pump a wastewater system pump, a storm drain system pump, or a flood prevention system pump? Because there are so many systems that have similar purposes, equipment can easily be misidentified with the wrong system. Misidentifying equipment with the wrong system affects system cost rollups and overall equipment system counts.

System-based identification designs are less flexible than an object-based design. An organization does not go to a manufacturer to buy a wastewater pump; it buys a centrifugal pump and places it into the wastewater system. Table 3.7 demonstrates that in order to parse the information from a database and find all of the pumps within a facility or organization, a system-based query would have to include all of the different possible system information from the database. Otherwise, to accurately get all of the information on pumps in a facility, an organization would have to perform specific text searches of the database

TABLE 3.7   System- versus Object-Based Equipment Identification Systems

System-Based Design Equipment System Table		Object-Based Design Equipment System Tables	
Code	Description	Code	System Description
X0001	Condensate Return System	X0001	Condensate Return System
X0002	Condensate Return System Centrifugal Pump	X0002	Chill Water System
X0003	Condensate Return System Axial	X0003	Domestic Water System
Y0001	Chill Water System		
Y0002	Chill Water System Centrifugal Pump	Code	Product Description
Y0003	Chill Water System Axial Pump	Y0010	Pump
		Y0011	Centrifugal Pump
		Y0012	Axial Pump
*	Each piece of equipment identified by system		
*	Additional man hours required to maintain list	X0002 + Y0011	
*	Equipment repeated for each system	Chill Water System Centrifugal Pump	

to get the results they needed. For example: If you search for just the word "pump" in a systems designed database, you will also get results such as fire "pumper," "pumped" effluent, "pumping" station, and so forth. The extra equipment would have be removed or specifically excluded from the query. In a similar query for pumps using an object-based approach, the query can just search for pumps using the equipment product code for the pump category "Y001."

The final conclusion is that a system-based design introduces errors and added complexity into a database used for identifying equipment. The data are not properly normalized because it is two pieces of information (data) placed in one box (data field). The inherent size, complexity, and costs do not make these types of designs good to use in equipment identification systems.

Object-Based Design

An object-based approach is significantly simpler and more flexible to use; therefore, it is more cost-effective and efficient. An object-based equipment design is one in which the equipment (object) and the systems (object) are maintained in separate tables (Table 3.7). The objects in each table are identified according to their design or function. For example, pumps would be identified by their types, such as centrifugal, axial flow, positive reciprocating, ejector, and so on. Systems would be identified by their purpose or function, such as fire suppression, condensate return, condensate supply, wastewater, and so on. The separate objects can then be linked together to create or describe new objects. For example, "centrifugal pump" in one table would be linked to a system object such as the "condensate return" or "domestic water" within another table in the database, resulting in condensate return centrifugal pump or domestic water centrifugal pump. Object-based design allows for the combination of objects to identify the relationship between component and systems. This ability allows an organization to parse its database by separate objects or a combination of objects based on the data needed. Data queries can quickly find all centrifugal pumps, all pumps, or all of the components related to a system such as the condensate return system. The data could then be quickly tabulated by system or product level. Because the equipment is identified at the product level, if the facility has a complete, all-disciplines, component-level inventory, then all of the components' energy usage within a system or space could be accurately determined for chargebacks, strategic plans, or even the development of an accurate curtailment plan. Because they can properly sort all of the product data, it would be easier for managers to tabulate all of the voltages, amps, horsepower, and efficiencies of all of the pumps within a facility or system. An object-based equipment identification system helps to ensure that the right data are placed in the right box.

Every facility should strive for an object-based component-level or complete inventory based on industry standards—because, if your company is not maximizing its interoperability, communication, costs, manpower, and efficiency, then your competition is. Industry standards will be discussed further in Chapter 4, "Industry Standards."

A brief discussion is necessary to explain how an equipment identification database (hardware/servers) should be set up. While there is a cloud computing, interconnection data highway, and so forth, the basic concept of centralized and decentralized database systems is important to understand.

Centralized versus Decentralized Databases

There are two basic methods to store your information in databases: centralized and decentralized. While typically this is the domain of your information and technology experts, it is important to understand how your data are being stored.

A centralized database is one in which all of the information is kept in a central database and then that information is accessed by the multiple applications that need that information (Figure 3.3). This should not be confused with a single physical database server. A centralized database could be spread across multiple servers and geographical locations.

A decentralized database is one in which all of the information is kept in separate databases or duplicated in different software packages (Figure 3.4).

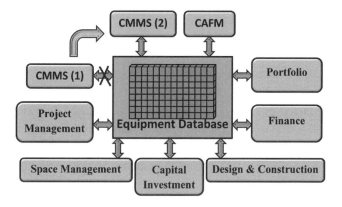

FIGURE 3.3 Centralized Database

A centralized database is preferable to a decentralized database. A common database ensures uniformity of the data, reduces the duplication of the data, improves the reliability of the data, and, thereby, increases the interoperability of the information. It is a more efficient method for an organization to determine its data needs and format, centralize the data, and then link its applications to that data. The benefit of a common database is further improved if industry standards are used. A central repository for all the data allows portability of the data from one application to another. For example, suppose an organization changes from one software application provider to another software application provider. In a centralized database model, the organization would just have to unlink the application from the database and reconnect the new application to the database.

A decentralized database system is one that uses the databases of separate applications and then tries to interlink, or road map, that data. Note: This is different from a singular database spread over multiple servers, hardware, or

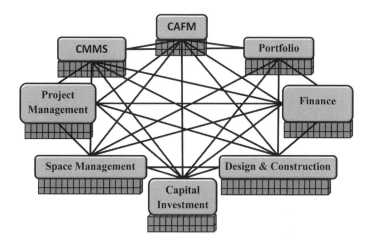

FIGURE 3.4 Decentralized Database

geographical areas, which is still deemed to be a centralized database. The problem created using different databases and applications to store the data is that the data are typically not interoperable because each application has a different data format. Multiple integrators have to be developed between the different software applications and the database, which creates data loss during the translations between the data exchanges and applications. Also, most applications have their own proprietary format, and in most companies these databases are not typically linked, which creates significant data duplication. Anyone who has transferred documents between applications, even using universal industry standard translators and protocols, can attest that there is rarely a 100% translation. Transfer a document between Microsoft Word and WordPerfect or between a PC and a Mac, and you can understand the problems. Further, for the data exchanges to happen and be effective, in a decentralized database, the data reference tables and integrators have to be developed and maintained by experts (cost). For example, it is not uncommon for large commercial real estate companies to have a portfolio management software program to determine the health and market value of their facilities, a strategic asset management package to project future facility costs, and a software package for the maintenance and operation of their facilities. All of these software packages use the exact same equipment data for projects, accounting, maintenance, operational costs, and so forth. If this information is not properly linked and synchronized, then there is data duplication and data loss, and the data quickly becomes obsolete in one or many of the programs. Using obsolete or inaccurate information is highly ineffective and wasteful in any organization.

What is important to remember is that the data and integrity of the data within the database is important to the operation and costs related to a facility. Errors and data loss within an application can be solved. But on the database side, the loss of the actual data or corruption of the data in the database is catastrophic to facility management and owner organizations, as shown in Chapter 2. Therefore, to minimize errors and costs, a facility management organization should consider a centralized database system.

COMPUTERIZED MAINTENANCE MANAGEMENT SYSTEMS (CMMS)

Computerized maintenance management systems (CMMS) and computer-assisted facility management (CAFM) are software programs designed to schedule and manage the maintenance tasks related to facilities. Maintenance is defined by tasks that have to be performed. The tasks are then used to create work orders that can be automatically scheduled for performance by the facility staff. The maintenance of a facility is very heavily related to the type and quality of equipment inventories. You have to know the amount and type of equipment within your facility in order to properly determine what maintenance is required.

There are basically two major designs of CMMS: location-based and object-based. A location-based system uses the facility rooms and spaces (locations) as the key database table to link and track all of the data within the program. The object-based CMMS program separates each set of data: space, facility, equipment, tasks, and the like, as separate objects that use the database to relate each piece of data to the others.

The basic crucial element for all CMMSs is their ability to provide an accurate, high-quality, well-organized object-based equipment inventory based on an industry standard for efficient and cost-effective facility management.

There are many analyses and books on the different CMMS systems in the industry. The main concept to understand is that it is very important to predefine the data fields your organization wants and the schema for those data points, before you start selecting a CMMS program. The industry spends millions of dollars data scrubbing information in order to transfer data from one data schema to another (transferring data from one CMMS to another CMMS schema). If, instead, you define and populate a database and then link that data to the CMMS your organization wants to use (centralized database), then when or if you have to migrate your data, you can just relink to the new CMMS. The data would not have to be scrubbed, thereby saving your organization millions of dollars. Obviously, this is not normally in the interest of the companies that develop CMMS programs; they have a capital incentive to lock you into their proprietary system. Therefore, it is important for facility management and owners to define and enforce the data schema and standards that all CMMS programs should be compliant with. This forces the CMMS programs to become more efficient and effective in order to adjust to the new market, thus benefiting all of facility management.

What typically occurs in the industry is that facility management analyzes the different CMMS programs and picks the one it believes is most beneficial to its organization. Interestingly, CMMS programs have a one-year return on investment, even though there is not a universal equipment inventory standard. When a facility transfers all of its data into the CMMS-program-defined proprietary database, the cost of transferring to a new CMMS program or of improving the design starts to become cost prohibitive. Most organizations are in this situation at this time. Facility management and owners have basically let information technology programmers—a significant portion of whom do not have facility management experience—define the data and schema that facility managers can use to operate their facilities. Doesn't it make more sense to define the data, industry standards, and schema before asking programmers to develop, or before selecting, the CMMS program?

CHAPTER 4

Industry Standards

In the previous chapter, the importance of data and data format, and the different equipment inventory types and systems were discussed. The conclusion was that the most beneficial equipment inventory system is an object oriented system based on industry standards. In this chapter, I discuss the different types of industry standards commonly used to identify equipment, and their pros and cons. The focus of this chapter is on standards for the identification and classification of equipment.

Why use industry standards? Plain and simple, data that are categorized and formatted using industry standards improves the interoperability between all of the systems and programs that are using the same standard. The more prevalent a standard, the more universal the communication is between two or more different systems. Systems can be software applications, databases, wireless communications, contracts, metrics, or basically any form of communication that would benefit from using the same language or standard. The reason that Morse code was understood by all of those who used it was that they all agreed on and used the same standard.

Another major advantage of using an industry standard for data related to equipment is that the standards reduce human entry errors, normalize the data, and allow the proper parsing and utilization of the information. For example, when I was tasked with normalizing an equipment data set of over 500,000 pieces of equipment, over 300,000 errors were found that had to be manually corrected. That is an enormous waste of manpower.

Take for example a small data set of equipment for the same facility: one taken without using a standard, and one taken using a standard (Table 4.1). The human errors in the inventory that did not use a standard should be evident. There are spelling errors, there is mixed usage in the classification of the types of equipment and equipment identification, and different conventions are used to name the same location. Compare this to the equipment inventory using a standard. With the latter, an organization could easily determine how many centrifugal pumps are in their inventory, what equipment is part of the fire suppression system, or which equipment is located in room 118.

There are some key features that should be considered when selecting any standard to use (see previous chapter for object-based discussion):

Is it an open standard?

Is it a commonly used standard?

Is the standard used in multiple related industries?

An open standard is one that allows the general public to submit and recommend modifications and improvements to the standard. Open standards tend to be able to evolve and improve over time. A key concept about open standards that should be understood is that they are typically free to

TABLE 4.1   Equipment Inventory: No Standard versus Standard

Equipment List: No Standard			Equipment List Using a Standard			Location		
Equipment	Equip. ID	Location	Equipment	System	Equip. ID	Floor	Space	Description
Pump	Pump-01	Mech. Room	Centrifugal Pump	Chill Water	P-001	1	104	Mechanical
Water Pump	PP-001	Mechanical	Sewage Ejector	Wastewater	P-002	1	104	Mechanical
Centr. Pump	P-02	Mech. Rm	Centrifugal Pump	Cooling Water	P-003	1	104	Mechanical
Valve	VLV-01	Rm 118	Ball Valve	Fire Suppression	BV-001	2	118	Kitchenette
Main Isolation	Valve-18	Kitchen	Gate Valve	Natural Gas	GTV-001	2	118	Kitchenette
Volve	V-017	118 Room	Ball Valve	Fire Suppression	BV-002	2	118	Kitchenette

all users. Confusion arises because most open standards do require a copyright agreement to be signed by an organization, to register to use the standard. OmniClass™ from Construction Specifications Institute (CSI) and Construction Specifications Canada (CSC) is a good example of this type of requirement. OmniClass™ is free, but CSI/CSC has to ensure the integrity of the standard for all users. Another misconception is that open standards allow any changes from anyone to be incorporated at any time. Industry standards have a strict modification and review process that includes industry vetting and voting on any changes. The standards themselves are typically on a review cycle ranging from every year to every five years. The purpose of this review process is to gradually introduce any changes of the standards into the community and give end users time to process those changes. I have heard many facility management organizations decide not to use a standard because they have determined that it is not "stable," that it is always undergoing change. This is actually counterproductive, because the organization should want a standard that continually improves. The improvements signify that the standard is being used by the industry and will therefore be adopted by more software and application solutions. When a change to an industry standard is adopted, a translation table is typically provided to transfer or upgrade any application or software using the standard. The translation is done in the background by the database programmer, and the transition should be seamless.

An open standard is very important to use because it ensures that your organization can add specialized equipment to the standard. Too often, an organization will reject a standard because it does not meet all of their needs, when in actuality they only had to help improve the standard and thereby benefit their organization and the industry as a whole. The argument of "we are specialized, different, or unique" is an easy copout from the effort required to improve an industry standard and it should not be tolerated in any corporation.

A commonly used standard tends to be usable, and it will therefore have more compatibility with other systems. However, it is important to note that the standard should not be obsolete. Morse code was a commonly used standard, and it is still in use today, but I wouldn't base my company's communication system on it.

When choosing a standard, it is important to know if the standard is prevalent in other related industries. In the context of this book, the main factor that should be considered when selecting a standard for equipment inventories is whether that standard is also used in the design and construction industry. Facility management and design and construction are very closely aligned.

The design and construction industry is also very knowledgeable and proactive in the use and development of industry standards. The additional benefit from using the same standard is that transfer of data from construction of a facility to the operations of the facility should be seamless.

INDUSTRY STANDARD ANALYSIS

The next portion of this chapter will evaluate the different standards that are commonly used to identify equipment.

MasterFormat®

MasterFormat® is an industry standard developed for work results maintained by the Construction Specifications Institute (CSI) and Construction Specifications Canada (CSC). This standard was primarily developed for organizing construction specifications. A secondary use of the standard is for cost estimating. OmniClass™ Table 22 is based on this standard and is also maintained by CSI/CSC. OmniClass™ will be discussed later in this book. MasterFormat® has been around the industry for a long time, and there are many corporations, software programs, and organizations that use MasterFormat® for equipment identification. RSMeans™ by Reed Construction Data is a premiere example of costing software.

MasterFormat® is an organizational framework based on work results, which are essentially the end results of construction processes, defined by CSI/CSC as "the permanent or temporary aspects of construction projects achieved through the application of a particular skill or trade to construction resources." When viewed in this context, work results are the combination of two types of data: the equipment or material and the labor or skill used to install that equipment or material. Material + Labor = Installed.

For example, a metal stair rail, an electrical conduit, a roof drain, and plumbing can all have the object "galvanized pipe" in common. How that pipe is installed is expressed as the work result; the actual product, though, is galvanized pipe. It is important to be able to separate the item or equipment from the action or work result. In this example, the complexity of trying to determine how much galvanized pipe is used in the facility is compounded by all of the possible different uses of that item.

MasterFormat® breaks down its information into installed construction elements and systems and is not an object-based standard (Table 4.2). For example, you can find centrifugal fire pumps, centrifugal domestic water pumps, and steam condensate pumps in OmniClass Table 22. The systems

TABLE 4.2 MasterFormat® Example

OmniClass™ Table 22 (MasterFormat®)	
OmniClass™ Number	**OmniClass™ Title**
22-21 24 00	Dry-Chemical Fire-Extinguishing Systems
22-21 24 13	Dry-Chemical Fire-Extinguishing Piping
22-21 24 16	Dry-Chemical Fire-Extinguishing Equipment
22-21 30 00	Fire Pumps
22-21 31 00	Centrifugal Fire Pumps
22-21 31 13	Electric-Drive, Centrifugal Fire Pumps
22-21 31 16	Diesel-Drive, Centrifugal Fire Pumps
22-21 32 00	Vertical-Turbine Fire Pumps
22-22 11 16	Domestic Water Piping
22-22 11 19	Domestic Water Piping Specialties
22-22 11 23	Domestic Water Pumps
22-22 11 23 13	Domestic-Water Packaged Booster Pumps
22-23 01 00	Operation and Maintenance of HVAC Systems
22-23 01 10	Operation and Maintenance of Facility Fuel Systems
22-23 01 20	Operation and Maintenance of HVAC Piping and Pumps
22-23 01 30	Operation and Maintenance of HVAC Air Distribution
22-23 01 30 51	HVAC Air Duct Cleaning

OmniClass™ Table 22 is a product of Construction Specifications Institute/Construction Specifications Canada. Version OmniClass_22_2006-05-02.

have been matched to the pump, even though the actual equipment in each case is a pump.

Because MasterFormat® is a quasi-system-based standard and is a combination of two data fields (equipment and labor) and sometimes three data fields (System + Equipment + Labor), it is not the proper tool to use to identify the different types of equipment. MasterFormat® could be used for classifying the different systems for the equipment, but it should not be used to identify the equipment itself.

UNIFORMAT II

UNIFORMAT II, ASTM E1557, is another commonly used industry standard for the classification and identification of equipment, and it is maintained by the American Society for Testing and Materials International (ASTM). This should not be confused with UniFormat™ developed and maintained by CSI/CSC.

UniFormat ™

UniFormat™, a publication of CSI and CSC, is the Uniform Classification System for organizing preliminary construction information into a standard order or sequence on the basis of functional elements. Functional elements, often referred to as systems or assemblies, are major components common to most buildings that usually perform a given function regardless of the design specification, construction method, or materials used (Construction Specifications Institute, www.csinet.org/uniformat).

UNIFORMAT II

1.1   This standard establishes a classification of building elements and related sitework. Elements, as defined here, are major components common to most buildings. Elements usually perform a given function, regardless of the design specification, construction method, or materials used. The classification serves as a consistent reference for analysis, evaluation, and monitoring during the feasibility, planning, and design stages of buildings. Using UNIFORMAT II ensures consistency in the economic evaluation of building projects over time and from project to project. It also enhances reporting at all stages in construction—from feasibility and planning through the preparation of working documents, construction, maintenance, rehabilitation, and disposal.

1.2   This classification applies to buildings and related site work. It excludes specialized process equipment related to a building's functional use but does include furnishings and equipment (ASTM E1557–05e1 Standard Classification for Building Elements and Related Sitework-UNIFORMAT II, "Scope," American Society for Testing and Materials, www.astm.org/Standards/E1557.htm).

UNIFORMAT II is a very strong and prevalent standard for the cost estimating of facilities; it is also very prevalent in the industry and is used by numerous companies and federal agencies to identify equipment. The history behind its adoption for equipment classification is simple: there were no other standards at the time that could have been used for the same purpose. Therefore, companies adapted this standard to fit their own needs. UNIFORMAT II is also prevalent in the industry for cost estimating, and therefore there is a familiarity with the code that leads organizations to want to use this same code to identify equipment. As previously noted in Chapter 3, this can be a costly mistake. But, as you will note, even in the scope of UNIFORMAT II it is stated: *"excludes specialized process equipment related to a building's functional use."* The analysis of this standard for this book is based on its use for equipment identification. The standard itself is an excellent standard to use for the purpose for which it was originally designed.

UNIFORMAT II has four hierarchical levels and is designed as an identification and construction system for cost estimations. The design is very similar to that of MasterFormat®. UNIFORMAT II is a mixed combination of various different types of data that combines systems, elements, and products. This standard is also heavily dependent upon a systems approach to classification. For example, take the code in UniFormat II: D2020: Domestic Water Distribution, D3040: Air Distribution System (Table 4.3); you can see the system structure. As previously noted, a systems-based approach is not an efficient means with which to identify equipment, and using such a system will result in additional cost to any organization.

UNIFORMAT II also included entries for equipment identification, based on its operational use. This equipment identification is commonly called level 4, after the level of code at which equipment identification occurs. For example, one instance of the code reviewed included WASTE PUMPS, FAN MOTOR, RFAN MOTOR, and SFAN MOTOR. A product such as a pump should not be identified by its purpose (WASTE PUMP). A facility manager needs to know the type of pump (centrifugal, positive reciprocating, pneumatic ejector, etc.) because the maintenance, operation, and parts are completely different for each type of pump. A better approach would be to relate the pump to the system in which it was installed (see Chapter 5, "Equipment Data Points," Equipment System Relationship section).

Another problem is that FAN MOTOR, RFAN MOTOR, and SFAN MOTOR are all the same product: an electric motor attached to a fan. First, this is an indication of an equipment assembly relationship (see Chapter 5, Equipment Assembly section), which implies that there is a fan involved with the motor. Second, electrical motors are not only used for fans. What if I replaced an "SFAN" motor, rebuilt that motor, and then placed that motor into a fan coil unit? Would that change it from an "SFAN" piece of equipment to something with another name? The type of equipment, electric motor, has not changed. Third, these three classifications all refer to the exact same type of equipment: "FAN MOTOR." An RFAN MOTOR, which I believe is a return fan motor, is the same as the SFAN MOTOR, a supply fan motor, except that the fan has been turned around 180 degrees in a piece of HVAC ductwork. The better way to address this same information is with an object-based approach: Identify the fan, then relate that fan to an electric motor (equipment assembly relationship), and then relate that assembly to either the return or the supply HVAC air distribution system (system relationship).

Another disadvantage of UNIFORMAT II is that there is not a significant number of level-4 components (Table 4.3). An iteration of the standard reviewed was found to have only 825 rows of actual code. Therefore, the

TABLE 4.3 UNIFORMAT II

Level 1	Level 2	Level 3	Level 4		
D	SERVICES				
	D20	PLUMBING			
		D2010	PLUMBING FIXTURES		
		D2020	DOMESTIC WATER DISTRIBUTION		
			D202003	DOMESTIC WATER EQUIPMENT	
		D2030	SANITARY WASTE		
			D203004	SANITARY AND VENT EQUIPMENT	
		D2040	RAINWATER DRAINAGE		
			D204003	RAINWATER DRAINAGE EQUIPMENT	
	D30	HVAC			
		D3030	COOLING GENERATING SYSTEMS		
			D303001	CHILLED WATER SYSTEMS	
			D303099	OTHER COOLING GENERATING SYSTEMS	
		D3040	DISTRIBUTION SYSTEMS		
			D304001	AIR DISTRIBUTION, HEATING & COOLING	
			D304002	STEAM DISTRIBUTION SYSTEMS	
		D3050	TERMINAL & PACKAGE UNITS		
			D305002	UNIT HEATERS	
			D305003	FAN COIL UNITS	
	D40	FIRE PROTECTION			
		D4020	FIRE SUPPRESSION WATER SUPPLY AND EQUIPMENT		
			D402001	FIRE PROTECTION WATER PIPING AND EQUIPMENT	
			D402002	FIRE PUMP	

UNIFORMAT II, American Society for Testing and Materials (ASTM), GSA Version 1975.

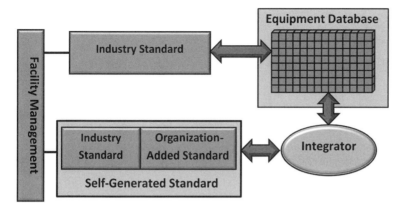

FIGURE 4.1   Modifying Standards

maximum number of products that could exist would be fewer than 825, taking out title and system categories such as Domestic Water Distribution. That is not a very large list of components for a user to choose from, to identify all of the different types of equipment in a facility. This is especially noticeable when compared to other standards that identify over 6,000 different types of components (OmniClass Table 23). The problem created is that any organization wanting to use UNIFORMAT II for identification of equipment would have to add the additional equipment to the standard to capture all of the equipment in a facility. When the equipment is added to the standard, it is no longer an industry standard but a quasi-industry/self-generated standard (Figure 4.1). The organization would also have to maintain their own version of the standard. The standard would no longer be compatible with industry standards and therefore not an efficient and effective method of equipment identification.

Another method to illustrate the problem with using UNIFORMAT II is a comparative analysis with an object-oriented industry standard (Table 4.4). When comparing UNIFORMAT II at the 4th and 5th levels to OmniClass™, it can be determined that UNIFORMAT II is technically the same concept as combining OmniClass™ Table 21 UniFormat™ and OmniClass™ Table 23 products into a single table. Having all of the information combined in one table, as in UNIFORMAT II, adds complexity to the table, costs manpower to maintain (because adding all the products to UNIFORMAT II would create a self-generated system), and introduces errors into the database. The more effective approach is to have the information properly separated into data elements based on the type of information and then use industry standards that support the individual elements.

Given the design and intended scope of UNIFORMAT II, its limited number of equipment types, and the fact that it is a systems-based standard, this standard—while excellent for cost estimating—is not the proper tool to use for the identification of equipment.

TABLE 4.4   UNIFORMAT II versus OmniClass™ Data Organization Design

Level 1		Level 2		Level 3		Level 4		Level 5
UNIFORMAT II with Additional Equipment								
D	**SERVICES**							
		D20	**PLUMBING**					
				D2010	**PLUMBING FIXTURES**			
				D2020	**DOMESTIC WATER DISTRIBUTION**			
						D202003	DOMESTIC WATER EQUIPMENT	
								Centrifugal Pump 0-50 HP
								Centrifugal Pump 50-100 HP

OmniClass Data Design (Object-Oriented)					
OmniClass Table 21		**OmniClass Table 23**			
Number	Title	Number	Title	Specification Unit	Specification Value
21-04 20 10	Domestic Water Distribution	23-27 17 12	Centrifugal Pump	Horse Power	40
21-04 20 10	Domestic Water Distribution	23-27 17 12	Centrifugal Pump	Horse Power	40

UNIFORMAT II, American Society for Testing and Materials (ASTM); OmniClass™ is a product of Construction Specifications Institute/Construction Specifications Canada.

The use of UNIFORMAT II to identify equipment in a database is a very poor application of this standard and will negatively impact your organization, because of the following:

- It is a systems-based identification system.
- Some equipment is identified according to its function, not its type.
- It has a small equipment product-type data set, which would have to be augmented by meshing it with another standard and/or adding missing organization equipment, creating a self-generated standard.
- It is not a true open standard.

The basic analysis is that UNIFORMAT II = OmniClass™ Table 21 + OmniClass™ Table 23, and it just makes more sense to split your data into two separate tables to better utilize the information within the database.

TABLE 4.5   United Nations Standard Products and Services Code (UNSPSC)

Segment	Segment Title	Family	Family Title	Class	Class Title	Key	Commodity	Commodity Title
40000000	Distribution and Conditioning Systems and Equipment and Components	40140000	Fluid and gas distribution	40141600	Valves	103529	40141603	Pneumatic valves
						103530	40141604	Safety valves
						103531	40141605	Solenoid valves
						103532	40141606	Relief valves
						103533	40141607	Ball valves
						103535	40141609	Control valves

UNSPSC is a product of the United Nations.

UNSPSC®

The United Nations Standard Products and Services Code (UNSPSC) is an international standard that was developed for the international coding of products and services. This standard is very extensive; you can identify anything from a rabbit to a check valve. The standard is also very close to being an object-based code. There are instances in the code in which some components are directly defined with a system-based approach, but the practice is not extensive. UNSPSC is a well-thought-out code.

As a standard for use in facility management, and specifically to classify equipment, UNSPSC is not adequate; it does not have, at this time, sufficient equipment types for identifying all of the equipment within a facility. UNSPSC also does not contain any data points related to building elements and work results that are needed for the construction or operation of a facility. The code is designed as a mixture of products and services.

This book stresses the importance of using a code that architects, design teams, construction, estimation, and facility operations can all use to capture and track components from cradle to grave. Whenever you have to develop integration between two different types of codes, there will be some inherent data loss. Therefore, it is preferable to have a single code that encompasses all of the needed data formats. A project manager who completes a project that upgrades a facility's fire safety system should not have to deal with data problems created by different codes in order to transfer the information to facility management. The fact that this standard is missing construction elements could cause problems.

Furthermore, at the time of this writing, UNSPSC is not a widely adopted standard, especially in the United States. Although UNSPSC is probably not the best tool to use to identify equipment within a facility, it is important to note that progress is being made to develop cross-reference tables from UNSPSC to some standards such as OmniClass™.

OmniClass™

The OmniClass Construction Classification System (known as OmniClass™ or OCCS) is a classification system for the construction industry. OmniClass is useful for many applications, from organizing library materials, product literature, and project information, to providing a classification structure for electronic databases. It incorporates other extant systems currently in use as the basis of many of its Tables—MasterFormat® for work results, UniFormat™ for elements, and EPIC (Electronic Product Information Cooperation) for structuring products (OmniClass, Construction Specifications Institute, www.omniclass.org/).

The OmniClass™ standard is a suite of tables designed as a faceted classification system for the construction industry (Table 4.6). The standard has various tables ranging from Table 11 - Construction Entities by Function to Table 49 - Properties.

An analysis of the complete set of tables reveals that the standard is set up to act like an object-oriented classification system. You are able to classify the facility type, space type, building elements, work results, phases, services, and so forth, and—most importantly to the topic of this book—you are able to classify products (equipment).

The current edition of "Table 23 - Products" covers almost 7000 products used in the construction and operation of buildings. This table is of vital interest to facility managers because these are the products that are required to be maintained, tracked, repaired, replaced, and operated during the complete building life cycle. Their specifications and maintenance instructions are used to establish maintenance schedules. Their spare parts lists are used to set up storeroom parts requirements and establish supply chains. Table 21 combined with Table 23 can provide a way of organizing and accessing useful data for failure modes and effects studies, and reliability-based maintenance programs (National Institute of Building Sciences, Whole Building Design Guide, www.wbdg.org/resources/omniclass.php).

TABLE 4.6 OmniClass™ Catalog of Tables

Table	Status	Release Date
Introduction - OmniClass Introduction	Release	3/28/2006
Table 11 - Construction Entities by Function	Release	3/28/2006
Table 12 - Construction Entities by Form	Release	3/28/2006
Table 13 - Spaces by Function	Pre Consensus Approved Draft	6/24/2010
Table 14 - Spaces by Form	Release	3/28/2006
Table 21 - Elements	Pre Consensus Approved Draft	2/11/2011
Table 22 - Work Results	Pre Consensus Approved Draft	4/11/2011
Table 23 - Products	Pre Consensus Approved Draft	6/24/2010
Table 31 - Phases	Release	3/28/2006
Table 32 - Services	Pre Consensus Approved Draft	6/24/2010
Table 33 - Disciplines	Release	3/28/2006
Table 34 - Organizational Roles	Release	3/28/2006
Table 35 - Tools	Draft	3/28/2006
Table 36 - Information	Pre Consensus Approved Draft	6/24/2010
Table 41 - Materials	Release	3/28/2006
Table 49 - Properties	Draft for Comment	6/24/2010

OmniClass™ is a product of Construction Specifications Institute/Construction Specifications Canada.

A review of the products table finds that the table is designed to identify products (equipment) in an object-oriented approach. The table also covers multiple disciplines related to facility management such as mechanical, architectural, electrical, plumbing, food services, security, fire life safety, child care, medical, and even historical preservation. The design to separate information by disciplines is different from separating data by systems. It is important to understand this difference when performing an analysis. OmniClass Table 23 (Table 4.7) is set up like a product catalog. When you go to a hardware store to buy a water pump, you go to the plumbing section of the store. You do not go to the domestic water system section, because it does not exist. The products in the store are basically separated into their respective disciplines. Ever notice that flooring, windows, and doors are typically found in the same area, the building envelope area? Note that there are gray areas, as in anything, such as kitchen and bath.

In 2010, an Inter-agency Federal Asset Classification Team (IFACT) project (www.wbdg.org/pdfs/bim_fs_ifact.pdf) was completed that improved the table by reducing system-based classifications and adding thousands of products to support the management and operation of federal facilities.

TABLE 4.7 OmniClass™ Table 23 - Products (2010-06-24)

OmniClass Number	OmniClass Title
23-13 39 31	Roof Membranes
23-13 39 31 11	Single Layer Roof Membranes
23-13 39 31 11 21	Ethylene Propylene Diene Monomer (EPDM) Single Layer Roof Membranes
23-13 41 17	Roof Vents
23-27 17 00	Pumps
23-27 17 11	Axial Split Pumps
23-27 17 13	Centrifugal Pumps
23-27 17 15	Diaphragm Pumps
23-27 21 00	Compressors
23-27 21 11	Axial Flow Compressors
23-27 21 13	Centrifugal Compressors
23-27 29 21 11	Aboveground Tank Containments
23-29 25 13	Fire Hydrants
23-29 25 13 11	Dry Barrel Fire Hydrants
23-29 25 13 13	Wet Barrel Fire Hydrants
23-33 25 00	Air Handling Units
23-33 25 11	Built Up Air Handling Units

OmniClass is a product of Construction Specifications Institute

OmniClass™ is, in simple terms, a standard for organizing all construction information. The concept for OmniClass is derived from internationally-accepted standards that have been developed by the International Organization for Standardization (ISO) and the International Construction Information Society (ICIS) subcommittees and workgroups from the early-1990s to the present.

In addition to the application of ISO 12006-2 in UniClass™, the object-oriented framework standardized by ISO/PAS 12006-3 has been adopted by ICIS members in their Lexicon program, and both standards are followed by groups in several other countries that are developing similar classification standards, including Norway, Netherlands, UK, and others, in concert with the Nordic chapter of the International Alliance for Interoperability (IAI), and the Japan Construction Information Center (JACIC), which is currently working to develop the Japanese Construction Classification System (JCCS), modeled in part on OmniClass™ (OmniClass, CSI/CSC website, www.omniclass.org/).

OmniClass™ is an open standard that is developed by consensus and with the participation of many organizations, firms, industry experts, and agencies from the United States and Canada. Because it is an open standard, if there is code missing for an item that an organization needs to identify or track, they can submit the recommendation to the OmniClass™ Development Committee for the next draft.

Now that we have established that OmniClass™ is an open object-oriented standard, it is important to determine the level of adoption of the standard in the industry. In the United States, OmniClass™ is the backbone standard for the National Building Information Modeling Standard™ (NBIMS), which is a standard under the buildingSMART alliance™. The standard is also a prevalent standard that can be used in Construction Operations Building Information Exchange™ (COBie), which is a standard for NBIMS and the Whole Building Design Guide under the National Institute of Building Sciences (NIBS). Building Information Modeling is a standard that has become very popular in the design and construction of facilities. OmniClass™ is also a combination, or unification, of multiple different standards used in the construction and costing industry: specifically MasterFormat® (Table 22 - Work Results) and UniFormat™ (Table 21 - Elements). UNIFORMAT II is based on UniFormat™.

A recent development related to OmniClass™ Table 23 - Products as a byproduct of the IFACT project was the development of a Reference Object Based Codes and Abbreviations Database (ROBCAD) (Table 4.8). ROBCAD is a reference table that cross-references National CAD Standard (NCS) and American Society of Mechanical Engineers (ASME) abbreviations and UNSPSC codes to the codes for OmniClass™ Table 23.

What this means to facility managers, and others who are identifying equipment, is that they can classify and identify their equipment using a consistent method.

For example, suppose you are inventorying a facility and have to capture a ball valve with a sequence number of 001. You identify the valve using the OmniClass™ products table as "Ball Valve: 23-27 31 13" and then cross-reference the abbreviation so as to label the valve BV-001.

Let's discuss another aspect of OmniClass™ as a suite of industry standard tables (Figure 4.2). Because the standard is a multifaceted suite of standards, the tables can be used to standardize a wide range of equipment data and still be compatible with each other. Figure 4.3 shows a graphical representation of some of the influences and uses of OmniClass™. The tables can be used for cost estimating, construction, architects, data formatting, and applications, and it is supported by multiple organizations that support industry

TABLE 4.8 OmniClass™ ROBCAD Example

NCS/ASME	OmniClass Number	Singular Name
RR	23-13 39 31 19	Roll Roof
RV	23-13 41 17 11	Roof Relief Vent
RV	23-13 41 17 13	Roof Ridge Vent
OVEN	23-21 21 13 31 19	Commercial Pastry Oven
OVEN	23-21 21 13 31 21	Commercial Pizza Oven
CBA	23-25 47 13 21 15	Blood Bank Analyzer
BGASA	23-25 47 13 21 17	Blood Gas Analyzer
COMPR	23-27 21 11	Axial Flow Compressor
COMPR	23-27 21 13	Centrifugal Compressor
BFV	23-27 31 17	Butterfly Valve
FLTV	23-27 31 23	Float Valve
GTV	23-27 31 25	Gate Valve
FPCONT	23-29 31 33	Fire Pump Controller
FPCONT	23-29 31 35	Jockey Pump Controller

OmniClass™ and ROBCAD are products of Construction Specifications Institute/Construction Specifications Canada.

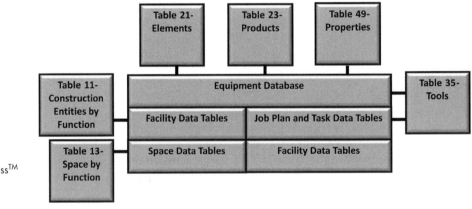

FIGURE 4.2 OmniClass™ Uses in Equipment Databases

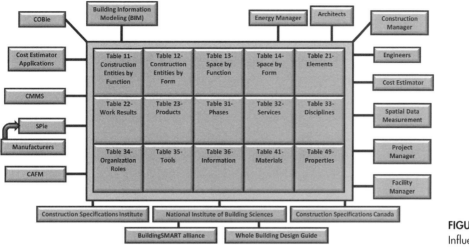

FIGURE 4.3 OmniClass Influences

standards and practices. As shown, there are numerous disciplines that use OmniClass™, and it is becoming more and more prevalent in the industry.

The conclusion is that OmniClass™ is an object-oriented, open, and commonly used standard that is used by multiple industries, especially the construction industry, and therefore it is the ideal standard for use by facility management for equipment inventories.

Other Industry Standards
Building Information Modeling (BIM)

Building Information Modeling is the process of designing a building collaboratively using one coherent system that has the capability of containing all disciplines in three-dimensional computer models, rather than as separate sets of drawings. The ability to design and construct a facility provides enormous gains in savings of cost and time, much greater accuracy in estimation, the avoidance of errors, and minimizing alterations and rework. While BIM software packages use databases, they use other standards to provide the consistency of information in the database for the identification of objects within the model. Another way to state this is that BIM provides for the graphical placement, dimensions, and location of a fan coil unit in a facility, but it does not provide an industry standard method for classifying data uniformly as to information such as the make, model, and serial number of that fan coil. OmniClass™ is the backbone standard for BIM recommended by the National Institute of Building Sciences (NIBS).

At the time of writing this book, there is a big discussion on how much information needs to be placed in the model. Building information models can get very large very quickly, with all of the layers and richness of information (terabytes).

There are typically multiple models and layers per each facility. The models are sometimes so packed with information that they are hard to open and view, even with today's technology. This problem will be solved in the future as technology advances. The real question, at this time, is does the equipment data have to be in the visual model? Besides BIM, equipment databases also have to be connected to CMMS, portfolio, financial, and capital investment software programs. Equipment information is one of the largest categories of information that has recently been added to the model to try to benefit facility management and owners.

The reality is that the vast majority of equipment information does not need to be in the actual model. The information can instead be linked to the model (Table 4.9). The model only needs to contain the minimal amount of information needed for users to positively identify the equipment within the model: equipment type, equipment acronym, and sequence number. The rest of the information is linked, using the BIM GUID for that graphical representation of the equipment in the model, to the equipment GUID in a properly formatted equipment database. The model can then access the information from the equipment database when needed. There is no reason to load the immense amount of equipment data into a model. In essence, a single BIM object would be linked to its entire facility equipment record.

Construction Operations Building Information Exchange (COBie)

Construction Operations Building Information Exchange (COBie) is a standard developed to capture and transfer design and construction submittals and handovers to facility management and operations in a digital format. The basic concept is that, instead of a truckload of paper being dropped off at a facility after construction, COBie would provide the format to digitize and catalog the data into a universal format that can be used to transfer the data electronically.

TABLE 4.9 BIM and Equipment GUID

Building Information Model			
BIM_GUID	**Acronym**	**Sequence Number**	
Yfe78…	P	189:AB	
Yfw8E…	GTV	14473	
Equipment Database			
BIM_GUID	**Equipment_GUID**	**Industry_Code_Description**	**Equipment_ID_Composite**
Yfe78…	o8ash05Rv…	Centrifugal Pump	ABC0000-P-189:AB
Yfw8E…	st7mnWq70…	Gate Valve	ABC0000-GTV-14473

For example: A BIM model would download the data into the COBie format, and then a computerized maintenance management system (CMMS) would download the COBie formatted data directly into its database. COBie provides a bidirectional transfer of data to and from the BIM and the CMMS. COBie provides the data format, but the default standard used to classify the data is OmniClass. COBie is one of the standards I recommend cross-referencing the equipment data fields with (see Chapter 5). COBie challenges and pilots can be found on the NIBS BuildingSMART alliance website: www.buildingsmart-alliance.org/index.php/newsevents/proceedings/cobiechallenge/.

Specifiers' Properties Information Exchange (SPIE)

Specifiers' Properties Information Exchange (SPIE) is an effort by the buildingSMART alliance to create a set of product templates that provides a universal format for manufacturers' data. Once manufactures' product data have been put into this universal format, it can be downloaded seamlessly into a building information model, COBie, or an equipment database, without data loss. Basically, the equipment cut sheets and specifications could be downloaded digitally into your database without personnel having to manually enter that information. SPIE is in its infant stages at this time, but has a huge potential to reduce data loss and save the industry significant resources. SPIE uses OmniClass™, MasterFormat® (OmniClass Table 22), and UniFormat™ (OmniClass Table 21) to sort and classify the product templates.

RESOURCES

ASTM E1557-09: Standard Classification for Building Elements and Related Sitework-UNIFORMAT II, "Scope," American Society for Testing and Materials, www.astm.org/Standards/E1557.htm.

National Institute of Building Sciences: www.nibs.org/.

Specifiers' Properties Information Exchange: www.buildingsmartalliance .org/index.php/projects/activeprojects/32.

Construction Operations Building Information Exchange: www.wbdg .org/resources/cobie.php.

Whole Building Design Guide: www.wbdg.org/.

Construction Specifications Institute: www.csinet.org/.

Construction Specifications Canada: www.csc-dcc.ca/.

OmniClass™: www.omniclass.org.

MasterFormat®: www.masterformat.com.

UniFormat™: www.csinet.org/uniformat.

CHAPTER 5

Equipment Data Points

One of the most important activities to accomplish when developing an equipment inventory is to determine exactly what information (data) about the equipment your organization needs. Developing this information is usually an ongoing evolutionary process. Every time new information is required, personnel have to be sent out to capture the data or modify an existing contract. Therefore, it is very important to determine up front the information and format needed by your organization. The formatting of the data, while a tedious process, is very important to ensuring that all the data are formatted the same way and accessible across the portfolio of your corporation.

This section deals with a significant number of the equipment data points that should be included in an equipment inventory system. These data points can be used to evaluate computerized management maintenance systems, capital portfolio systems, and equipment inventory collection programs, and as an attachment to contracts for data needed. There are obviously numerous other data points that a facility manager needs that are not related to equipment, for example, room square footage and wall height. Because this guide is focused on equipment, these other data points will not be covered in

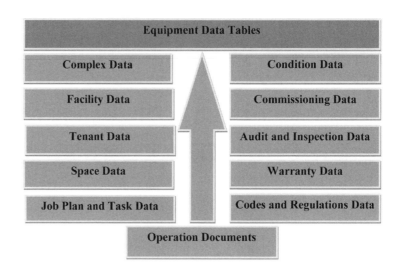

FIGURE 5.1 Equipment
Inventory Tables

this guide. Related data should then be combined into defined table sets and parsed (Figure 5.1)

It is important for an organization to understand how it plans to label equipment and the resulting format for that data. In Chapter 6, "Equipment Identification and Tags," I cover equipment identification recommendations. I based some of the following data points on my recommended format.

Because data format is critical to the success of any equipment inventory or database program, I always try to recommend using industry standards whenever possible. At the time of this writing; the vast majority of the data points I propose are still in the process of being included in industry standards. I recommend that, whenever possible, data points from multiple systems should be unified under a single industry standard to reduce integration errors in database systems (see Chapter 4, "Industry Standards").

UNIQUE IDENTIFIERS

A discussion of global unique identifications, unique identifications, and primary database keys is needed prior to continuing. Identifiers are used to uniquely identify a set of data within a database. Basically, the data are pinned to this single unique identifier, allowing the database to know what information belongs together (Figure 5.2). Universally unique identifiers (UUIDs) are normally computer-generated identifiers and are so complex that the odds of replication of the same unique identifier for two pieces of data would be approximately 1 in 14 trillion. Hence, they are universally unique. Globally unique identifier (GUID) is Microsoft's implementation of UUIDs. For this guide, the text will refer to UUIDs as GUIDs only, so that users do not confuse UUIDs with UIDs discussed shortly. A date-and-time-based hexadecimal GUID has a statistically lower chance of replication; this would not occur until sometime in the later decades of 3000 AD. A GUID is not normally humanly understandable: for example, AfYh01DE817JmW01. A unique identification (UID) is an identifier that is unique to an organization, corporation, or the like. There is a statistically better chance of replication when using a unique identifier because they are normally human developed and assigned. Creating database identifiers that includes an equipment acronym and generated asset number starting at 0000001, is an example of a UID. For example, the first air handler would be identified as AHU-0000001 and the second as AHU-0000002 in the database. So imagine that you have multiple facilities in your portfolio, and each facility started using UIDs starting at 0000001. When you try to combine the data from all of the facilities into a single database for better efficiency, the result is that there will be a large number of duplicate UIDs (AHU-0000001s), which will cause conflicts in your database. Some organizations will add building numbers, room numbers, or wing designations to their UID to try to make them universally unique. This in itself is a bad practice and will cause errors. The equipment is restricted by the information included in its UID. For example, when equipment is moved from one building, room, or wing to the next building, room, or wing, the equipment will have to have a new identifier assigned to it. Reassigning identifiers is a complex and time-consuming process that ultimately will lead to data loss. When you change the UID of a data set in a database, all of the tables and data linked to that data set have to be changed also. An organization should avoid developing its own unique database identification system.

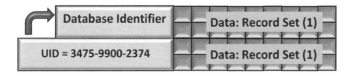

FIGURE 5.2 GUID and UID Examples

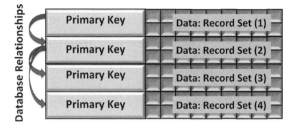

FIGURE 5.3 Primary Key Examples

"Primary key" is a computer database term that denotes the unique database field that all other data for a specific record or table within that database is attached to (Figure 5.3). One table in a database is connected or linked to another table in a database using these primary keys. Primary keys are required to be unique for each record and table within that database. A primary key can be a UID or GUID.

Because the primary keys and unique identifiers can be hidden in the database and therefore would not be seen by the end users, there really is no reason to make them recognizable by using a human understandable UID (Table 5.1). There is significant confusion on this part by facility managers. Facility managers believe that the data set has to have a special name so they know what that data set is; AHU-001. Realistically, the data AHU (equipment acronym) and 001 (equipment sequence number) should be stored in the database as separate data elements. The database program will still display the information AHU-001 to the facility manager (Table 5.2). How that data record is pinned (primary key) in the database should not be a concern for facility management's use or identification of the data—with the exception that using a GUID is better than a UID.

TABLE 5.1 Unique Identification and Primary Key Example Data Set

Equipment Database							
Type	Primary Key	Facility Number	Equipment Acronym	Equipment Sequence	Equipment Priority	Floor	Room Number
GUID	AfYh01DE817JmW01	ABC0000	AHU	1	2	8	8140
UID	AHU-0000002-UID	ABC0000	AHU	2	3	7	7120

TABLE 5.2 User Displayed Data

Facility Number	Equipment Acronym	Equipment Sequence	Equipment Priority	Floor	Room Number
ABC0000	AHU	1	2	8	8140
ABC0000	AHU	2	3	7	7120

The following is a list of all the data fields discussed in this section:

Equipment Data Fields

Equipment Zone GUID

Equipment Zone Description

Equipment GUID

Industry Code Description

Industry Code Number

Equipment Operation
Description

Equipment Acronym

Equipment Sequence
Number

Equipment Identification
Composite

Equipment Space

Equipment Plot Point (N)

Plot Point X

Plot Point Y

Plot Point Z

Equipment Location
Description

Previous Equipment
Identification

Previous Equipment GUID

Equipment Organization
Asset Number

Equipment Power Supply

Equipment System
Description

Equipment System Code

Equipment Assembly

Equipment Control

Equipment Alarm

Equipment Indication

Equipment Failure Impact

Equipment Space
Relationship

Equipment Priority

Equipment Continued
Operation

Equipment Owner

Equipment Curtailment

Equipment Operation
Schedule

Equipment Normal
Operations Status

Equipment After-Hours
Operations Status

Equipment Status

Equipment Failure Status

Equipment Tag Condition

Equipment Security Level

Equipment Manufacturer

Equipment Model Name

Equipment Model Number

Equipment Serial Number

Equipment Manufactured
Date

Equipment Manufacturer
Shelf Life

Equipment Installed Date

Equipment Life Expectancy

Equipment Age

Equipment Operation Age

Equipment Purchased Con-
dition

Equipment Installation Cost

Equipment Specification
Purpose

Equipment Specification
Unit

Equipment Specification
Value

Complex Data Fields

Complex GUID

Complex Number

Complex Name

Site Plot Point (N)

Plot Point X

Plot Point Y

Plot Point Z

Complex Address

Facility Data Fields

Facility GUID

Facility Number

Facility Name

Facility Alias Name

Facility Owner

Facility Designation

Facility Design Function

Facility Design Code

Facility Use Function

Facility Use Code

Facility Plot Point (N)

Plot Point X

Plot Point Y

Plot Point Z

Facility Organization
Location Code

Facility Address

Facility Priority

Space Data Fields

Architectural Zone GUID

Architectural Zone
    Description

Space GUID

Floor Number

Blueprint Room Number

Organization Room Number

Space Design Function

Space Design Code

Space Use Function

Space Use Code

Space Description

Space Identification
    Composite

Space Priority

Tenant Data Fields

Tenant GUID

Tenant Name

Tenant Organization Name

Tenant Department Name

Tenant Code

**Job Plan and Task Data
Fields**

Job Plan GUID

Job Plan Identification

Job Plan Title

Job Plan Description

Job Plan Type

Job Plan Tool

Job Plan Tool Code

Job Plan Document

Job Task GUID

Job Task Sequence Number

Job Task Identification
    Composite

Job Task Status

Job Task Status Related
    Cause

Job Task Performer

Job Task Frequency

Job Task Frequency Units

Job Task Inspection
    Percentage

Job Task Season

Job Task Start Date

Job Task Time Standard

Job Task Time Standard
    Units

Job Task Tool

Job Task Tool Code

Condition Data Fields

Condition Assessment
    GUID

Condition Assessment
    Short Description

Condition Assessment
    Provider

Condition Assessment Date

Condition Assessment
    Document

Condition Equipment
    GUID

Equipment Condition

Equipment Condition
    Related Cause

Equipment Life Used

Equipment Life Remaining

Condition Observation

Condition Recommendation
    Type

Condition Recommendation

Commissioning Data Fields

Commissioning GUID

Commissioning Short
    Description

Commission Provider

Commission Date

Commissioning Document

Commissioning Equipment
    GUID

Commission Observation

Commission
    Recommendation

Commissioning Set Point
    Position

Commissioning Set Point
    Unit

Commissioning Set Point
    Value

Commissioning Set Point
    Comment

**Audit and Inspection Data
Fields**

Audit GUID

Audit Type

Audit Provider

Audit Date

Audit Short Description

Audit Document

Audit Equipment GUID

Equipment Compliance

Compliance Regulations

Audit Observation

Audit Recommendation

Audit Resolution

Audit Resolution Date

Warranty Data Fields

Warranty GUID

Warranty Short Description

Warranty Number

Warranty Provider Name

Warranty Provider Contact
Information

Warranty Installer Name

Warranty Installer Contact
Information

Warranty Start Date

Warranty End Date

Extended Warranty Available

Extended Warranty Number

Extended Warranty
Provider Name

Extended Warranty Provider
Contact Information

Extended Warranty Start
Date

Extended Warranty End
Date

Substantial Completion Date

Warranty Document

Extended Warranty
Document

**Code and Regulations Data
Fields**

Code GUID

Code Type

Code Source

Code Title

Code Designation

Code Comments

Code Enforcement

Code Document

**Operations Documents
Data Fields**

Operation Document
GUID

Operation Document
Type

Operation Document Short
Description

Operation Document

Operation Video

EQUIPMENT DATA POINT DISCUSSIONS

In the following section, I will discuss each of the different data points from
the previous list. I tried to logically group each set of data into its own related
data tables. The purpose of grouping the data was to reduce the amount of
data replication within any equipment database system. For example, the name
of the facility should only have to be entered once into the database and then
it can be associated with all of its related equipment. Otherwise, a person
would have to enter the facility name every time he or she entered a new piece
of equipment, which in turn would substantially increase the size of the database itself. Another reason to separate the data into their own separate tables
is for modularity and parsing of the data. For example, facility information
such as building number, city, and state should be in a table separate from the
one for equipment data within the same relational database. All of the equipment in that building has the same facility information. The advantage is that
if I change the facility data, I do not have to go into the database and change
every equipment record to reflect that change. I can globally apply the change

to all of the equipment within that facility. Each logical grouping of data requires its own database unique identifier. The unique identifier fields, GUID, are there to remind the facility manager that they need a placeholder in their database to pin that data. Because unique identifiers were discussed already, I will not go in detail for each GUID data point listed in this section.

It is highly recommended that Attachment 1: Equipment Data Usage and Cross Reference Worksheet is used during the review of the following data points.

Each recommended data point also has a suggested data field name provided in brackets: for example, Equipment GUID and its data field name [Equipment_GUID]. The data field names provided are only suggestions for use by organizations preparing databases from scratch or that need to fill in gaps in their current system. There are numerous industry codes being developed and each has its own way of developing and assigning data field names. Because most industry standards at the time of this writing do not include all of the data fields needed for equipment inventory, there needs to be a way to capture the data in a uniform format. Once you capture the information in a uniform format, that information can then be cross-referenced or mapped to any needed industry standard format (Table 5.3).

The hope is that in the future all of the database field names for all data points can be developed into a universal standard. This book would then be revised to replace the recommended database field names with industry standard database field names. Until then a cross map, as shown in Table 5.3, can be developed.

TABLE 5.3　Equipment Data Fields (Book) to Industry Standard Data Field Cross Map

Equipment Data Fields (Book)	Industry Standard Data Fields
Equipment_GUID	ComponentID
Industry_Code_Number	ComponentCode
Industry_Code_Description	ComponentDescrip(1)
Equipment_Operation_Description	ComponentDescrip(2)
Equipment_Acronym	ComponentAbbrev
Equipment_Sequence	ComponentSeq
Equipment_ID_Composite	ComponentLabel
Space_GUID	SpaceID
Architectural_Zone_GUID	ZoneID
Floor_Number	FloorNumber
Blueprint_Room_Number	RoomNumber(1)
Prg_Room_Number	RoomNumber(2)

EQUIPMENT DATA TABLE FIELDS

The equipment data field table represents the equipment information that is important to the operation of a facility. This table is the main data table that the other data tables would be associated with in the relational database. The data points developed for this guide are considered a work in progress, and while extensive, it is understood that they are not all inclusive and future development is expected and welcome. It should be noted that an organization does not have to implement all of these data points to have an effective equipment inventory system. The implementation should be a stepped approach based on what is most productive for a specific organization, with the realization that, as computer programs and systems improve, organizations will be able to expand their level of equipment information. Owners and organizations should expect a lot of this information to come from design and construction for new or renovated facilities. The most important point is for owners and organizations to know what information they need and in what format they want that information. Figure 5.4 shows the equipment data set and the related reference tables recommended in this guide.

Equipment Zones

Equipment zones are the designated mechanical, electrical, plumbing (MEP), or equipment areas within a facility that serve a specific operational purpose

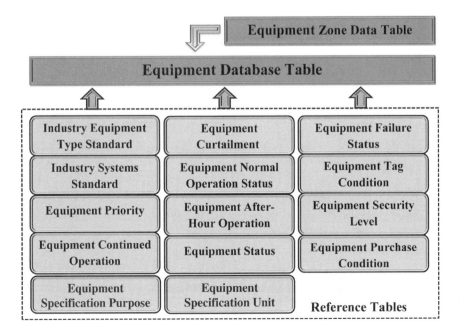

FIGURE 5.4 Equipment Data Tables

based on the building's design. Equipment zones would be the heating zones, cooling zones, and the like that are based on the orientation and design of the facility. It should be noted that zones are not to be confused with systems. Zones are a set or group of equipment and/or systems that is designed to meet a specific operational requirement in the design of a building. Systems are a group of equipment designed to perform a specific function in the facility. For example, fire safety systems are designed to protect the building from a fire and mitigate damage. ZONE A HVAC is a group of equipment designed to heat or cool a specific section of a building within predetermined design parameters. ZONE A HVAC could include the heating and ventilation system, steam distribution system, and building exhaust system. Equipment system grouping is covered later on in the chapter.

A distinction must be made between equipment zones and architectural zones. Equipment zones are groups of equipment that perform a specific operational function designed into a building. An architectural zone consists of spaces that are grouped together in a specific manner to create an architectural structure within a facility. For example, an architectural zone would be the logical grouping of all the spaces that are contained within a wing of a hospital. The hospital wing would be an architectural zone. Architectural zones are defined in the spaces data table section. It is conceivable that there could be multiple heating and cooling equipment zones within a single architectural zone.

The equipment zone data are developed as a separate table, not included in the equipment data table, because an equipment zone can contain multiple pieces of equipment. Therefore, instead of replicating the zone data in each equipment data record, the zone data are set up in their own data table.

Equipment Zone GUID

[EQUIPMENT_ZONE_GUID]

The equipment zone GUID is a defined space in the database for the unique identifier attached to all related equipment zone data (Table 5.4).

TABLE 5.4   Equipment Zone GUID Example

Equipment Zone GUID	Equipment Zone Description
Ty3bX0871...	Zone A Heating and Ventilation
7K9eFwk10...	Sector 5 Exhaust Zone
19tE088P3...	E Ring Slice 2 120 VAC Electrical Distribution
9AYg3e704...	Train A

Equipment Zone Description

[EQUIPMENT_ZONE_DESCRIPTION]

The equipment zone description is the designated place for personnel to input the description of the zone. It is important to have predefined nomenclature for each of the zones because in a database "Zone A HVAC" is seen differently from "ZONE A Heating and Ventilation." A computer does not know that the two zone descriptions refer to the same type of equipment, and therefore any data mining done could be skewed because of the inconsistent usage. If the facility staff performs a data search for all "ZONE A HVAC" equipment, the results will not include the equipment related to the "ZONE A Heating and Ventilation." Therefore, it is important to review the descriptions and ensure all descriptions are spelled and annotated correctly and that there is only one entry for each zone (Table 5.5).

TABLE 5.5 Equipment Zone Description Data Example

Equipment Zone GUID	Equipment Zone Description
Ty3bX0871...	Zone A Heating and Ventilation
7K9eFwk10...	Sector 5 Exhaust Zone
19tE088P3...	E Ring Slice 2 120 VAC Electrical Distribution
9AYg3e704...	Train A

Equipment GUID

[EQUIPMENT_GUID]

The equipment GUID is a defined space in the database for the unique identifier used to link all related equipment data (Table 5.6).

TABLE 5.6 Equipment GUID Data Examples

Equipment_GUID	Industry_Code_Number	Industry_Code_Description	Equipment_Operation_Description
o8ash05Rv...	23-27 17 13	Centrifugal Pump	Supply to Cooling Tower CT-03
A8FDy9w54...	23-33 25 11 11	Built Up Indoor Air Handling Unit	Supplies Rooms 3310, 3120, 3130
fw565r713...	23-35 15 11 13 13	Single Speed Three Phase AC Motor	
qrv35t47j...	23-27 29 19 11 15	Multiple Walled Vented Tank	Fuel Oil
st7mnWq70...	23-27 31 25	Gate Valve	Fuel Oil Tank TNK-02 Isolation
Giqre9732...	23-35 13 17 15 11	Power Dry Step Down Transformer	Supplies Power to EPB-LP17

Industry Code Description

[INDUSTRY_CODE_DESCRIPTION]

As previously mentioned, it is very important to use industry standards whenever possible. One of the first things that have to be accomplished when taking an equipment inventory is to identify the type or classification of each piece of equipment as it is entered into the database. The most effective means to identify a class or type of equipment is to use an industry standard so that the architect, engineer, budget analyst, and facility manager can ensure they are all talking about the same type of equipment. Most industry standards related to the product types of equipment are broken up into two data fields; Coded Number and Product Description. Per Chapter 4.0 the recommended industry standard for equipment types is OmniClass™ Table-23 Products.

The Industry Code Description data field captures the product type description that is related to the Industry Code Number (Table 5.7). Using industry codes and descriptions is important because this normalizes the data across your database and aligns the data with that used elsewhere in the industry. It also ensures that your data tables are correctly formatted and the same information is used across your organization. Allowing personnel to manually enter the descriptions, instead of selecting from a reference table, can cause significant problems when your organization tries to mine the data (Table 5.8). A database sees "centrifugal pump" differently from "pump" or "centrif-pump." Manual entry of data can result in spelling errors, format errors, and even database problems if special characters such as @, *, - are utilized. Imagine trying to get useful data out of a non-normalized database and then having to make executive and strategic decisions. The product titles used in the example tables of this chapter, such as "Boiler",are from the ROBCAD table. The ROBCAD table removes the plural from the titles of the productslisted in OmniClass™ Table 23. ROBCAD, discussed in chapter 4, is the cross-reference of OmniClass™ Table 23 products to NCS/ASME acronyms. The plurals were removed toallow facility managers to singularly identify equipment such asa"pump" instead of OmniClass™ Table 23 "pumps."

TABLE 5.7   Industry Code Cross-Reference to Equipment Database Data Example

Equipment_GUID	Industry_Code	Industry_Code_Description	Equipment_Acronym
o8ash05Rv…	23-27 17 13	Centrifugal Pump	P
fw565r713…	23-35 15 11 13 13	Single Speed Three Phase AC Motor	MOT
qrv35t47j…	23-27 29 19 11 15	Multiple Walled Vented Tank	TNK
st7mnWq70…	23-27 31 25	Gate Valve	GTV
k3Het683q…	23-27 29 19 13 15	Single Walled Vented Tank	TNK
T3hg26J3Y…	23-21 45 11 11 11	Fine Art Painting	FAPTG
Fe09Tw56s…	23-29 25 19 11	Stored Pressure Fire Extinguisher	FE

OmniClass™ Table 23 - ROBCAD		
NCS/ASME	OmniClass™ Number	OmniClass™ Title
P	23-27 17 13	Centrifugal Pump
TNK	23-27 29 19 11	Multiple Wall Tank
GTV	23-27 31 25	Gate Valve

TABLE 5.8 Industry Code Example

OmniClass™ Table 23 (ROBCAD)		
NCS/ASME	OmniClass™ Number	OmniClass™ Title
P	23-27 17 11	Axial Split Pump
P	23-27 17 13	Centrifugal Pump
TNK	23-27 29 19	Tank
TNK	23-27 29 19 11	Multiple Wall Tank
TNK	23-27 29 19 13	Single Walled Tank
V	23-27 31 00	Valve
BFP	23-27 31 11	Backflow Preventer
BV	23-27 31 15	Ball Valve
FLTV	23-27 31 23	Float Valve
GTV	23-27 31 25	Gate Valve
GLV	23-27 31 27	Globe Valve
HYD	23-29 25 13 13	Wet Barrel Fire Hydrant
CH	23-33 21 13 19 11	Packaged Rotary Screw Chiller
AHU	23-33 25 17	Modular Air Handling Unit
AHU	23-33 25 17 13	Modular Rooftop Air Handling Unit
XFMR	23-35 13 15 15	Electrical Network Step Up Transformer

OmniClass™ Table 23 and ROBCAD are products of Construction Specification Institute/Construction Specification Canada

Industry Code Number

[INDUSTRY_CODE_NUMBER]

The industry code number data field is used to capture the industry digital code that is related to the product type description (Table 5.7). It is important to be able to cross-reference the industry codes used to define equipment type to allow the organization to cross-reference their equipment across their portfolio and the industry. This ensures that the correct information is captured and, ultimately, can be used for statistics and comparisons. For example: An architect enters in his design that he or she installed a centrifugal pump, with an industry code of "23-27 17 13." The construction manager can then verify that the correct type of equipment was installed, and when construction is complete the code can be used to download the data into the correct area of a database for facility management to use. The organization could then use the code to see specifically how many centrifugal pumps are installed across their portfolio.

OmniClass™ is the recommended industry standard to use to properly identify the type of equipment (See Chapter 4, "Industry Standards").

Equipment Operation Description

[EQUIPMENT_OPERATION_DESCRIPTION]

The purpose of the equipment operation description field is to allow design and construction personnel, engineers, or the facility management team to manually add additional text to the equipment that further identifies the function or purpose of equipment that was installed in the facility (Table 5.9). A facility could literally have hundreds, if not thousands, of ball valves installed in a single facility. The ability to differentiate the purpose of each of those valves is very important to the operation of any facility—for example, Fuel Oil Tank T-02 Isolation Ball Valve. In the example, the "Ball Valve" comes from the industry code product type and the "Fuel Oil Tank T-02 Isolation" would be the additional added text in the equipment operation description data field (Table 5.10).

TABLE 5.9   Equipment Operation Description Data Example

Industry_Code_Number	Industry_Code_Description	Equipment_Operation_Description	Equipment_Acronym
23-27 17 13	Centrifugal Pump	Supply to Cooling Tower CT-03	P
23-33 25 11 11	Built-Up Indoor Air-Handling Unit	Supplies Rooms 3310, 3120, 3130	AHU
23-27 31 25	Gate Valve	Fuel Oil Tank TNK-02 Isolation	GTV
23-35 13 17 15 11	Power-Dry Step-Down Transformer	Supplies Power to EPB-LP17	XFMR
23-35 29 17	Molded-Case Circuit Breaker	Feed from XFMR-022	CB
23-27 11 21 13	Level Control Module	Fuel Oil DayTank TNK-01	LCM
23-27 11 11 19	Temperature Indicator	Security Control Room 191	TI

TABLE 5.10   Equipment Operation Description Examples

Equipment Operational Description	Industry Code Description
Main Gas Line Isolation	Ball Valve
Reactor Coolant Pump-01 Isolation	Ball Valve
Boiler BLR-05B Draft	Centrifugal Fan
The Kiss	Fine Art Sculpture
Lighting Room 4120, 4132, 4144	Circuit Breaker
Main Entrance	Glass Revolving Door
Blood Analysis	Centrifuge

It is important to note that the industry code description and equipment operation description be two different data fields for a specific reason. It is not uncommon for a piece of equipment, such as a motor, to be replaced in a system. The equipment would then be sent out for repairs or to be rebuilt and then sit on a shelf to be used in another system. The product type of the motor never changes, but the equipment operation description could. The equipment operation description should be kept as concise as possible.

Equipment Acronym

[EQUIPMENT_ACRONYM]

Acronyms have been used to identify and label equipment ever since human beings started constructing buildings. Acronyms became prevalent when a shorthand identification system was needed to annotate equipment when drawing blueprints. For example: AHU on a blueprint stands for "air handling unit." The equipment acronym field is used to capture that abbreviation (See Table 5.9). Acronyms are commonly used for equipment identification in the field and are shorthand for the equipment type (AHU-001). Some organizations use preventive maintenance guide cards, self-made acronym lists, or industry standards. (See the discussion in Chapter 3, "Equipment Inventory Types and Systems.") It is recommended that you use industry standards such as the National CAD Standards™ (NCS) and/or the American Society of Mechanical Engineers (ASME) list of approved abbreviations (see Chapter 4, "Industry Standards"). The Construction Specification Institute (CSI) has a table (ROBCAD) that already cross-references NCS/ASME acronyms to OmniClass™ Table 23 Products. The purpose of using an industry standard is to ensure that the acronyms used by facility management and owners are the same acronyms you would typically find on your blueprints and documents. When using a self-generated list of acronyms, you introduce human error into system. The deviation from industry standards creates significant costs for any organization because you have to train personnel on your system, you have to cross-reference the organization's unique system to industry standards, and you have to pay for upkeep on the system. If BR2 were used to identify all of the boilers in your organization, you would need to train people that BR2 is a boiler, your blueprints would need to be converted, and the data from the architects for new construction could not easily be cross-referenced to your database. Using proprietary self-generated identification systems is a waste of resources.

Equipment Sequence Number

[EQUIPMENT_SEQUENCE]

The equipment sequence number is the sequential number assigned to the equipment according to the design and construction of a facility (Table 5.11). Because there are multiple instances of the same type of equipment, such as multiple ball valves, within a facility, it is necessary to sequentially number the equipment. For example, in VLV-001 the 001 indicates that the valve has been labeled with the sequential number 001 and that other valves exist within a facility. Because there are a wide variety of ways in which to number something—001, 21A, 6AB, SR51—it is important to predefine a convention that is used on all of your equipment, especially for new construction. During design and construction, the equipment sequence number, in the United States, is normally based on the rules defined by the National CAD Standards (NCS). The sequential number is normally assigned during design and construction, and this is the best time to capture this information. For existing buildings, the number entered into the database should be the same as the one listed on blueprints and other construction documentation. Ad hoc self-numbering should be avoided. If an organization has multiple segmented sequence numbers, for example 7-A-8, you should develop a convention for handling the segments.

(continued)

[EQUIPMENT_SEQUENCE] (*continued*)

A good recommendation is to use a colon for separating the segments. The reason for using a colon is that the common convention in the industry of using dashes to separate the different segments of information in equipment identifiers (for example, AHU-7-A-8-ABC0000) makes it harder for human beings and computers to determine when one data field stops and another one starts. Is the 7-A-8 one piece of information or multiple different pieces of information? Is 7 the floor number or the sequence number? A dash is also commonly used between segments as a normal method for separating data fields in a database. If you use a colon in the preceding example, it becomes AHU-7:A:8-ABC0000. A computer and human operator can now easily define that AHU is the acronym, 7:A:8 is the equipment sequence number, and ABC0000 is the facility number. Note that not using a colon makes the equipment sequence number 7A8, which can be construed as 7A-8 or 7-A-8 or 7-A8.

TABLE 5.11   Equipment Sequence Number Data Example

Industry_Code_Description	Equipment_Acronym	Equipment_Sequence	Equipment_ID_Composite
Centrifugal Pump	P	189:AB	ABC0000-P-189:AB
Built-Up Indoor Air-Handling Unit	AHU	050	ABC0000-AHU-050
Single-Speed Three-Phase AC Motor	MOT	978	ABC0000-MOT-978
Multiple-Walled Vented Tank	TNK	02	ABC0000-TNK-02
Gate Valve	GTV	14473	ABC0000-GTV-14473
Power-Dry Step-Down Transformer	XFMR	022	ABC0000-MCC-8A-XFMR-022

In Table 5.11, the equipment sequence number for ABC0000-P-189:AB shows a proper use of colons in the equipment sequence of 189:AB. When the equipment identification label of ABC0000-P-189:AB is then used, facility management is able to properly identify what the different portions of the identification stand for.

Equipment Identification Composite

[EQUIPMENT_ID_COMPOSITE]

It is very important to the personnel operating a building that their equipment be labeled in the fields (See Chapter 6, "Equipment Identification and Tags," and Table 5.12). You cannot turn on chiller number one if you do not know which of the six chillers in your facility is number one. If the equipment information has been properly segmented into its related data fields, based on the concepts in this book, it will be easier for an organization to combine these different fields to make their equipment tags (see Chapter 6, "Equipment Identification and Tags"). The equipment identification composite field is used to capture the combination of the desired data fields and place the resulting information into an easy-to-use single data field (Table 5.13). For example, Facility Number + Equipment Acronym + Equipment Sequence Number would result in ABC0000-AHU-001, which equates to air handling unit number 001 in building numbered ABC0000. Technically, the displayed information, ABC0000-AHU-001, could be produced by programming software to only show these fields to the user without having to add an extra data field to the database for an equipment identification composite. The advantages of having this extra data field are ease of sorting and exporting database information and easy exporting of the equipment identification number for labeling equipment by the end users. Making it easier for staff to perform sorts and exports reduces their costs and training requirements. It is important to point out that the composite field is a text data field, which is filled by using the concatenation of multiple other fields. If I wanted to sort all of the valves in a specific facility in a database, I could sort by the single equipment identification composite field or instead sort by combining the equipment acronym and facility number or name. Both methods have their value, but the additional field provides a little more flexibility and simplicity. When designing or constructing a new facility, it is very important to predefine the equipment identification format prior to constructing the portion of facility that labels the equipment and develops the record set of drawings. This will reduce the costs to an organization from having to relabel the equipment and update the drawings.

TABLE 5.12 Equipment Identification Composite Data Example

Industry_Code_Description	Equipment_Acronym	Equipment_Sequence	Equipment_ID_Composite
Centrifugal Pump	P	189:AB	ABC0000-P-189:AB
Built Up Indoor Air Handling Unit	AHU	050	ABC0000-AHU-050
Single Speed Three Phase AC Motor	MOT	978	ABC0000-MOT-978
Multiple Walled Vented Tank	TNK	02	ABC0000-TNK-02
Gate Valve	GTV	14473	ABC0000-GTV-14473
Power Dry Step Down Transformer	XFMR	022	ABC0000-MCC-8A-XFMR-022

TABLE 5.13 Equipment Identification Composite Examples

Data Fields	Equipment Identification Composite
Facility Number + Equipment Acronym + Equipment Sequence	ABC0000-AHU-001
Equipment Acronym + Equipment Sequence + Facility Name	VLV-AB:7:8-ABC0000
Equipment Acronym + Equipment Sequence	FAN-098B
Equipment Acronym + Equipment Sequence + Equipment Zone	VLV-8746-Train A

Equipment Space

The equipment space, or location, is captured by selecting the space from the space data tables. The space data should be developed before taking equipment inventory so that personnel can just select the space from a drop-down table. The space GUID is the data field that should be captured in the equipment data tables to create the relationship between the equipment and space data tables (Table 5.14). The user is not expected to pick from a list of GUIDs, especially since the user would not be able to discern what space the GUIDs represent. Instead, a programmer would develop a drop-down menu from the space table database showing floor, room number, and so forth, and when the user selects the correct space, the program itself will enter the GUID that represents that space into the database.

TABLE 5.14   Equipment Identification Composite Examples

Equipment_ID_Composite	Space_GUID	Equipment_Plot_Point	Equipment_Plot_Altitude	Equipment_Plot_Latitude	Equipment_Plot_Longitude
ABC0000-P-189:AB	f9th35Dg1…				
ABC0000-AHU-050	N37d075h2…	Reference	800	−0.140716667	37.56385
ABC0000-MOT-978	N37d075h2…	Reference	800	−0.140716667	37.56385
ABC0000-TNK-02	092Thuq23…	Reference	800	−0.140716667	37.56385
ABC0000-GTV-14473	092Thuq23…	Reference	800	−0.140716667	37.56385

Equipment Plot Point

[EQUIPMENT_PLOT_POINT(N)] (N denotes that multiple fields are possible.)

The equipment plot points are used to map equipment within a complex or facility. These data points were included in the data set for equipment to enable facility management to track equipment location in a facility or within a site boundary. For example, a complex could put in the coordinates for the street lamps on the site so that proper tracking and maintenance could occur.

The equipment plot point data field is used to number or name the different groupings of geological location coordinates for altitude, latitude, and longitude. There are numerous ways in which to identify a specific point on the earth. For simplicity, this guide includes only the basic data points for altitude, latitude, and longitude. The concept, as in connect the dots, is to capture as many plot points as necessary to accurately to be able to draw a line that defines the equipment boundary within the facility or complex. A single set of plot points could also be used to pinpoint a piece of equipment's location. Table 5.15 is shown as an example; note that all of the plot points would be different in real life. The same plot point is used in all cases just to show what the data would look like.

The data field points included is as follows:

Equipment Plot Point	[Equipment_Plot_Point(N)]
Equipment Plot Altitude	[Equipment_Plot_Altitude(N)]
Equipment Point Latitude	[Equipment_Plot_Latitude (N)]
Equipment Point Longitude	[Equipment_Plot_Longitude (N)]

TABLE 5.15   Equipment Plot Points Examples

Equipment_ID_Composite	Space_GUID	Equipment_Plot_Point	Equipment_Plot_Altitude	Equipment_Plot_Latitude	Equipment_Plot_Longitude
ABC0000-P-189:AB	f9th35Dg1…				
ABC0000-AHU-050	N37d075h2…	Reference	800	−0.140716667	37.56385
ABC0000-MOT-978	N37d075h2…	Reference	800	−0.140716667	37.56385
ABC0000-TNK-02	092Thuq23…	Reference	800	−0.140716667	37.56385
ABC0000-GTV-14473	092Thuq23…	Reference	800	−0.140716667	37.56385

Equipment Location Description

[EQUIPMENT_LOCATION_DESCRIPTION]

The equipment location description is a field provided to the staff to enable them to make a comment about the location of a piece of equipment within a space or area (Table 5.16). For example, valve is located 15 feet in the air behind the air expansion tank in the North corner of the room. This field should not be used to capture the floor and room number (see Space Data Fields) but to augment the information for more efficient operations.

TABLE 5.16 Equipment Location Description Examples

Equipment_ID_Composite	Space_GUID	Equipment_Location_Description
ABC0000-MOT-978	N37d075h2...	Inside AHU-50 north side
ABC0000-GTV-14473	092Thuq23...	Between TNK-02 and south wall 2 feet off the floor
ABC0000-MCC-8A-XFMR-022	32Siqw87s...	Left-side transformer, mounted 5 feet off the floor, east side of the space
ABC0000-LCM-05	092Thuq23...	Module is mounted next to tank space door, right side, 4 feet off floor
ABC0000-LDET-22	092Thuq23...	Mounted on top of TNK-01, 15 feet off floor
ABC0000-SW-22	092Thuq23...	Inside Tank TNK-01
ABC0000-P-018	092Thuq23...	Next to TNK-01

Previous Equipment Identification

[PREVIOUS_EQUIPMENT_ID]

When adopting or transferring to a new equipment data schema and identification, it is very important for facility management to be able to cross-reference the old equipment data to the new (Table 5.17). The previous equipment identification data field is used to capture the identification of previous existing equipment. Regulations require the history of some equipment to be kept for a predetermined time. This field allows the organization to convert to a more efficient equipment inventory system and still maintain the existing history (Table 5.18).

TABLE 5.17 Previous Equipment Data Example

Industry_Code_Description	Equipment_ID_Composite	Previous_Equipment_ID	Previous_Equipment_GUID
Centrifugal Pump	ABC0000-P-189:AB	P01-189-AB	ABC0000101
Built-Up Indoor Air Handling Unit	ABC0000-AHU-050	AirHand-50	ABC0000001
Single-Speed Three-Phase AC Motor	ABC0000-MOT-978	M3-978	ABC0000002
Multiple-Walled Vented Tank	ABC0000-TNK-02	FOTK-2	ABC0007001
Gate Valve	ABC0000-GTV-14473	V-14-FOTK-2	ABC0007002
Power-Dry Step-Down Transformer	ABC0000-MCC-8A-XFMR-022		ABC0060001
Electrical Panel Board	ABC0000-XFMR-022-EPB-LP17	ELEC0090090913	ABC0060058
Molded-Case Circuit Breaker	ABC0000-EPB-LP17-CB-MAIN	ELEC0078914875	ABC0060059
Molded-Case Circuit Breaker	ABC0000-EPB-LP17-CB-01	ELEC0078914876	ABC0060060

(continued)

[PREVIOUS_EQUIPMENT_ID] (continued)

TABLE 5.18 Previous Equipment Identification Examples

Equipment Identification Composite	Previous Equipment Identification
ABC0000-AHU-001	AirHand-001
VLV-AB:7:8-ABC0000	V-AB-7-8
FAN-098B	F82-098B-50HP
VLV-8746-Train A	Valve-A-8746-4-Inch

Previous Equipment GUID

[PREVIOUS_EQUIPMENT_GUID]

The previous equipment GUID is a data field that allows your database managers to connect and cross-map the existing data from the old equipment database to the new equipment database (Table 5.19). In most instances, the old database can be maintained, and this field used to cross-reference data to the new equipment database. Cross-referencing the data will allow you to archive information and still be able to move your organization to an industry standard equipment information system without losing information.

TABLE 5.19 Previous Equipment GUID Data Example

Industry_Code_Description	Equipment_ID_Composite	Previous_Equipment_ID	Previous_Equipment_GUID
Centrifugal Pump	ABC0000-P-189:AB	P01-189-AB	ABC0000101
Built Up Indoor Air Handling Unit	ABC0000-AHU-050	AirHand-50	ABC0000001
Single Speed Three Phase AC Motor	ABC0000-MOT-978	M3-978	ABC0000002
Multiple Walled Vented Tank	ABC0000-TNK-02	FOTK-2	ABC0007001
Gate Valve	ABC0000-GTV-14473	V-14-FOTK-2	ABC0007002
Power Dry Step Down Transformer	ABC0000-MCC-8A-XFMR-022		ABC0060001
Electrical Panel Board	ABC0000-XFMR-022-EPB-LP17	ELEC0090090913	ABC0060058
Molded Case Circuit Breaker	ABC0000-EPB-LP17-CB-MAIN	ELEC0078914875	ABC0060059
Molded Case Circuit Breaker	ABC0000-EPB-LP17-CB-01	ELEC0078914876	ABC0060060

Equipment Organization Asset Number

[EQUIPMENT_ORG_ASSET_NUMBER]

The equipment organization asset number is a data field that allows the storage of any organization-specific self-generated number that is associated with a piece of equipment (Table 5.20). For example, corporation ABC performs an independent equipment inventory on an old facility without consulting blueprints and starts numbering equipment for financial and accounting purposes, starting at ABC000001. This field is used to capture that unique asset number. This type of identification is found typically in information technology departments for numbering computers, printers, and servers, and the like.

TABLE 5.20 Equipment Organization Asset Number Data Example

Equipment_ID_Composite	Equipment_Org_Asset_Number	Equipment_Power_Supply	Equipment_System_Code
ABC0000-P-189:AB	ABC0000101	ABC0000-MCC-8A-CB-18	21-51 51 18 11
ABC0000-AHU-050	ABC0000001	Tye2u98te…	21-51 51 16
ABC0000-MOT-978	ABC0000002	9fn09graO…	21-51 51 16
ABC0000-TNK-02	ABC0007001		21-51 71 11 14
ABC0000-GTV-14473	ABC0007002		21-51 71 11 14

Using a self-generated asset number is a very useful way to manually inventory a large existing facility. This allows multiple personnel to independently inventory the facility without having to worry about conflicting equipment sequence numbers. Conflicting equipment sequence numbers is a huge problem when a facility does not have blueprints to reference. For example, suppose that your team sends out five people to inventory a facility. Each person starts identifying equipment and capturing data. Because there are no blueprints for this facility, the team will generate all of the equipment sequence numbers from scratch. Because they are using asset tags, they gather all of the information and then come back to the office to download their data. Once the data are downloaded for all five members, they can then start adding equipment sequence numbers without duplicating the numbers. When labels are ordered, the correct tags can then be placed on the correct equipment by cross-referencing the asset number to the correct piece of equipment in the database. When inventorying a facility without using these asset numbers, the five members run the risk of having a lot of duplicate equipment sequence numbers, and this causes data conflicts in the database. For example, one of the team members identifies the first ball valve she encounters with an equipment sequence number of 001. Another member of the team identifies the first ball valve he encounters with an equipment sequence number of 001, and so on. Now, when all of the team members combine their data, you have two ball valves with the equipment sequence number of 001. Even if you correct these errors in the database, you still have to ensure that the information is corrected in the field. Therefore, you are taking multiple trips out to the field to fix the data repeatedly. Using a web-based centralized equipment inventory collection program (which doesn't exist at the time of writing this book) could solve this problem if everyone were able to maintain connectivity. This data field could also be used to capture tenant equipment identification numbers for cross-referencing.

Equipment Power Supply

[EQUIPMENT_POWER_SUPPLY]

The ability to capture where power comes from for equipment is vitally important to facility management. There are numerous codes and regulations that require equipment power be secured and locked out prior to repairs or maintenance. Sadly, a vast number of facilities do not have this information. The equipment power supply data field is used to link equipment to the component that supplies it electrical power (Table 5.21). For example, if a motor (MOT-001) is supplied electrical power from circuit breaker 04 (CB-04) on electrical panel box LP:19 (EPB-LP:19), the circuit breaker (EPB-LP:19-CB-04) would be the electrical power supply for the motor. While the circuit breaker equipment identification composite EPB-LP:19-CB-04 could be loaded into this data field, it is recommended that the GUID associated with the circuit breaker information be loaded instead. Either method is acceptable depending on the design of the database. Remember, facility management will not see the GUID. The database software should instead show the staff the equipment identification composite information. The GUID is used to just link the two separate data records.

TABLE 5.21   Equipment Power Supply Data Example

Equipment_ID_Composite	Equipment_Org_Asset_Number	Equipment_Power_Supply	Equipment_System_Code
ABC0000-P-189:AB	ABC0000101	ABC0000-MCC-8A-CB-18	21-51 51 18 11
ABC0000-AHU-050	ABC0000001	Tye2u98te...	21-51 51 16
ABC0000-MOT-978	ABC0000002	9fn09graO...	21-51 51 16
ABC0000-MCC-8A-XFMR-022	ABC0060001	ABC0000-MCC-8A-CB-05	21-51 71 11 14
ABC0000-XFMR-022-EPB-LP17	ABC0060058	Giqre9732...	21-51 71 11 14

This field provides the ability to develop an electrical breaker book within a database and is vitally important to safety, emergency response, and the reduction of wasted resources spent recreating this information. Because it is important to link electrical information to equipment, it is highly recommended that an organization inventory the electrical distribution system before inventorying the mechanical systems (See Chapter 7, "Inventorying Equipment"). Inventorying the electrical system first will eliminate the need to back fill the information later, which rarely happens.

Equipment System Relationship

Identifying the system related to a piece of equipment is a very important part of the operation of a facility. System performance and cost rollups are a typical performance measure used to determine the overall health of a facility. The different equipment systems are typically designated during design and construction (Table 5.22). Industry codes and standards should be used whenever possible (see Chapter 4, "Industry Standards"). Instead of having personnel manually enter the system code every time they inventory a piece of equipment, it is better to keep the system code and description in a separate

TABLE 5.22 Equipment System Data Example

Equipment_ID_Composite	Equipment_System_Code	Equipment_System_Description
ABC0000-P-189:AB	21-51 51 18 11	Heating and Cooling Distribution for Single Facility
ABC0000-AHU-050	21-51 51 16	Air Distribution
ABC0000-MOT-978	21-51 51 16	Air Distribution
ABC0000-TNK-02	21-51 71 11 14	Electric Service and Distribution for Single Facility
ABC0000-GTV-14473	21-51 71 11 14	Electric Service and Distribution for Single Facility
ABC0000-MCC-8A-XFMR-022	21-51 71 11 14	Electric Service and Distribution for Single Facility
ABC0000-XFMR-022-EPB-LP17	21-51 71 11 14	Electric Service and Distribution for Single Facility

reference table so that it can be updated and used in a pull-down menu. The table can then be used as a drop-down menu so that personnel can select the code and system from a list (Table 5.23). The use of a reference table ensures that the data are uniform and usable. It is also recommended that industry standards, the same ones the architects use to define systems in design and construction, be used to define the systems in a facility. OmniClass™ Table-21 (CSI/CSC) Elements is the recommended table to use to identify the different systems that make up a facility.

TABLE 5.23 Equipment System Reference Table Examples

OmniClass™ Table 21*	
OmniClass™ Number	OmniClass™ Title
21-51 51 00	Heating, Ventilating and Air Conditioning (HVAC)
21-51 51 16	Air Distribution
21-51 51 16 11	Ventilation
21-51 31 11 17	Domestic Water Distribution

* The industry code used in this example is OmniClass™, which is a product of the Construction Specification Institute.

Equipment System Description

[EQUIPMENT_SYSTEM_DESCRIPTION]

The data field equipment system description is used to capture the nomenclature of the system that is directly related to the equipment system code (See Table 5.22). A reference table or industry code should be used by personnel to designate the system name, instead of allowing them to type in the information. Using predetermined names prevents human error and data inconsistencies. OmniClass™ Table-21 (CSI/CSC) Elements is the recommended table to use to identify the different systems that make up a facility.

(continued)

[EQUIPMENT_SYSTEM_DESCRIPTION] (*continued*)

Equipment should be related to the lowest hierarchical system level of the reference table or industry code. When developing a system reference table or using an industry code, each system should be related to others in a hierarchical order. For example, an "HVAC Duct Fan" would be associated with the "Ventilation" system. In the reference table, the "Ventilation" system would be associated with the "Air Distribution" system, which would then be associated with the "Heating Ventilation and Air Conditioning" (HVAC) system. In most industry standards the hierarchical level of order from ventilation to air distribution to HVAC is already established. Associating equipment with the lowest hierarchical system allows facility management to select data by bringing up the smaller set of ventilation system components, a larger set of air distribution components, or all of the HVAC system components. While it is possible for equipment to belong to multiple systems, the system that the equipment was designed to support should be the one selected.

Equipment System Code

[EQUIPMENT_SYSTEM_CODE]

Industry standards typically use a description related to a numeric code to develop their data tables. The equipment system code is the data field used to capture the digital code related to the system classification an equipment component is associated with (Table 5.22).

Equipment Assembly

[EQUIPMENT_ASSEMBLY]

Equipment rarely consists of a single component (Figure 5.5). Large equipment is usually made up of individual components that each has its own maintenance and tracking requirements. The term "assembly" is used to describe this association of equipment. The equipment assembly data field is used to capture these associations that a component has with other components (Table 5.24). Another commonly used name for this assembly relationship is a parent-child relationship. For example, an air handling unit typically contains a couple of dampers, a motor, and a blower (Figure 5.5). The motor, dampers, and blower are said to have an assembly relationship with the air handling unit assembly. In simpler terms, the motor is a part of the air handling unit.

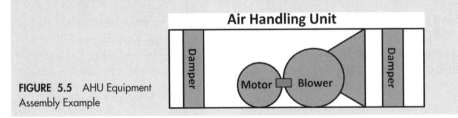

FIGURE 5.5 AHU Equipment Assembly Example

TABLE 5.24 Equipment Assembly Data Example

Equipment_GUID	Equipment_ID_Composite	Equipment_Power_Supply	Equipment_Assembly
A8FDy9w54...	ABC0000-AHU-050	Tye2u98te...	
fw565r713...	ABC0000-MOT-978	9fn09graO...	A8FDY9w54...
qrv35t47j...	ABC0000-TNK-02		
st7mnWq70...	ABC0000-GTV-14473		ABC0000-TNK-02
Giqre9732...	ABC0000-MCC-8A-XFMR-022	ABC0000-MCC-8A-CB-05	
POq8723F4...	ABC0000-XFMR-022-EPB-LP17	Giqre9732...	ABC0000-MCC-8A-XFMR-022
Dpo0984kf...	ABC0000-EPB-LP17-CB-MAIN		POq8723F4...
9fn09graO...	ABC0000-EPB-LP17-CB-01		ABC0000-XFMR-022-EPB-LP17
Pv4ghT671...	ABC0000-LDET-22		k3Het683q...
6Fweih1G4...	ABC0000-SW-22		k3Het683q...
k3Het683q...	ABC0000-TNK-01		
9gd937Qju...	ABC0000-MOACTR-02		Xy398gnTy...
Xy398gnTy...	ABC0000-CHKV-02		

Assembly data are very important to the operation of a facility. Each of the separate components in an assembly affects how the complete assembly operates, each has different maintenance requirements, and each has different financial and tracking requirements. For example, the vast majority of personnel entering data into service call programs are administrative personnel instead of facility maintenance personnel. Administrative personnel would probably not know that a motor failure would affect an air handler. If that air handler was supplying the air conditioning to a critical data server, this lack of knowledge and association of components could have a significant cost impact on an organization. When an executive team is projecting future cost improvements and financial repairs, the team might only be provided the information that a motor replacement is required in one of their facilities. The team may not be informed of the impact that motor has on the air handler. Because the assembly data affect multiple faucets of the organization, it is important to capture the data.

Because there are multiple types of relationships/associations of equipment within a facility, some addressed later in this chapter, the equipment assembly data field is used to capture the design or installation relationship for the equipment. Industry standard practice is to relate a component to the equipment it is designed to support, based on the installed purpose for that component. For example, a tamper switch on a fire control valve is installed to monitor the position of the valve. A tamper switch is typically associated with the valve and a fire control panel that issues an alarm when the valve is out of its normal position. Because the installed purpose of the tamper switch is to monitor the position of the valve, the assembly relationship for the tamper switch is the fire control valve. The relationship between the switch and the fire control panel would be covered in equipment control, alarm, or indication relationships data sets discussed later in this chapter.

Typically, equipment is only associated with one assembly or parent. A parent assembly though can contain multiple pieces of equipment as subassemblies or children. For example, the air handling unit is the parent and the motor, dampers, and blower are its children (subassemblies). Because of this, the parent equipment data are what is entered into this data field. Some call it the "one level up" relationship approach. The motor, dampers, and blower would have the air handling unit data placed in their equipment assembly data field (Table 5.25).

Typically, larger equipment is the main assembly and is not typically part of another assembly. A large facility boiler is an example of an assembly that is not part of another assembly. While the boiler could be a part of the heating ventilation system of a building, it is important to not confuse systems with equipment assemblies. A good question to ask when taking an inventory is, "Is this equipment a part of an assembly?" If the equipment is not part of an assembly, leave this data field blank.

The two schools of thought on what data should be entered into this data field are to enter the GUID of the parent assembly or to enter the equipment identification composite of the parent assembly. While both methods would

TABLE 5.25 Equipment Assembly Examples

Equipment	Equipment GUID	Equipment Assembly
Boiler (BLR-01)	X7yter77we...	N/A
Boiler Draft Fan (FAN-872)	9Tfjkhqwoi...	X7yter77we...
Air Handling Unit (AHU-007)	pLw9gh3...	N/A
Heating Coil (COIL-008)	K53Ygte...	pLw9gh3...
Heating Coil Inlet Isolation Ball Valve (BV-007A:H)	qW9d02...	K53Ygte...
Heating Coil Outlet Isolation Ball Valve (BV-007B:H)	M0y2gfy...	K53Ygte...
Feeder (ABC0000-FDR-1A)	Ku3ju5y...	N/A
Network Protector (ABC0000-FDR-1A-NTWK-002)	H8ydtsu...	Ku3ju5y...
Switchboard (ABC0000-NTWK-002-SWBD-52:A)	7g9Ughey...	H8ydtsu...
Air Circuit Breaker (ABC000-SWBD-52:A-ACB-001)	0Wou73...	7g9Ughey...
Air Circuit Breaker (ABC000-SWBD-52:A-ACB-002)	P73bHt...	7g9Ughey...

work, I recommend entering the GUID and basically link the parent and child equipment data records. I in no way suggest that personnel taking inventory out in the field enter the long and meaningless string of GUID information each time they want to capture this relationship. What I suggest is that the parent equipment information be captured first and entered into the equipment database. Once the parent data are captured, a drop-down list of equipment that exists within the database could be used to associate the parent with its children by selecting the parents' equipment identification for the children. The software package used should enter the GUID of the parent into the equipment assembly data field for the child. No matter which method is used, a drop-down list of existing equipment should always be used to prevent human error.

In Table 5.24 you can see that the motor ABC0000-MOT-978 is linked to the air handler ABC0000-AHU-050 by the GUID for the AHU A8FDY9w54... to the motor.

In Table 5.25 you can see the relationship of the product in its assembly. For example, FAN-872 is an assembly of BLR-01 by the GUID X7yter77we... entered into the Equipment Assembly field.

Electrical distribution systems pose a unique problem and challenge to facility management. A circuit breaker has a direct relationship with the circuit breaker panel in which it is installed. But, how do you relate that an electrical panel is directly fed from a transformer or feeder? You cannot use the system relationship because then you are just relating each piece of equipment singularly to a system name and not showing the association between the electrical panel and the transformer. All electrical components are part of the electrical distribution system. You cannot use zones because they are areas of electrical distribution based on design and also are not named according to the actual components. For example, a group of electrical components would be related in an equipment zone called ZONE A Electric. Because of these problems and instead of developing a new data field, I recommend using the equipment assembly data field to also denote the association of one electrical component to another. For example, in Figure 5.6 the air circuit breakers are an assembly of the switchboard. The switchboard is powered from the network protector, which is, in turn, powered from the feeder. In most situations, the feeder would be the end point for a facility. The advantage of being able to relate the electrical distribution components in this manner is that it gives personnel the ability to trace forward and backward the entire electrical distribution system (See Chapter 6, "Equipment Identification and Tags"). In this example, a technician can determine that air circuit breaker 002 (ABC000-SWBD-52:A-ABC-002) is part of switchboard 52:A (SWBD-52:A). The switchboard is powered from (ABC0000-NTWK-002-SWBD-52:A) network protector 002 (NTWK-002),

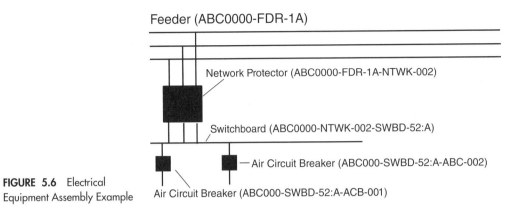

Feeder (ABC0000-FDR-1A)

Network Protector (ABC0000-FDR-1A-NTWK-002)

Switchboard (ABC0000-NTWK-002-SWBD-52:A)

Air Circuit Breaker (ABC000-SWBD-52:A-ABC-002)

FIGURE 5.6 Electrical
Equipment Assembly Example

Air Circuit Breaker (ABC000-SWBD-52:A-ACB-001)

and it in turn is powered from (ABC0000-FDR-1A) feeder 1A. This is very important information to a technician troubleshooting an emergency electrical fault in the field.

Equipment Control

[EQUIPMENT_CONTROL(N)] (N denotes that multiple fields are possible.)

The equipment control data field is used to capture any control associations that one piece of equipment has with another piece of equipment (Table 5.26). What controls that piece of equipment?

TABLE 5.26 Equipment Control Data Example

Equipment_GUID	Industry_Code_Description	Equipment_ID_Composite	Equipment_Control	Equipment_Control
hdJwe0023...	Building Automated System	ABC0000-BAS-01	Le76Fieyh...	
Le76Fieyh...	Level Control Module	ABC0000-LCM-05	7feT38s61...	9gd937Qju...
Pv4ghT671...	Level Detector	ABC0000-LDET-22	Le76Fieyh...	
6Fweih1G4...	Level Switch	ABC0000-SW-22	Pv4ghT671...	
7feT38s61...	Centrifugal Pump	ABC0000-P-018		
k3Het683q...	Single Walled Vented Tank	ABC0000-TNK-01		
9gd937Qju...	Motor Operated Valve Actuator	ABC0000-MOACTR-02	7feT38s61...	

For example (Figure 5.7): A level switch (SW-22) is installed to monitor the level of a tank and send a control signal to start a pump (P-18) when the level in the tank gets low. The level switch has a control relationship with the pump. Note: The level switch, because of its installed purpose, has an

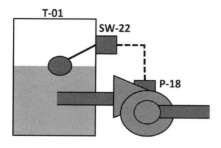

FIGURE 5.7 Tank Equipment Control Example

equipment assembly relationship with the tank. It was installed to monitor or control the level in the tank. Control relationships are vitally important for impact analysis and risk assessments. A technician needs to know the data, especially during troubleshoot, repairs, and maintenance. The technician turns off power to calibrate the level switch, what happens to the pump? Does the level switch fail low on a loss of power? Could the tank overflow?

Again, as with the equipment assembly data fields, the parent association is entered into the equipment control data field. Using the same one level up relationship scheme as the other relationship data fields simplifies the overall database usage for end users and programmers. There is a higher probability of having multiple relationships when designating controls. Equipment can have a many-to-many control relationship. A component can control multiple pieces of equipment (Control Module) or be controlled by multiple pieces of equipment (Alarm Module). Because of this possibility, only the control relationship is captured. Note: The inverse of the control relationship would be the controlled relationship. When multiple control relationships exist, a data field has to be populated for each instance. The method to determine what equipment belongs in the control relationship field is to ask, "What does this equipment supply a control signal to. . . .?" As previously mentioned in the equipment assembly data field, it is recommended that a GUID be used to link the associated equipment that is controlled.

Example (Figure 5.8 and Table 5.27): Level switch (SW-22) supplies a level control signal to a level control module (LCM-05). A pump (P-18) is controlled by the level control module based on the level from the level control switch. The level control module also controls the motor operated check valve (CHKV-02). The motor operated check valve supplies a control signal to the pump that prevents the pump from starting until the valve is fully open. When the level of the tank gets low a signal is sent to the level control module. The level control module then sends a signal to open the motor operated check valve and start the pump to raise the level back to the normal band. Table 5.27 is an example of what the database for this relationship might look like.

TABLE 5.27　Equipment Control Examples

Equipment	Equipment GUID	Equipment Control	Equipment Control
Level Control Module (LCM-05)	Le9fdty…	23rFtu3…	Zvqu876L…
Level Switch (SW-22)	0Ftq4n9…	Le9fdty…	
Centrifugal Pump (P-18)	23rFtu3…		
Motor Operated Check Valve (CHKV-02)	Zvqu876L…	23rFtu3…	

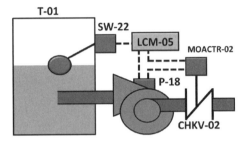

FIGURE 5.8　Tank Equipment Control Relationship

Equipment Alarm

[EQUIPMENT_ALARM(N)] (N denotes that multiple fields are possible.)

The equipment alarm data field is very similar to the equipment control data fields except that you are capturing the association that a component has with another piece of equipment based on an alarm function. What alarms are caused by the equipment? For example, a level switch is installed to monitor the level of a tank, and when the tank level gets low the switch sends an alarm signal to a building automated system (BAS). Therefore, the level switch has an alarm relationship with the building automated system. Again, the parent association is entered into the equipment alarm data field. Using the same one level up relationship scheme as the other relationship data fields simplifies the overall database usage for end users and programmers.

Equipment can have a many-to-many relationship in relation to alarms. A component can send an alarm signal to multiple pieces of equipment (proactive) or the equipment can alarm based on inputs from multiple pieces of equipment (reactive). Because of this possibility, only the proactive alarm relationship is captured. When multiple proactive alarm relationships exist, a data field has to be populated for each instance. The method to determine what equipment belongs in the alarm relationship field is to ask, "This equipment supplies an alarm signal to. . . ."

For example (Figure 5.9): A level switch (SW-22) supplies an alarm signal to a level control alarm module (LCM-05). A motor-operated check valve (CHKV-02) supplies an alarm signal to the level control module. The level control module (LCM-05) supplies an alarm signal to the building automated system (BAS-001). Table 5.28 and Table 5.29 show an example of how the alarm relationships could be related in a database.

TABLE 5.28 Equipment Alarm Examples

Equipment	Equipment GUID	Equipment Alarm
Building Automated System (BAS-001)	Xg4De39…	
Level Control Module (LCAM-05)	Le9fdty…	Xg4De39…
Level Switch (LSW-22)	0Ftq4n9…	Le9fdty…
Motor-Operated Check Valve (CHKV-02)	Zvqu876L…	Le9fdty…

TABLE 5.29 Equipment Alarm Data Example

Equipment_GUID	Industry_Code_Description	Equipment_ID_Composite	Equipment_Alarm
hdJwe0023…	Building Automated System	ABC0000-BAS-01	
Le76Fieyh…	Level Control Module	ABC0000-LCM-05	hdJwe0023…
Pv4ghT671…	Level Detector	ABC0000-LDET-22	Le76Fieyh…
6Fweih1G4…	Level Switch	ABC0000-SW-22	
9gd937Qju…	Motor-Operated Valve Actuator	ABC0000-MOACTR-02	Le76Fieyh…

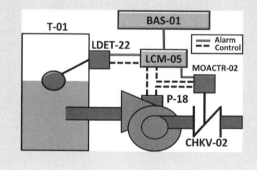

FIGURE 5.9 Tank Alarm Relationship Example

Equipment Indication

[EQUIPMENT_INDICATION(N)] (N denotes that multiple fields are possible)

The equipment indication data fields are similar to those for equipment control and alarm. For example, a temperature indicator is installed to monitor the temperature of air exhausting from an air handling unit. The temperature indicator sends a signal to the building automated system. The temperature indicator has an indication relationship with the building automated system. This relationship is set up and determined the exact same way as the control and alarm relationships.

Equipment can have a many-to-many relationship in relation to indications. A component can send an indication signal to multiple pieces of equipment (proactive) or have multiple indications from multiple pieces of equipment (reactive) like a building automated system. Because of this possibility,

(continued)

[EQUIPMENT_INDICATION(N)] (N denotes that multiple fields are possible) (*continued*)

only the proactive indication relationship is captured. When multiple proactive indication relationships exist, a data field has to be populated for each instance. The method to determine what equipment belongs in the indication relationship field is to ask, "This equipment supplies an indication signal to. . . ."

For example (Table 5.30), a temperature control module (TCM-092) gets temperature signals from three temperature indicators (TI-191, TI-316A, and TI-316B). The temperature indicators would be said to have an equipment indication relationship with the temperature control module. Each of the temperature indicators would have the GUID or equipment identification number for the temperature control module placed in their equipment identification data fields. In the example (Table 5.30), GUIDs are used instead of equipment identification composites.

TABLE 5.30 Equipment Indication Data Example

Equipment_GUID	Industry_Code_Description	Equipment_ID_Composite	Equipment_Indication	Equipment_Failure_Impact
5Hgsoih8s...	Temperature Control Module	ABC0000-TCM-092		olAYr9HD1...
dTrbn32ht...	Temperature Indicator	ABC0000-TI-191	5Hgsoih8s...	5Hgsoih8s...
Keb5g28Bt...	Temperature Indicator	ABC0000-TI-316A	5Hgsoih8s...	5Hgsoih8s...
23Jjfrt47a...	Temperature Indicator	ABC0000-TI-316B	5Hgsoih8s...	5Hgsoih8s...
olAYr9HD1...	Air Conditioner	ABC0000-ACU-191		

Equipment Failure Impact

[EQUIPMENT_FAILURE_IMPACT(N)] (N denotes that multiple fields are possible.)

The equipment failure impact data field is used to capture the impact of an equipment failure on other components. This relationship can be closely tied to the control relationship, and in many instances it is the same information. This data field is used to capture the primary component-to-component relationship of a failure. There are typically multiple levels of equipment affected by a single component failure. The first level or failure, primary impact, would be those components directly affected by the failure (Figure 5.10). When those components fail they affect the next level of components, called the secondary impacted components. This effect, essentially a domino effect, continues on until there are no more components to affect. For example, a control module fails, causing a valve to fail closed. Because a valve failed closed, a pump interlocked with the valve shuts off. The first, or primary, level of impact between the control module and the valve is the only one considered when entering data into inventory. The secondary failure impact of the valve on the pump will be captured when the valve is inventoried.

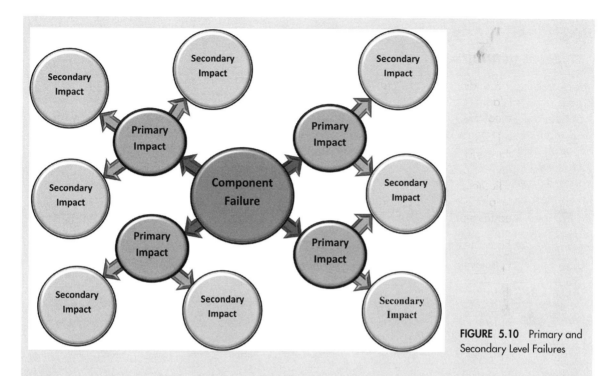

FIGURE 5.10 Primary and Secondary Level Failures

Example (Figure 5.11), a temperature control module (TCM-092) controls the temperature in rooms 191, 316A, and 316B. The control module receives temperature indication from temperature indicators (TI-191, TI-316A, TI-316B) and controls air conditioning units (ACU-191, RAC-316A, RAC-316B) to maintain room temperatures. Room air conditioners (RAC-316A, RAC-316B) have the ability to send control signals to air handler units (AHU-051, AHU-052) for added cooling when they are

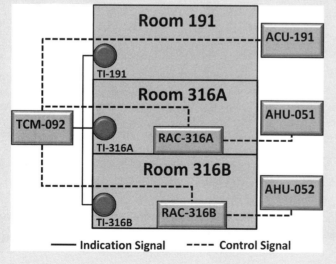

FIGURE 5.11 Room Control Failure Example

(continued)

[EQUIPMENT_FAILURE_IMPACT(N)] (N denotes that multiple fields are possible.) (*continued*)

unable to maintain room temperature. The temperature control module fails high to ensure that cooling is always supplied to the data center rooms 316A and 316B. Therefore, if the temperature control module fails, all of the air conditioner units (ACU-191, RAC-316A, and RAC-316B) fail to the cooling mode. This is considered to be the primary level or immediate failure impact of the temperature control module. The secondary impact would be the air handler units (AHU-051, AHU-052) starting because the room air conditioners (RAC-316A and RAC-316B) are running at maximum cooling and are still receiving a high signal from the failed temperature control module. The room air conditioners, therefore, send a start signal to the air handling units (secondary impact).

Equipment can have a many-to-many relationship to what they impact. A component can have an impact on multiple pieces of equipment or can be affected by multiple pieces of equipment. Because of this possibility, only what a component directly affects is captured. When multiple impact relationships exist, a data field has to be populated for each instance (Table 5.31).

TABLE 5.31 Equipment Failure Impact Data Example

Equipment_GUID	Equipment_ID_Composite	Equipment_Failure_Impact	Equipment_Failure_Impact	Equipment_Failure_Impact
A8FDy9w54...	ABC0000-AHU-050			
fw565r713...	ABC0000-MOT-978	A8FDY9w54...		
qrv35t47j...	ABC0000-TNK-02			
st7mnWq70...	ABC0000-GTV-14473	qrv35t47j...		
Giqre9732...	ABC0000-MCC-8A-XFMR-022	POq8723F4...		
POq8723F4...	ABC0000-XFMR-022-EPB-LP17			
Dpo0984kf...	ABC0000-EPB-LP17-CB-MAIN	POq8723F4...		
9fn09graO...	ABC0000-EPB-LP17-CB-01	fw565r713...		
5Hgsoih8s...	ABC0000-TCM-092	oIAYr9HD1...	WEdbe803d...	Y4udhjRw6...
dTrbn32ht...	ABC0000-TI-191	5Hgsoih8s...		
Keb5g28Bt...	ABC0000-TI-316A	5Hgsoih8s...		
23Jjfrt47a...	ABC0000-TI-316B	5Hgsoih8s...		
oIAYr9HD1...	ABC0000-ACU-191			
WEdbe803d...	ABC0000-RAC-316A	497Ghe2t1...		
497Ghe2t1...	ABC0000-AHU-051			
Y4udhjRw6...	ABC0000-RAC-316B	Just2t37h...		
Just2t37h...	ABC0000-AHU-052			

It is important to note that the electrical power relationships are captured in the equipment power supply data fields. Therefore, the loss of an electrical distribution component or subcomponent would not need to be included in the failure impact data fields.

Equipment Space Relationship

[EQUIPMENT_SPACE_REL (N)] (N denotes that multiple fields are possible.)

The equipment space relationship, not to be confused with the equipment location, is used to capture the association that equipment has with a space or room. For example (Table 5.32), an air handling unit provides the air conditioning to spaces 113A, 113B, and 114. The air handler has a relationship with these spaces. Therefore, if the air handling unit was lost, these spaces would lose air conditioning. The air handler itself is physically located in the mechanical room identified as 02:220: Mechanical. The understanding of what equipment supplies or affects which spaces is important to understanding the operation of a facility, troubleshooting problems, and properly setting up chargebacks. Not all components will have a space relationship. Each of the affected space would have their space GUID placed in the space relationship data field for that equipment. In the example in Table 5.32, GUIDs are used instead of space identification composites.

TABLE 5.32   Equipment Space Relationship Data Example

Equipment_GUID	Equipment_ID_Composite	Equipment_Space_Rel (1)	Equipment_Space_Rel (2)	Equipment_Space_Rel (N)
o8ash05Rv...	ABC0000-P-189:AB			
A8FDy9w54...	ABC0000-AHU-050	Y7hru8yhR...	I4h83pK09s...	T41s1ssiL...

Space_GUID	Architectural_Zone_GUID	Floor_Number	Blueprint_Room_Number	Org_Room_Number
Y7hru8yhR...	19tE0oP32...	1	113	113A
I4h83pK09s...	19tE0oP32...	1	113	113B
T41s1ssiL...	19tE0oP32...	1	114	114

Equipment Priority

[EQUIPMENT_PRIORITY]

Equipment prioritization is a very important aspect of developing an asset management system. Identifying the equipment within a facility is only half of the equation when it comes to managing equipment. The other half is establishing how to properly use that equipment information. Computer systems and facility management have to know the different priorities of their equipment in order to be able to operate efficiently. When scheduling work for equipment, an equipment priority is used to schedule the work and denote to facility staff the importance of that maintenance. Both the staff and the system need to know whether the equipment is for emergency use, mission-critical use, or affects public safety, and so forth. The only way to accomplish this is to prioritize the equipment properly. For example, a technician receives two similar work orders to fix two similar pieces of equipment at different locations. In this scenario, the only way the technician knows which equipment to work on

(continued)

[EQUIPMENT_PRIORITY] (*continued*)

first is if the equipment has been properly prioritized. If the equipment does not have a priority, the technician might go to the wrong equipment first and could have to be rerouted when the error is found. The amount of wasted resources spent rerouting technicians is significant. The impact of not prioritizing equipment even affects executive strategic planning and decisions. The executive team needs to know where to wisely spend their capital funds and what the most useful impact on their business is. Do I fix aging equipment that is critical to my operation before I fix equipment that is nonessential? How would this be accomplished if the equipment has not been prioritized? Common practice in the industry is to send out a call for project requests from their departments when there are extra discretionary funds at the end of a budgetary year. At that point, companies with a large portfolio of facilities will typically receive a lot of requests for repair and equipment improvement projects. If the equipment is not prioritized then how are the most profitable projects selected? It is amazing how many projects are funded because of when the project was submitted rather that because of what was vital to the profitability and operation of the company.

As of the writing of this book, there are no industry standards for equipment priorities. The U.S. Coast Guard does have a very extensive criticality matrix that could be adopted for this purpose. Personally, I prefer using a letter system over a numbering system because of the number of human interactions with the information. There are numerous instances in the industry in which facilities start labeling everything a "1" priority. What exactly does a "1" mean? Are life-threatening and equipment failures both a "1" and to which do I respond to first? Instead, by using a human-understandable lettering system (Table 5.33), once you prioritize the equipment with a lettered system, you can develop a reference table that assigns a number to each priority level that a computer can understand (Table 5.34). This allows you to adjust the importance of the equipment according to the facility, without having to change the priority on each piece of equipment. An example of the data is shown in Table 5.35.

TABLE 5.33   Equipment Priority Data Example

Equipment_GUID	Industry_Code_Description	Equipment_ID_Composite	Equipment_Priority
o8ash05Rv…	Centrifugal Pump	ABC0000-P-189:AB	BOE
A8FDy9w54…	Built-Up Indoor Air Handling Unit	ABC0000-AHU-050	MCE
st7mnWq70…	Gate Valve	ABC0000-GTV-14473	MCE
POq8723F4…	Electrical Panel Board	ABC0000-XFMR-022-EPB-LP17	BOE
HGdb5028d…	Molded-Case Circuit Breaker	ABC0000-EPB-LP17-CB-02	NEE
Ohe33jG2x…	Traction Passenger Elevator	ABC0000-ELEV-15	ELS
Mnc07Vz23…	Portable Post and Railing Barrier	ABC0000-RLGBARR-P17	PHS
Nfk43lud3…	Aboveground Primary Tank Containment	ABC0000-ASTPCON-02	ENE
eF9hwj12b…	Intrusion Detection Buried Cable	ABC0000-BLID-A74	SCE
y7G4H3j28…	Computed Tomography CT Complete Stationary Unit	ABC0000-CT-M9	MED

TABLE 5.34 Equipment Priority Examples

Code	Priorities	Description
ELS	Emergency/Life Safety Equipment	Equipment whose purpose is for emergency or life safety. For example, an emergency generator that supports life safety systems, or emergency lighting. Another example is an elevator that is used for building evacuation that is powered by emergency power.
FSE	Fire Safety Equipment	Equipment that supports fire safety and suppression.
PHS	Public Health and Safety Equipment	Equipment that is used to protect the health and safety of the public. For example: A biohazard containment door or confined space barricade.
PSE	Personnel Safety Equipment	Equipment that is used directly for personnel safety. For example, harness hooks on a roof used by maintenance personnel.
MCE	Mission Critical Equipment	Equipment that is essential to operate to support the mission of an organization. For example, an air conditioning unit that supplies a critical data center.
MED	Medical	Equipment that is used for medical purposes.
SCE	Security Equipment	Equipment used for the physical security of a facility. For example, cameras, key cards, and the like.
ENE	Environmental Safety Equipment	Equipment that is used to protect the environment. For example, a berm around a tank that prevents the release of the tank contents to the environment in the advent of a tank failure.
PLO	Plant Operation	Equipment that is essential for plant operation.
PRO	Production	Equipment that is essential for production operations.
BOE	Building Operations Equipment	Equipment that is essential to the operation of a building. For example, the normal power system that is required for the normal operation of a building.
ESE	Essential Support Equipment	Equipment that is deemed essential to support building operation. For example, an air dryer for a compressed air system. While the compressed air system would be coded building operations equipment required to operate the pneumatic valves of an HVAC system, the dryer supports that function but is of a lower category. The system could operate without the dryer for a short time.
NEE	Nonessential Equipment	Any equipment that is not categorized as above. For example, a water fountain.

TABLE 5.35 Internal Computer Reference Table Example

Code	Number	Code	Number
ELS	1	ENE	3
FSE	1	PLO	4
PHS	1	PRO	5
PSE	2	BOE	6
MCE	2	ESE	7
MED	2	NEE	8
SCE	3		

Equipment Continued Operation

[EQUIPMENT_COOP]

Continuity of Operations (COOP) is a United States federal initiative, required by presidential directive, to ensure that agencies are able to continue performance of essential functions under a range of adverse circumstances (e.g., a chemical attack). Federal regulations require government agencies to track and maintain COOP-related equipment. While the equipment COOP field is unique to government organizations, any organization would benefit from ensuring they understand and categorize equipment that allows them to continue their operation during adverse conditions. For example, what is the ability of a facility to maintain critical operations after an earthquake? The COOP equipment was developed as a separate field from equipment priorities because equipment can have an installed purpose or priority and could also be COOP equipment. For example, a fire damper should be related to the fire safety systems and have a priority for fire safety equipment. If the fire damper is also used to isolate a building from a chemical attack, then it would also be COOP equipment (Table 5.36). Interestingly, federal regulations require historical fine arts, such as paintings and sculptures, to be tracked by the COOP program. The purpose being that if the building is on fire, someone should grab the priceless Monet on the way out.

TABLE 5.36 Equipment Continued Operation Data Example

Equipment_GUID	Equipment_ID_Composite	Equipment_Priority	Equipment_COOP
o8ash05Rv...	ABC0000-P-189:AB	BOE	No
A8FDy9w54...	ABC0000-AHU-050	MCE	No
fw565r713...	ABC0000-MOT-978	MCE	No
qrv35t47j...	ABC0000-TNK-02	MCE	Yes
st7mnWq70...	ABC0000-GTV-14473	MCE	Yes
Giqre9732...	ABC0000-MCC-8A-XFMR-022	BOE	No
0Gdhew765...	ABC0000-FDMPR-07	FSE	Yes
T3hg26J3Y...	ABC0000-FAPTG-02	NEE	Yes

Equipment Owner

[EQUIPMENT_OWNER]

It is important for budgeting, facility management, and strategic planning to determine who owns and is responsible for maintaining and tracking equipment within a facility. The purpose of the equipment owner data field is to capture this type of information (Table 5.37). Items like chargebacks, contracts, insurance, maintenance costs, and risk assessments are all dependent on knowing who owns the equipment. For example, suppose that a tenant adds two portable 5-ton air conditioners to its data center. Who pays for the electrical load created by these units? If one of the air conditioners fails and catches fire because maintenance was not performed on the unit, who is responsible? Is there a clause in the contract that allows facility management to maintain the equipment if requested? The full legal name of the organization that owns the equipment should be entered into the data field. Abbreviations and acronyms should be avoided because they tend to create confusion.

TABLE 5.37 Equipment Owner Data Example

Equipment_GUID	Equipment_ID_Composite	Equipment_COOP	Equipment_Owner
o8ash05Rv...	ABC0000-P-189:AB	No	ABC Corporation
hdJwe0023...	ABC0000-BAS-01	No	ABC Corporation
olAYr9HD1...	ABC0000-ACU-191	No	Security Tech
WEdbe803d...	ABC0000-RAC-316A	No	JBC Organization
T3hg26J3Y...	ABC0000-FAPTG-02	Yes	Smithsonian
Gj09Ht123...	ABC0000-FASCLPTR-07	Yes	AB Hayes Art

Equipment Curtailment

[EQUIPMENT_CURTAILMENT]

Curtailment is a period of time in which an electric utility asks corporations to reduce their peak electrical load. The equipment curtailment data field would be used to capture the different curtailment levels at which equipment would be secured (Table 5.38). The reason utilities ask companies to reduce their electrical load during peak times periods is because the electrical grid could be close to its capacity for carrying the load or there is a shortage of generating capacity by the utility company. Failure to assist in curtailments could cause brownout and blackouts. Curtailment levels are differing levels at which different equipment in a facility would be secured based on the load requirements of the electrical grid (Table 5.39). The curtailment levels would be accumulative and build upon each other as more stringent curtailments are required. For example, a nonessential curtailment level would be a request from a utility company for the facilities to voluntarily shut off nonessential loads like unused lighting, fountains, drinking water fountains, and so forth. A heighted curtailment level from a utility might indicate that the electric grid is getting close to its limit and facilities should reduce load as much as possible without affecting their operation, turning off equipment such as domestic chilling and hot water systems, air conditioning in unoccupied spaces, including the nonessential loads. An imminent curtailment level request from a utility company might indicate that if facilities do not start curtailment of loads, there will be a high possibility of rolling brownouts. The facility could then start shutting down equipment such as three out of four elevators in an elevator bank, mechanical room air conditioning, heightened loads, and the nonessential loads. Then there is a critical curtailment level in which blackouts are predicted. The facility should start reducing load as much as possible, be ready to start and load emergency generators, and protect personnel and mission-critical equipment. Knowing what equipment can be secured and at what levels can result a significant savings in resources and impact on the organization. At the time of writing this guide, there is no national unified curtailment level response designated by the industry. The most opportune time to determine

(continued)

[EQUIPMENT_CURTAILMENT] (continued)

the different levels at which equipment can be secured and still maintain the function of the facility is probably during commissioning. Commissioning is also the best time to determine the facility operational energy baselines. A reference table for the different levels should be developed and used to populate this data field to prevent human data-entry errors.

TABLE 5.38   Equipment Curtailment Data Example

Equipment_GUID	Equipment_ID_Composite	Equipment_COOP	Equipment_Curtailment
o8ash05Rv...	ABC0000-P-189:AB	No	3
A8FDy9w54...	ABC0000-AHU-050	No	2
qrv35t47j...	ABC0000-TNK-02	Yes	4
Giqre9732...	ABC0000-MCC-8A-XFMR-022	No	1
hdJwe0023...	ABC0000-BAS-01	No	4
T3hg26J3Y...	ABC0000-FAPTG-02	Yes	N/A

TABLE 5.39   Curtailment Level Examples

Curtailment Level	Description
1	Nonessential. The electrical grid is close to capacity. Secure nonessential loads.
2	Essential. The electrical is close or at capacity and utility is starting peak generators. Secure nonessential and reduce essential loads.
3	Imminent. The electrical grid is at full capacity possible brownouts are expected. Reduce load at facility as much as possible to not impact operations.
4	Critical. The electrical grid is at or above full capacity. Immediate curtailment is required, startup emergency generators, and protect critical loads.

Equipment Operation Schedule

[EQUIPMENT_OPERATION_SCHEDULE]

This field is a placeholder for the method used to designate the operating schedule for equipment required for building operation plans. Building operation plans are used to determine when equipment is required to be running to maintain normal weekday, weekend, night, startup, and shut down operations of a building. Knowing when equipment is supposed to be running versus what is actually running in the field is important to facility management and owners when trying to reduce operational costs, developing chargebacks, and evaluating and troubleshooting building operations. For example, an organization has a facility with a very high electrical usage at night. It needs to know what equipment should be running at night versus what is actually running at night. Because there are multiple ways to include a schedule in a database and every piece of equipment can have multiple schedules, the data fields for developing a schedule are not included in this book. For example, equipment could run only every third Thursday of a month, or daily, or monthly, or only during winter months. The data fields, equipment normal operations status, and equipment after-hours operations status are included in the book because they assist in developing building operation plans and are an additional data set beyond that associated with the equipment schedules.

Equipment Normal Operations Status

[EQUIPMENT_NORM_OP]

One of the best ways to understand the operation of a facility and develop methods for cost savings is for facility management to understand what equipment is running during normal operations (Table 5.40). This status field simplifies the process by allowing facility management to designate whether equipment is running during normal operations, YES, or not running during normal operations, NO.

TABLE 5.40   Equipment Normal Operations Status Data Example

Equipment_GUID	Equipment_ID_Composite	Equipment_Norm_Op	Equipment_After_Op
o8ash05Rv…	ABC0000-P-189:AB	Yes	No
A8FDy9w54…	ABC0000-AHU-050	Yes	No
fw565r713…	ABC0000-MOT-978	Yes	No
qrv35t47j…	ABC0000-TNK-02		
st7mnWq70…	ABC0000-GTV-14473		
hdJwe0023…	ABC0000-BAS-01	Yes	Yes
Le76Fieyh…	ABC0000-LCM-05	Yes	Yes

Equipment After-Hours Operation Status

[EQUIPMENT_AFTER_OP]

One of the best ways to develop methods for cost savings is for facility management to understand what equipment is supposed to be running outside of normal operating hours (Table 5.41). This status field helps simplify the process by simply allowing facility management to designate whether equipment is supposed to be running after hours, YES, or not running, NO. The reason that there is a separate after-hours status and a normal operation status is because some equipment is required to be running during normal and after-hours operations. Therefore, both statuses have to be captured.

TABLE 5.41   Equipment After-Hours Operation Status Example

Equipment_GUID	Equipment_ID_Composite	Equipment_Norm_Op	Equipment_After_Op
o8ash05Rv…	ABC0000-P-189:AB	Yes	No
A8FDy9w54…	ABC0000-AHU-050	Yes	No
fw565r713…	ABC0000-MOT-978	Yes	No
qrv35t47j…	ABC0000-TNK-02		
st7mnWq70…	ABC0000-GTV-14473		
hdJwe0023…	ABC0000-BAS-01	Yes	Yes
Le76Fieyh…	ABC0000-LCM-05	Yes	Yes

Equipment Status

[EQUIPMENT_STATUS]

The equipment status is used to capture the position that the equipment is required to be in for normal building operation of the facility (open/closed, on/off, standby/throttled, abandoned/removed) based on commissioning, operation, or design (Table 5.42). Understanding the normal position of the equipment is important because it allows operations to be able to determine deviations or changes in the normal position of the equipment. For example, suppose that a technician in the field is troubleshooting a low chill water flow situation in the facility. The technician finds a chill water bypass valve throttled open. Is the bypass valve the problem? What is its normal position? Did design or commissioning purposely have the bypass valve throttled open to improve building operation performance? The technician and facility management has no way to know the normal position of that valve unless that information is captured somewhere. Another reason to capture the status of equipment is that there are likely in the industry thousands of pieces of equipment that have been abandoned in place or removed for which organizations are still paying a contractor to maintain. There is currently no industry standard for equipment status. A reference table should be developed and used to provide standard user entries into the database to prevent human entry errors (Table 5.43).

TABLE 5.42   Equipment Status Data Example

Equipment_GUID	Equipment_ID_Composite	Equipment_Status	Equipment_Failure
o8ash05Rv...	ABC0000-P-189:AB	ON	FOF
st7mnWq70...	ABC0000-GTV-14473	NO	FC
Giqre9732...	ABC0000-MCC-8A-XFMR-022	ON	FOF
POq8723F4...	ABC0000-XFMR-022-EPB-LP17	ON	FOF
Dpo0984kf...	ABC0000-EPB-LP17-CB-MAIN	ON	FTP
Le76Fieyh...	ABC0000-LCM-05	ON	FLO
5Hgsoih8s...	ABC0000-TCM-092	ON	FHI

TABLE 5.43   Equipment Status Examples

Equipment Status	Abbrev	Description
Open	NO	Normally open
Close	NC	Normally closed
Throttled: (N)	NT	Normally throttled. (N) equal the number of turns.
On	ON	Equipment is normally running.
Off	OFF	Equipment is normally secured.
Standby	STBY	Equipment is designed as standby equipment and could be running if main equipment is secured.
As Needed	AS	Equipment is used as needed to perform a specific function usually for a short time period.
Passive	PASS	Installed equipment is passive and has no operational status. For example, indicators and tanks.
Abandoned	AIP	Equipment is abandoned in place.
Removed	REM	Equipment is removed and no longer used.

Equipment Failure Status

[EQUIPMENT_FAILURE]

The equipment failure status is used to capture the failure position or default position of equipment when a loss of power or motive forces occurs (Table 5.44). The failure status is normally based on the manufacturer, design, construction, or commissioning of the facility. Knowing the failure position of a piece of equipment can be vital to your organization. For example, there is a big difference in a normal seeking automatic transfer switch (ATS) and a power-seeking automatic transfer switch. On a loss of normal electrical power, a normal seeking ATS will always return to its designated main source of electrical power when power to that source is restored. A power-seeking ATS, on the other hand, will remain on the alternate power source, even when normal power is restored, until the alternate power source is lost. Knowing what type of ATS is installed in the facility can be very important when switching power sources around. The failure position of equipment could also have a significant impact when performing maintenance and troubleshooting. For example, a technician is sent out to perform a routine fuel oil tank level switch calibration. If the level switch failure position is fails low, meaning that when power is removed from the switch it indicates a low tank level, then when the technician removes power from that switch the automatic tank makeup equipment would automatically start to fill the tank. The technician would need to secure and isolate the automatic tank makeup system prior to performing the maintenance. Otherwise, the fuel oil makeup system will continually feed fuel to the tank until the level switch is returned to service or the tank overflows. The release of fuel oil to the environment is a very costly scenario for any organization. There is currently no industry standard for equipment failure status. Failure designations can be found for electrical and instrument and control equipment on their equipment specification sheets. A reference table should be developed and used to provide standard user entries into the database to prevent human entry errors (Table 5.45).

TABLE 5.44 Equipment Failure Status Data Example

Equipment_GUID	Equipment_ID_Composite	Equipment_Status	Equipment_Failure
o8ash05Rv...	ABC0000-P-189:AB	ON	FOF
st7mnWq70...	ABC0000-GTV-14473	ON	FC
Giqre9732...	ABC0000-MCC-8A-XFMR-022	ON	FOF
POq8723F4...	ABC0000-XFMR-022-EPB-LP17	ON	FOF
Dpo0984kf...	ABC0000-EPB-LP17-CB-MAIN	ON	FTP
Le76Fieyh...	ABC0000-LCM-05	ON	FLO
5Hgsoih8s...	ABC0000-TCM-092	ON	FHI

(continued)

[EQUIPMENT_FAILURE] (continued)

TABLE 5.45 Equipment Failure Status Examples

Equipment Failure Status	Abbrev	Description
Fail Open	FO	The equipment fails open. Normally this would be reserved for mechanical equipment like a valve or a damper. An electrical component that fails open, such as a circuit breaker, should be considered to fail in the off position. Industry consistently though expresses electrical contacts as failing open or closed.
Fail Close	FC	The equipment fails closed. Normally, this would be reserved for mechanical equipment like a valve or a damper. An electrical component that fails closed, such as a circuit breaker, should be considered to fail in the on position. Industry consistently though expresses electrical contacts as failing open or closed.
Fail On	FON	Equipment fails to the on position. This is a typical setup for emergency standby equipment required for event mitigation.
Fail Off	FOF	Equipment fails to the off position.
Fail Trip Free	FTP	Equipment fails to the trip-free position and has to be physically reset prior to operation. This is a common failure status for molded case electrical circuit breakers like the ones in homes.
Fail As Is	FAS	When equipment fails to as is, it means that the position stays the same as when it lost its power. Therefore, a running pump that fails as is on a loss of power will turn back on when power is restored.
Fail Low	FLO	Equipment fails low.
Fail Mid Position	FMD	Equipment fails to the middle position.
Fail High	FHI	Equipment fails high.
Power Seeking	PWR	Power-seeking devices will swap to an alternate power source when their normal power source is lost. When normal power is restored, the device does not swap back to the normal source.
Normal Seeking	NOR	Power seeking devices will swap to an alternate power source when their normal power source is lost. When normal power is restored, the device swaps back to the normal source.

Equipment Tag Condition

[EQUIPMENT_TAG]

The equipment tag condition field is used in the database to simply denote whether or not a component has a physical tag and what the condition of the tag is (Table 5.46). The different types of tag conditions should be developed and preloaded into a reference table instead of allowing personnel to enter or develop their own (Table 5.47). Using a reference table allows the data to be used and parsed in a more consistent fashion and reduces human input errors.

TABLE 5.46 Equipment Tag Condition Data Examples

Equipment_GUID	Equipment_ID_Composite	Equipment_Tag	Equipment_Security_Level
o8ash05Rv...	ABC0000-P-189:AB		
A8FDy9w54...	ABC0000-AHU-050	Installed	None
fw565r713...	ABC0000-MOT-978	No Tag	None

Equipment_GUID	Equipment_ID_Composite	Equipment_Tag	Equipment_Security_Level
qrv35t47j...	ABC0000-TNK-02	Installed	Classified
st7mnWq70...	ABC0000-GTV-14473	Replace	
Giqre9732...	ABC0000-MCC-8A-XFMR-022	Installed	
POq8723F4...	ABC0000-XFMR-022-EPB-LP17	Installed	
Dpo0984kf...	ABC0000-EPB-LP17-CB-MAIN	No Tag	
9fn09graO...	ABC0000-EPB-LP17-CB-01	No Tag	

TABLE 5.47 Equipment Tag Condition Reference Table Examples

Tag Condition	Description
Installed	Tag is installed and in good condition.
No Tag	The component has no tag and one needs to be ordered.
Replace	Tag is in poor condition and needs to be replaced.
Mislabeled	Tag is wrong and equipment is mislabeled.

Equipment Security Level

[EQUIPMENT_SECURITY_LEVEL]

There are facilities in which allowing access to equipment information to unintended personnel or the public would have adverse consequences to a company. For example, a bank institution might have air handling units and ventilations ducts associated with their secure vaults that they would not want to be common knowledge. The security department at an industry headquarters might not want general access to the type and location of security devices. At the same time, they want to use a common format for all of their equipment data and use a centralized database to improve their efficiency. There are two schools of thought on this subject: (1) do not capture this information or (2) capture the information on a separate secured server. The problem with not capturing secure equipment is simple; you cannot manage or ensure the proper maintenance is being performed on the equipment. The problem with number two is that you have to maintain a completely separate database and software program for that equipment, even though the same technicians work on all of the equipment (secure and unsecure). The better option is to tag the secure equipment information in the database and only allow access to that data per technician logon and security level.

The equipment security level allows the equipment information security levels to be set so that software and databases can ensure that only the personnel who have the proper level of access can see the information (Table 5.48). The different types of security level should be developed and preloaded into a reference table instead of allowing personnel to enter or develop their own (Table 5.49). Using a reference table allows the data to be used and parsed in a more consistent fashion and reduces human input errors.

(continued)

[EQUIPMENT_SECURITY_LEVEL] (continued)

TABLE 5.48   Equipment Security Level Data Example

Equipment_GUID	Equipment_ID_Composite	Equipment_Security_Level	Equipment_Manufacturer
A8FDy9w54...	ABC0000-AHU-050	None	AC Company
fw565r713...	ABC0000-MOT-978		Motors RUS
qrv35t47j...	ABC0000-TNK-02	Classified	KD Manufacturing
Xy398gnTy...	ABC0000-CHKV-02	Classified	Valves 2Go
1789gt435...	ABC0000-GENENG-01	Classified	ElectricCo
5Hgsoih8s...	ABC0000-TCM-092	Secret	Control Inc.
dTrbn32ht...	ABC0000-TI-191	Classified	Control Inc.
Keb5g28Bt...	ABC0000-TI-316A	Secret	Control Inc.

TABLE 5.49   Equipment Security Level Reference Table Example

Security Level
None
Classified
Secret
Top Secret

Equipment Specifications

A discussion of attributes and specifications is important at this stage. The two definitions are frequently comingled, and this leads to confusion when developing contracts and databases. Per Webster's dictionary, a specification is "a detailed listing or description of the required properties of some object proposed to be built or bought." Typically, when related to equipment, specifications are those properties that define the design and operational parameters of a component. For example, a motor is defined by horsepower, frequency, amperage, voltage, and so forth. Notice that equipment sequence number, acronym, location, and the like are not listed as a specification. Specifications are normally defined and developed by the manufacturer of the component. Webster defines an attribute as "that which is attributed; a quality which is considered as belonging to, or inherent in, a person or thing; an essential or necessary property or characteristic." So an attribute is something that defines a necessary characteristic. While specifications are necessary characteristics of a component, an easier way to separate the two is to define attributes as properties that create a unique instance of a component and specifications are the design properties of that component. An instance is something so uniquely defined that it is the only one that exists within a set of defined circumstances. For example, air conditioners as a whole are not unique and are made by many different manufacturers and with many different designs. The minute an air conditioner is purchased and then installed in a facility, ACUNIT-001, it becomes an instance. There is no other ACUNIT-001 designed by XYZ manufacturer with ABC serial number within that facility. Each person in the world is an instance that is defined by attributes and meets certain design specifications.

There are specifications that are universal for all equipment, such as make, model, and manufacturer, which make up the core information about the component. Because these specifications are universal, separate data fields have been defined for them.

Equipment Manufacturer

[EQUIPMENT_MANUFACTURER]

This data field is used to capture the name of the equipment manufacturer (Table 5.50). It is not only important to facility management to capture the manufacturer, model, and serial numbers of equipment, but this information is also important to other departments within an organization. The project management, safety, environmental, sustainability, energy, and even the portfolio divisions can make use of this information. For example, a large corporation has received a manufacture recall of all Triton Series ELS fire dampers manufactured by JB Corporation with serial numbers starting 378NX. The management team needs to know how many of the dampers are in their portfolio. The safety team needs to devise contingency fire plans when the dampers are being replaced. The project team needs to know suitable replacement dampers that meet the same specifications and which facilities will be affected. The budget team needs to know who to charge for the projects, staff costs, and at what level the organization or the manufacturer will pay for the costs.

TABLE 5.50 Equipment Manufacturer Data Example

Equipment_GUID	Equipment_ID_Composite	Equipment_Manufacturer	Equipment_Model_Name
o8ash05Rv...	ABC0000-P-189:AB	Pump Corp	PSC
A8FDy9w54...	ABC0000-AHU-050	AC Company	Troy
fw565r713...	ABC0000-MOT-978	Motors RUS	SSE
qrv35t47j...	ABC0000-TNK-02	KD Manufacturing	
st7mnWq70...	ABC0000-GTV-14473	Valves 2Go	Titan
Giqre9732...	ABC0000-MCC-8A-XFMR-022	ElectricCo	Series 1100
POq8723F4...	ABC0000-XFMR-022-EPB-LP17	ElectricCo	Series 2400

Equipment Model Name

[EQUIPMENT_MODEL_NAME]

The equipment model name and number are separated into two fields. The fields are separated because it is not uncommon to find multiple pieces of equipment with the same model name but different model numbers. The easiest example is the car industry. There are multiple versions of a pickup model named F150 that have model numbers ES, LS, and so on. This data field is used to capture only the model name (Table 5.51).

TABLE 5.51   Equipment Model Name Data Example

Equipment_GUID	Equipment_ID_Composite	Equipment_Manufacturer	Equipment_Model_Name
o8ash05Rv...	ABC0000-P-189:AB	Pump Corp	PSC
A8FDy9w54...	ABC0000-AHU-050	AC Company	Troy
fw565r713...	ABC0000-MOT-978	Motors RUS	SSE
st7mnWq70...	ABC0000-GTV-14473	Valves 2Go	Titan
Giqre9732...	ABC0000-MCC-8A-XFMR-022	ElectricCo	Series 1100
POq8723F4...	ABC0000-XFMR-022-EPB-LP17	ElectricCo	Series 2400
Dpo0984kf...	ABC0000-EPB-LP17-CB-MAIN	ElectricCo	Series 240

Equipment Model Number

[EQUIPMENT_MODEL_NUMBER]

The equipment model number data field is used to capture the designated manufacturer product model number. For example, if you brought an Atlas Series 3400 valve model 24 ball valve, Atlas would be the manufacturer, Series 3400 would be the model name, and 24 would be the model number. This data field is used only to capture the model number (Table 5.52).

TABLE 5.52   Equipment Model Number Data Example

Equipment_GUID	Equipment_ID_Composite	Equipment_Model_Name	Equipment_Model_Number
o8ash05Rv...	ABC0000-P-189:AB	PSC	1148
A8FDy9w54...	ABC0000-AHU-050	Troy	21500
fw565r713...	ABC0000-MOT-978	SSE	19778
st7mnWq70...	ABC0000-GTV-14473	Titan	589
Giqre9732...	ABC0000-MCC-8A-XFMR-022	Series 1100	1105
POq8723F4...	ABC0000-XFMR-022-EPB-LP17	Series 2400	2400E
Dpo0984kf...	ABC0000-EPB-LP17-CB-MAIN	Series 240	240MDX

Equipment Serial Number

[EQUIPMENT_SERIAL_NUMBER]

This data field is used to capture the equipment serial number, which is the manufacturer's serial number, usually found on the equipment label plate or purchase order (Table 5.53).

TABLE 5.53 Equipment Serial Number Data Example

Equipment_GUID	Equipment_ID_Composite	Equipment_Serial_Number	Equipment_Manf_Date
o8ash05Rv...	ABC0000-P-189:AB	97409189236y49	1/17/1992
A8FDy9w54...	ABC0000-AHU-050	38748-8378237-2387	4/22/2000
fw565r713...	ABC0000-MOT-978	4748437d-2q39872	10/26/1998
qrv35t47j...	ABC0000-TNK-02	3247670	11/9/1999
st7mnWq70...	ABC0000-GTV-14473	97409714-3-243-23	6/6/1995
Giqre9732...	ABC0000-MCC-8A-XFMR-022	54-98710-61	2/19/1999
POq8723F4...	ABC0000-XFMR-022-EPB-LP17	12548-5408-4	5/5/1998
9fn09graO...	ABC0000-EPB-LP17-CB-01	524-dh-09308	7/18/1999

Equipment Manufactured Date

[EQUIPMENT_MANF_DATE]

The manufacture date is used to capture the actual date that the equipment was manufactured (Table 5.54). The manufacture date is important to organizations when determining the applicability of the manufacturer's warranty, useful life, and shelf life of equipment. It is recommended to use the standard month-date-year format: MM/DD/YYYY.

TABLE 5.54 Equipment Manufactured Date Data Example

Equipment_GUID	Equipment_ID_Composite	Equipment_Serial_Number	Equipment_Manf_Date
o8ash05Rv...	ABC0000-P-189:AB	97409189236y49	1/17/1992
A8FDy9w54...	ABC0000-AHU-050	38748-8378237-2387	4/22/2000
fw565r713...	ABC0000-MOT-978	4748437d-2q39872	10/26/1998
qrv35t47j...	ABC0000-TNK-02	3247670	11/9/1999
st7mnWq70...	ABC0000-GTV-14473	97409714-3-243-23	6/6/1995
Giqre9732...	ABC0000-MCC-8A-XFMR-022	54-98710-61	2/19/1999
POq8723F4...	ABC0000-XFMR-022-EPB-LP17	12548-5408-4	5/5/1998
9fn09graO...	ABC0000-EPB-LP17-CB-01	524-dh-09308	7/18/1999

Equipment Manufacturer Shelf Life

[EQUIPMENT_SHELFLIFE]

Shelf life is the maximum amount of time, usually in years, which a piece of equipment can sit on a shelf before being installed and still be covered by the manufacturer's guarantees. The shelf life field is used to capture the maximum shelf life allowed for a component, based on the manufacturer's information, which still allows the warranty to be valid (Table 5.55). Maximum shelf life can normally be found in the equipment documentation. For example, suppose that a technician wants to install a motor that has a maximum shelf life of 10 years. The date is 2010 and the motor manufacture date was 1995. Therefore, today's date minus the equipment manufacture date would equate to 15 years that this motor has been sitting on a shelf (actual shelf life). Actual shelf life minus the equipment manufacturer shelf life would state that the motor is 5 years beyond the manufacturer's recommendation. The manufacturer needs to be contacted for a variation letter or to determine the validity and ownership of warranties. You have a multimillion dollar facility built and your construction manager gets a special deal on air conditioners. Are you covered or responsible for the contractor installing equipment that is significantly past its shelf life? What are your quality assurance inspection procedures? The manufacturer's recommended maximum shelf life would be entered into this data field.

TABLE 5.55   Equipment Manufacturer Shelf Life Data Example

Equipment_GUID	Equipment_ID_Composite	Equipment_Manf_Date	Equipment_ShelfLife	Installed_Date
o8ash05Rv...	ABC0000-P-189:AB	1/17/1992	5	3/18/2000
A8FDy9w54...	ABC0000-AHU-050	4/22/2000		4/22/2000
fw565r713...	ABC0000-MOT-978	10/26/1998	10	4/22/2000
qrv35t47j...	ABC0000-TNK-02	11/9/1999		11/9/1999
st7mnWq70...	ABC0000-GTV-14473	6/6/1995	10	11/18/1999
9fn09graO...	ABC0000-EPB-LP17-CB-01	7/18/1999	5	1/20/2000
hdJwe0023...	ABC0000-BAS-01	3/28/1999	2	2/20/2000
Le76Fieyh...	ABC0000-LCM-05	11/23/1999	5	12/15/1999
olAYr9HD1...	ABC0000-ACU-191	9/9/1989	8	5/10/2000
WEdbe803d...	ABC0000-RAC-316A	5/7/2001	8	8/20/2005

Equipment Installed Date

[INSTALLED_DATE]

The equipment installed date field is used to capture the date that the piece of equipment was actually installed in the facility (Table 5.56). Installed dates are very important to facility management and owners to determine life expectancy of equipment, scheduling future long-term budgets, warranties, and so forth. For example, an organization installs a pump that is designed to operate, with proper maintenance, for 25 years. If the pump was installed in the year 2010, the facility management and executive team could then schedule the funds and replacement costs for the pump tentatively for the year 2035.

TABLE 5.56 Equipment Installed Date Data Example

Equipment_GUID	Equipment_ID_Composite	Equipment_Manf_Date	Equipment_ShelfLife	Installed_Date
o8ash05Rv...	ABC0000-P-189:AB	1/17/1992	5	3/18/2000
A8FDy9w54...	ABC0000-AHU-050	4/22/2000		4/22/2000
fw565r713...	ABC0000-MOT-978	10/26/1998	10	4/22/2000
qrv35t47j...	ABC0000-TNK-02	11/9/1999		11/9/1999
st7mnWq70...	ABC0000-GTV-14473	6/6/1995	10	11/18/1999
9fn09graO...	ABC0000-EPB-LP17-CB-01	7/18/1999	5	1/20/2000
hdJwe0023...	ABC0000-BAS-01	3/28/1999	2	2/20/2000
Le76Fieyh...	ABC0000-LCM-05	11/23/1999	5	12/15/1999
olAYr9HD1...	ABC0000-ACU-191	9/9/1989	8	5/10/2000
WEdbe803d...	ABC0000-RAC-316A	5/7/2001	8	8/20/2005

Equipment Life Expectancy

[LIFE_EXPECTANCY]

The equipment life expectancy field is used to capture, in years, the manufacturers or industry's projected expected life span of this type of equipment (Table 5.57). Life expectancy of equipment is typically based on the amount of time equipment can be expected to last while in operation and does not normally take into account the length of time it was sitting on a shelf. This information, when compared to the installed date, is vital for the proper strategic planning and budgeting of the facility. When entering a numeric value into this field, it should be assumed that the number is in years.

TABLE 5.57 Equipment Life Expectancy Data Example

Equipment_GUID	Equipment_ID_Composite	Life_Expectancy	Equipment_Age
o8ash05Rv...	ABC0000-P-189:AB	25	17
A8FDy9w54...	ABC0000-AHU-050	20	9
fw565r713...	ABC0000-MOT-978	25	11
qrv35t47j...	ABC0000-TNK-02	35	10
st7mnWq70...	ABC0000-GTV-14473	20	14
Giqre9732...	ABC0000-MCC-8A-XFMR-022	25	10
hdJwe0023...	ABC0000-BAS-01	10	10
Le76Fieyh...	ABC0000-LCM-05	15	10
Just2t37h...	ABC0000-AHU-052	20	9

Equipment Age

[EQUIPMENT_AGE]

Equipment age captures the current age of the equipment and displays this age in years (Table 5.58). The age of the equipment can be entered to the database or the database programmers can automatically calculate the age by using the current date and subtracting the manufactured date. Having a quick reference to the age of the equipment in the facility can be beneficial to projecting staffing and future strategic planning. For example, if the age of a piece of equipment is past its life expectancy, an organization can determine to increase the level of maintenance on the equipment or replace the equipment, depending on its condition.

TABLE 5.58 Equipment Age Data Example

Equipment_GUID	Equipment_ID_Composite	Life_Expectancy	Equipment_Age
o8ash05Rv...	ABC0000-P-189:AB	25	17
A8FDy9w54...	ABC0000-AHU-050	20	9
fw565r713...	ABC0000-MOT-978	25	11
qrv35t47j...	ABC0000-TNK-02	35	10
st7mnWq70...	ABC0000-GTV-14473	20	14
hdJwe0023...	ABC0000-BAS-01	10	10
Le76Fieyh...	ABC0000-LCM-05	15	10
Just2t37h...	ABC0000-AHU-052	20	9

Equipment Operation Age

[EQUIPMENT_OPS_AGE]

The equipment operation age captures the length of time equipment has been in service (Table 5.59). The data can be hand entered into the database itself or it could be calculated by using the current date and subtracting the installed date. The equipment operation age data is the age used to determine when that equipment reaches the end of its life expectancy. For example, suppose that a pump manufactured in 1992 has a life expectancy of 25 years based on manufacturers' recommendations. The pump was installed and placed in service in the year 2000. In 2010, the actual age of the equipment is 18 years, according to the date on which it was manufactured. However, because life expectancy is actually based on the number of years a piece of equipment is in operation, the equipment's operation age is 10 years (10 years in operation). Shelf life is not taken into account when determining life expectancy. Therefore, the facility should expect another 15 years of operation out of the equipment.

TABLE 5.59 Equipment Operation Age Data Example

Equipment_GUID	Equipment_ID_Composite	Equipment_Age	Equipment_Ops_Age
o8ash05Rv...	ABC0000-P-189:AB	17	9
A8FDy9w54...	ABC0000-AHU-050	9	9
fw565r713...	ABC0000-MOT-978	11	9
qrv35t47j...	ABC0000-TNK-02	10	10
st7mnWq70...	ABC0000-GTV-14473	14	10
hdJwe0023...	ABC0000-BAS-01	10	9
Le76Fieyh...	ABC0000-LCM-05	10	10
Just2t37h...	ABC0000-AHU-052	9	9

Equipment Purchased Condition

[PURCHASED_CONDITION]

The equipment purchased condition data field is used to designate what the condition of the equipment was when it was installed (Table 5.60). Most owners are under the impression that any equipment they have purchased and installed is brand new. When in reality, equipment that is installed in older facilities is often no longer made, and it is therefore cheaper to rebuild or buy refurbished equipment than it would be to replace a whole system. Therefore, it is important to know what the condition of the equipment was when it was installed. There is no industry standard for purchase condition of equipment. A reference table should be developed and used to provide standard user entries into the database to prevent human entry errors (Table 5.61).

TABLE 5.60 Equipment Purchase Condition Data Example

Equipment_GUID	Equipment_ID_Composite	Purchased_Condition	Equipment_Installation_Cost
o8ash05Rv...	ABC0000-P-189:AB	Rebuilt	$45,000.00
qrv35t47j...	ABC0000-TNK-02	New	$23,112.23
st7mnWq70...	ABC0000-GTV-14473	New	$3,994.94
9fn09graO...	ABC0000-EPB-LP17-CB-01	New	$165.00
1789gt435...	ABC0000-GENENG-01	New	$453,988.53
Ohe33jG2x...	ABC0000-ELEV-15	New	$89,000.00
T3hg26J3Y...	ABC0000-FAPTG-02		Priceless
Gj09Ht123...	ABC0000-FASCLPTR-07		Priceless

TABLE 5.61   Equipment Purchase Condition Examples

Purchase Condition	Description
New	Equipment is new from the manufacturer or distributor.
Rebuilt	Equipment was been rebuilt. Rebuilt means a complete overhaul of the equipment to as new a condition as possible. Machining, milling, and rewinding of equipment are typical.
Refurbished	Refurbished equipment is equipment in which seals, gaskets, and degraded parts are replaced but no major rebuilding has been performed.
Used	Used equipment has had no replacement or rebuilding of parts.

Equipment Installation Cost

[EQUIPMENT_INSTALLATION_COST]

Equipment installation cost is used to capture the actual cost of the equipment at the time of its installation (Table 5.62). You should not use this field to capture the labor and other related installation costs of the equipment. Equipment installation cost is important for capital depreciation, taxes, project estimations, and strategic planning.

TABLE 5.62   Equipment Installation Cost Data Example

Equipment_GUID	Equipment_ID_Composite	Purchased_Condition	Equipment_Installation_Cost
o8ash05Rv...	ABC0000-P-189:AB	Rebuilt	$45,000.00
qrv35t47j...	ABC0000-TNK-02	New	$23,112.23
st7mnWq70...	ABC0000-GTV-14473	New	$3,994.94
9fn09graO...	ABC0000-EPB-LP17-CB-01	New	$165.00
1789gt435...	ABC0000-GENENG-01	New	$453,988.53
Ohe33jG2x...	ABC0000-ELEV-15	New	$89,000.00
T3hg26J3Y...	ABC0000-FAPTG-02		Priceless
Gj09Ht123...	ABC0000-FASCLPTR-07		Priceless

Equipment Specification Purpose

[SPEC_PURPOSE (N)] (N denotes that multiple fields are possible.)

Every product has its own unique specifications that are based on the specific type of equipment. For example, the product specifications for a motor are different from those for a manual ball valve. For a motor you need to know the horsepower, amperage, voltage, and the like. For a manual ball valve, you need to know size of the valve, valve seat material, and so on. Because there are literally thousands of different types of equipment that require different specification parameters, there are literally millions of possible combinations of specifications. Instead of defining the millions of possible specifications that could be used, I have broken the data down into three data fields that can be used for any of the combinations: equipment specification purpose, specification unit, and specification value data fields. The data fields can then be replicated to cover all the specifications related to each specific piece of equipment. For example, if I designed a system for a 40-horsepower, 240-volt, 3-phase motor, the equipment specification purpose would be design; the specification units would be Horsepower, Voltage, Phase; the equipment specification values would be 40, 240, and 3.

The equipment specification purpose is used to denote the purpose for that specification (Table 5.63), whether it was a design specification, manufacturer's specification, operating characteristics, tested values, or so on. The importance of this field is to allow owners and facility management to know what was the intent of that specification. The different types of specification purposes should be developed and preloaded into a reference table instead of allowing personnel to enter or develop their own. Using a reference table for design, tested, installed, and the like allows the data to be used and parsed in a more consistent fashion and reduces human input errors (Table 5.64).

TABLE 5.63 Equipment Specification Purpose Data Example

Equipment_ID_Composite	Spec_Purpose (1)	Spec_Unit (1)	Spec_Value (1)	Spec_Purpose (2)	Spec_Unit (N)	Spec_Value (N)
ABC0000-P-189:AB	Design	Horse Power	50	Installed	Horsepower	50
ABC0000-AHU-050	Design	SCFM	45000	Installed	SCFM	52000
ABC0000-MOT-978	Design	Horse Power	40	Installed	Horsepower	50
ABC0000-TNK-02	Design	Gallon	7000	Installed	Gallon	7500
ABC0000-GTV-14473	Design	Size Inch	4	Design	Seat Material	Carbon Steel
ABC0000-XFMR-022-EPB-LP17	Design	Voltage AC	240	Installed	Voltage AC	240
ABC0000-EPB-LP17-CB-MAIN	Design	Voltage AC	240	Design	Amperage	500
ABC0000-EPB-LP17-CB-01	Design	Voltage AC	240	Design	Amperage	100
ABC0000-EPB-LP17-CB-02	Design	Voltage AC	240	Design	Amperage	100
ABC0000-EPB-LP17-CB-03	Design	Voltage AC	240	Design	Amperage	100
ABC0000-LCM-05	Design	Voltage DC	24	Installed	Voltage DC	24
ABC0000-P-018	Design	Horse Power	5	Design	Voltage AC	240
ABC0000-TNK-01	Design	Gallon	500	Installed	Gallon	650
ABC0000-MOACTR-02	Design	Horse Power	1.5	Design	Voltage AC	240

TABLE 5.64 Specification Purpose Type Examples

Specification Purpose Types
Design
Installed
Tested
Operation
Calibrated

Equipment Specification Unit

[SPEC_UNIT (N)] (N denotes that multiple fields are possible.)

Every product has its own unique specifications that are based on the specific type of equipment. For example, the product specifications for a pump are different from those for a check valve. Because there are literally thousands of different types of equipment that require different specification parameters, the equipment specification unit and value data fields are used to capture each variant based on the type of equipment. The equipment specification unit is used to capture the unit of measure or property for the specification: horsepower, British thermal units, temperature, pressure, and so on. For example, if I have a 240-voltage alternating current (VAC) 500-ampere circuit breaker, the units would be voltage, alternating current, and amperes (Table 5.65). Using a reference table to ensure that specification units are always entered the same way is important. Currently, there is only one industry standard that I know of, OmniClass™ Table 49, that has a compilation of these types of units. At the time of writing this book, OmniClass™ Table 49 – Properties was in a draft form (Table 5.66).

TABLE 5.65 Equipment Specification Unit Data Example

Equipment_ID_Composite	Spec_Purpose (1)	Spec_Unit (1)	Spec_Value (1)	Spec_Purpose (2)	Spec_Unit (N)	Spec_Value (N)
ABC0000-P-189:AB	Design	Horse Power	50	Installed	Horsepower	50
ABC0000-AHU-050	Design	SCFM	45000	Installed	SCFM	52000
ABC0000-MOT-978	Design	Horse Power	40	Installed	Horsepower	50
ABC0000-TNK-02	Design	Gallon	7000	Installed	Gallon	7500
ABC0000-GTV-14473	Design	Size Inch	4	Design	Seat Material	Carbon Steel
ABC0000-XFMR-022-EPB-LP17	Design	Voltage AC	240	Installed	Voltage AC	240
ABC0000-EPB-LP17-CB-MAIN	Design	Voltage AC	240	Design	Amperage	500
ABC0000-EPB-LP17-CB-01	Design	Voltage AC	240	Design	Amperage	100
ABC0000-EPB-LP17-CB-02	Design	Voltage AC	240	Design	Amperage	100
ABC0000-EPB-LP17-CB-03	Design	Voltage AC	240	Design	Amperage	100
ABC0000-LCM-05	Design	Voltage DC	24	Installed	Voltage DC	24
ABC0000-P-018	Design	Horse Power	5	Design	Voltage AC	240
ABC0000-TNK-01	Design	Gallon	500	Installed	Gallon	650
ABC0000-MOACTR-02	Design	Horse Power	1.5	Design	Voltage AC	240

TABLE 5.66 Equipment Specification Unit Examples

OmniClass™ Table 49 - Properties	
Number	Title
49-71 19 13	Length
49-71 19 15	Width
49-71 51 21 11	Minimum Temperature
49-71 51 21 13	Maximum Temperature
49-71 75 25	Gage Pressure
49-71 75 33	Static Pressure Differential
49-91 41 11	Amperage
49-91 41 13	Voltage

OmniClass™ Table-49 is a product of Construction Specification Institute/Construction Specification Canada. Version OmniClass_49_2010-06-04 DRAFT

Equipment Specification Value

[SPEC_VALUE(N)] (N denotes that multiple fields are possible.)

The equipment specification value is the numerical value associated with the specification unit for that type of equipment. For example, if I have a 40-horsepower, 240-volt, 3-phase motor, the equipment specification units would be Horsepower, Voltage, Phase; the equipment specification values would be 40, 240, and 3 (Table 5.67). Values do not have to be only numerical. It is possible to be creative with the values field to capture items like valve seat material carbon steel, where the specification unit is valve seat material and the value is carbon steel.

TABLE 5.67 Equipment Specification Value Data Example

Equipment_ID_Composite	Spec_Purpose (1)	Spec_Unit (1)	Spec_Value (1)	Spec_Purpose (2)	Spec_Unit (N)	Spec_Value (N)
ABC0000-P-189:AB	Design	Horsepower	50	Installed	Horsepower	50
ABC0000-AHU-050	Design	SCFM	45000	Installed	SCFM	52000
ABC0000-MOT-978	Design	Horsepower	40	Installed	Horsepower	50
ABC0000-TNK-02	Design	Gallon	7000	Installed	Gallon	7500
ABC0000-GTV-14473	Design	Size Inch	4	Design	Seat Material	Carbon Steel
ABC0000-XFMR-022-EPB-LP17	Design	Voltage AC	240	Installed	Voltage AC	240
ABC0000-EPB-LP17-CB-MAIN	Design	Voltage AC	240	Design	Amperage	500
ABC0000-EPB-LP17-CB-01	Design	Voltage AC	240	Design	Amperage	100
ABC0000-EPB-LP17-CB-02	Design	Voltage AC	240	Design	Amperage	100
ABC0000-EPB-LP17-CB-03	Design	Voltage AC	240	Design	Amperage	100
ABC0000-LCM-05	Design	Voltage DC	24	Installed	Voltage DC	24
ABC0000-P-018	Design	Horsepower	5	Design	Voltage AC	240
ABC0000-TNK-01	Design	Gallon	500	Installed	Gallon	650
ABC0000-MOACTR-02	Design	Horsepower	1.5	Design	Voltage AC	240

COMPLEX DATA FIELDS

Where the equipment is located is important to operations for tracking, allocation of resources, and proper financial planning. Location information is broken down from the macro level, complex, down to the micro level of space. The complex data field is used to capture information about a complex, campus, or group of facilities (Figure 5.12). Only the information that is important for locating equipment is included in this book. While there is other information that is important about a complex that an organization might like to add, this book is focused on equipment. It is recommended that an organization add any other necessary data fields to those defined. When dealing with a complex of multiple buildings, the financial aspects of the group as a whole are important. The term "complex" is synonymous with the terms "site," "base," or "campus."

FIGURE 5.12   Complex
Data Tables

Complex GUID

[COMPLEX_GUID]

The complex GUID is a defined space in the database for the unique identifier used to link all related complex data (Table 5.68). GUIDs are normally hidden from the end user and do not need to be user understandable. The complex GUID would be then linked to the associated equipment in the database.

TABLE 5.68   Complex GUID Data Example

Complex_GUID	Complex_Number	Complex_Name	Site_Plot_Point	Site_Plot_Altitude
T98fU12bV...	0001	Policy Plaza Complex	Reference	800
K7f23Yu89...	0002	High Headquarter		
9zx4We12q...	0003	Warm Storage Complex		
P7yhtiu34...	0004	University of Town		
I09fT435x...	0005	Forward Research Base		

Equipment Database				
Equipment_GUID	Industry_Code_Description	Equipment_ID_Composite	Complex_GUID	Facility_GUID
o8ash05Rv...	Centrifugal Pump	ABC0000-P-189:AB	T98fU12bV...	Ik6hfd9Ar...
A8FDy9w54...	Built-Up Indoor Air Handling Unit	ABC0000-AHU-050	T98fU12bV...	Ik6hfd9Ar...
fw565r713...	Single-Speed Three Phase AC Motor	ABC0000-MOT-978	T98fU12bV...	Ik6hfd9Ar...
qrv35t47j...	Multiple-Walled Vented Tank	ABC0000-TNK-02	T98fU12bV...	Ik6hfd9Ar...

Complex Number

[COMPLEX_NUMBER]

Most companies or organizations that have a large number of facilities will develop a building and a complex numbering system for tracking purposes. The complex number data field is for the number that identifies the complex in the organizations' portfolio (Table 5.69). The complex number is typically used by portfolio or finance departments. It is important to have the necessary information that links the equipment data needed for the finance and portfolio departments to the complex at which the costs occurred. Example: RPUID = Real Property Unique ID.

TABLE 5.69 Complex Number Data Example

Complex_GUID	Complex_Number	Complex_Name	Site_Plot_Point	Site_Plot_Altitude
T98fU12bV...	0001	Policy Plaza Complex	Reference	800
K7f23Yu89...	0002	High Headquarter		
9zx4We12q...	0003	Warm Storage Complex		
P7yhtiu34...	0004	University of Town		
I09fT435x...	0005	Forward Research Base		

Complex Name

[COMPLEX_NAME]

The complex name is the assigned name for the complex per an organization's portfolio management division (Table 5.70). For example, State Polytechnic Institute Campus

TABLE 5.70 Complex Name Data Example

Complex_GUID	Complex_Number	Complex_Name	Site_Plot_Point	Site_Plot_Altitude
T98fU12bV...	0001	Policy Plaza Complex	Reference	800
K7f23Yu89...	0002	High Headquarter		
9zx4We12q...	0003	Warm Storage Complex		
P7yhtiu34...	0004	University of Town		
I09fT435x...	0005	Forward Research Base		

Site Plot Point

[SITE_PLOT_POINT(N)] (N denotes that multiple fields are possible.)

The site plot points are used to map out the site boundary of the complex (Table 5.71). These data points were included in the data set for equipment to enable facility management to track equipment location in relation to the site boundary. The site boundary is typically used to determine who is responsible for the equipment. For example, when looking at the water utility line, typically a facility is responsible for the water line between the utility meter, normally located close to the site boundary, and the facility. From the water meter back to the utility, it is the utility's responsibility. Therefore, it is important to know where your site boundaries are.

(continued)

[SITE_PLOT_POINT(N)] (N denotes that multiple fields are possible.) (continued)

TABLE 5.71   Site Plot Point Data Example

Complex_Name	Site_Plot_Point	Site_Plot_Altitude	Site_Plot_Latitude	Site_Plot_Longitude
Policy Plaza Complex	Reference	800	−0.140716667	37.56385
	0001	801	−0.140716667	37.56385
	0002	803	−0.140716667	37.56385
	0003	800	−0.140716667	37.56385
	0004	815	−0.140716667	37.56385

The site plot point data field is used to number or name the different groupings of geological location coordinates: altitude, latitude, and longitude. There are numerous ways in which to identify a specific point on the earth. For simplicity, this guide only includes the basic data points for altitude, latitude, and longitude. The plot point data field is used to number or define the purpose of that set of plot points. The concept, as in connect the dots, is to capture as many plot points as necessary to accurately to be able to draw a line that defines the site boundary of the facility or complex.

The data field points included are:

Site Plot Point	[Site_Plot_Point(N)]
Site Plot Point Altitude	[Site_Plot_Altitude(N)]
Site Plot Point Latitude	[Site_Plot_Latitude (N)]
Site Plot Point Longitude	[Site_Plot_Longitude (N)]

Complex Address

The following data points are used to capture the address of the complex. These data fields are self-explanatory and are not discussed in this guide. These fields were developed for the United States and can be modified for other countries. The address of the complex and facilities are important for shipping, code and regulation compliance, taxes, and the like.

Complex Country	[Complex_Country]
Complex Address	[Complex_Address]
Complex City	[Complex_City]
Complex State	[Complex_State]
Complex Zip	[Complex_ZipCode]

FACILITY DATA FIELDS

The facility data fields are the minimum information about a facility needed for an equipment inventory. Figure 5.13 shows the facility table and any recommended reference tables. "Facility" is synonymous with the terms "structure," "garage," "park," and "building." The term "facility" was selected because of the usage of the term in facility management. There are more types of information about a facility that a facility management staff needs to know, such as gross square footage, rentable square footage and so on, that is not included in this guide. This book focuses on the data needed strictly for equipment.

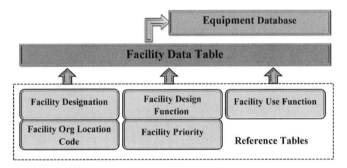

FIGURE 5.13 Facility Data Tables

Facility GUID

[FACILITY_GUID]

The Facility GUID is a defined space in the database for the unique identifier used to link all related facility data (Table 5.72). GUIDs are normally hidden from the end user and do not need to be user understandable. The Facility GUID would be linked to the associated equipment in the database.

TABLE 5.72 Facility GUID Data Example

Facility_GUID	Facility_Number	Facility_Name	Facility_Owner
LKFDh3wie...	DC0001	JMC	ABC Corporation
KJB8D0itW...	DC0002	Daily Federal	JKL Corporation
lk6hfd9Ar...	DC0003	Fairview	ABC Corporation

Equipment Database			
Equipment_GUID	Industry_Code_Description	Equipment_ID_Composite	Facility_GUID
o8ash05Rv...	Centrifugal Pump	ABC0000-P-189:AB	lk6hfd9Ar...
A8FDy9w54...	Built-Up Indoor Air Handling Unit	ABC0000-AHU-050	lk6hfd9Ar...
fw565r713...	Single-Speed Three-Phase AC Motor	ABC0000-MOT-978	lk6hfd9Ar...
qrv35t47j...	Multiple-Walled Vented Tank	ABC0000-TNK-02	lk6hfd9Ar...

Facility Number

[FACILLITY_NUMBER]

The facility number is the organization's self-generated number that uniquely identifies the facility in that organizations portfolio (Table 5.73). Facility numbers are typically used by financial and portfolio departments to track facility finances and metrics.

TABLE 5.73   Facility Number Data Example

Facility_GUID	Facility_Number	Facility_Name	Facility_Alias	Facility_Owner
LKFDh3wie…	DC0001	JMC		ABC Corporation
KJB8D0itW…	DC0002	Daily Federal	Building 2	JKL Corporation
lk6hfd9Ar…	DC0003	Fairview	AB Headquarters	ABC Corporation

Facility Name

[FACILITY_NAME]

The Facility Name is the legal or portfolio name of the facility (Table 5.74). For example: White House. Capturing the proper name for the facility improves the ways in which equipment data can be grouped to determine the operational characteristics of different facilities.

TABLE 5.74   Facility Name Data Example

Facility_GUID	Facility_Number	Facility_Name	Facility_Alias	Facility_Owner
LKFDh3wie…	DC0001	JMC		ABC Corporation
KJB8D0itW…	DC0002	Daily Federal	Building 2	JKL Corporation
lk6hfd9Ar…	DC0003	Fairview	AB Headquarters	ABC Corporation

Facility Alias Name

[FACILITY_ALIAS(N)] (N denotes that multiple fields are possible.)

The facility alias name is used to capture any other name for the facility besides the approved corporate or legal name (Table 5.75). Example: A corporation might have in their portfolio the "John J Warehouse," but the building is known by the tenants and city as the "Wharf Market." Capturing this information allows the resources used to cross-reference the information to deal with documents or invoices addressed to either of these names quickly.

TABLE 5.75 Facility Name Alias Data Example

Facility_GUID	Facility_Number	Facility_Name	Facility_Alias	Facility_Owner
LKFDh3wie...	DC0001	JMC		ABC Corporation
KJB8D0itW...	DC0002	Daily Federal	Building 2	JKL Corporation
lk6hfd9Ar...	DC0003	Fairview	AB Headquarters	ABC Corporation

Facility Owner

[FACILITY_OWNER(N)] (N denotes that multiple fields are possible.)

The facility owner is a text designation of the organization, corporation, or person who owns the facility (Table 5.76). There are instances in which there are multiple owners of a facility. In such scenarios, all of the owners should be captured. Capturing the owner's name allows the proper decisions for, tax relief, charges, finances, and the like to be properly assigned to the responsible party.

TABLE 5.76 Facility Owner Data Example

Facility_GUID	Facility_Number	Facility_Name	Facility_Alias	Facility_Owner
LKFDh3wie...	DC0001	JMC		ABC Corporation
KJB8D0itW...	DC0002	Daily Federal	Building 2	JKL Corporation
lk6hfd9Ar...	DC0003	Fairview	AB Headquarters	ABC Corporation

Facility Designation

[FACILITY_DESIGNATION]

The facility designation field is used to denote the disposition of the facility within the corporation's portfolio (Table 5.77). This field would be used to denote whether the building is leased, owned, under construction, decommissioned, and so forth (Table 5.78). This allows an organization to parse its data based on the status of their buildings. There currently is not an industry standard, that I am aware of, that defines the different designations. A reference table should be developed for the different facility designations to allow users to select their designations and thereby prevent human entry errors.

TABLE 5.77 Facility Designation Data Example

Facility_GUID	Facility_Number	Facility_Name	Facility_Owner	Facility_Designation
LKFDh3wie...	DC0001	JMC	ABC Corporation	Owned
KJB8D0itW...	DC0002	Daily Federal	JKL Corporation	Leased
lk6hfd9Ar...	DC0003	Fairview	ABC Corporation	Owner

(continued)

[FACILITY_DESIGNATION] (*continued*)

TABLE 5.78   Facility Designation Examples

Facility Designation	Description
Owned	Facility is owned by the organization.
Leased	This facility is leased by the organization.
Decommissioned	This facility is no longer in use and awaiting disposition.
Condemned	This facility is condemned and is not to be used.
Construction	This facility is under construction.

Facility Design Function

[FACILITY_DESIGN_FUNCTION]

Determining the design function of the facility is important in measuring the performance and operation of that facility. Capturing what the actual design function of the facility will allow the owner and facility manager to examine how the facility performs in relation to its peers and within a portfolio. This information is related to equipment in that a major part of determining how a facility performs is also determining what equipment was installed to support the design function. For example, if I have two facilities that were designed as office buildings and use the same type of constant volume control equipment, can I determine what my projected operating costs would be for those types of facilities? The facility design function data field is used to capture what the actual construction design function of the facility was (Table 5.79). The facility function types should be standardized for selection by the user as a reference table to prevent user and human error (Table 5.80). It is recommended that you use OmniClass™ Table 11 Construction Entities by Function for this purpose (See Chapter 4, "Industry Standards").

TABLE 5.79   Facility Design Function Data Example

Facility_Number	Facility_Name	Facility_Design_Code	Facility_Design_Function	Facility_Use_Code
DC0001	JMC	11-11 11 21	Training Center	11-12 27 21
DC0002	Daily Federal	11-17 11 17	Multi-tenant Office Building	11-17 11 17
DC0003	Fairview	11-17 11 17	Multi-tenant Office Building	11-17 11 11

TABLE 5.80   Facility Function Types

OmniClass™ Table 11 Construction by Function	
Number	Title
11-11 11 21	Training Center
11-11 21 14	Broadcasting Facility
11-12 11 11	Daycare Facility

OmniClass™ Table 11 Construction by Function	
Number	Title
11-12 11 14	Preschool Facility
11-12 24 11	University
11-12 27 11	Biomedical Research Facility
11-12 27 14	Chemical Research Facility
11-12 27 21	Computing Research Facility
11-13 11 11	Administrative Government Facility
11-13 11 14	Regulatory Agency Facility
11-13 11 17	Courthouse
11-13 11 24	Police Station
11-13 11 27	Post Office
11-13 21 11	Military Headquarters
11-13 24 11	Hospital
11-14 11 11	General Purpose Library
11-17 11 11	Headquarters Office
11-17 11 14	Regional Administrative Office
11-17 11 17	Multi-tenant Office Building

CSI/CSC OmniClass™ Table 11 is a product of Construction Specification Institute/Construction Specification Canada, Version OmniClass_11_2006-03-28

Facility Design Code

[FACILITY_DESIGN_CODE]

The facility design code is used to capture the code related to the design function type. In the Table 5.79 Facility Design Function Data Example, the code is the OmniClass™ number related to the title, function, designated for the facility.

Facility Use Function

[FACILITY_USE_FUNCTION]

The functional use of a facility is as important in measuring the performance and operation of a facility as the design function. It is not uncommon to find a warehouse that has been converted to a computer data center or even offices. Knowing the use of the facility, combined with the design function of the facility, gives owners and facility managers a better understanding of the operation

(continued)

[FACILITY_USE_FUNCTION] (*continued*)

and equipment usage within that facility. The facility use function data field is used to capture what the actual utilization of the facility is (Table 5.81). The facility use types should be standardized for selection by the user as a reference table to prevent user errors. It is recommended that you use the same table used for the design function of the facility, OmniClass™ Table 11 Construction Entities by Function for this purpose (See Chapter 4, "Industry Standards").

TABLE 5.81   Facility Use Function Data Example

Facility_Number	Facility_Name	Facility_Design_Function	Facility_Use_Code	Facility_Use_Function
DC0001	JMC	Training Center	11-12 27 21	Computing Research Facility
DC0002	Daily Federal	Multi-tenant Office Building	11-17 11 17	Multi-tenant Office Building
DC0003	Fairview	Multi-tenant Office Building	11-17 11 11	Headquarters Office

Facility Use Code

[FACILITY_USE_CODE]

The facility use code is used to capture the code related to the use function type. In Table 5.81 Facility Use Function Data Example, the code is the OmniClass™ number related to the title, function, designated for the facility.

Facility Plot Point

[FACILITY_PLOT_POINT(N)] (N denotes that multiple fields are possible.)

The facility plot points are used to map out the boundary of the facility. These data points were included in the data set to enable an organization to map the boundaries of a facility on a site or complex.

The facility plot point data field is used to number or name the different groupings of geological location coordinates: altitude, latitude, and longitude. There are numerous ways in which to identify a specific point on the earth. For simplicity, this guide only includes the basic data points for altitude, latitude, and longitude. The plot point data field is used to number or define the purpose of that set of plot points. The concept, as in connect the dots, is to capture as many plot points as necessary to accurately to be able to draw a line that defines the boundary of the facility. Table 5.82 shows an example of how the data would look; note that the same plot point was used for all the data for simplicity and the real-world data would be different for each point in the database.

The data field points included is as follows:

Facility Plot Point   [Facility_Plot_Point(N)]
Facility Plot Point Altitude   [Facility_Plot_Altitude(N)]

Facility Plot Point Latitude   [Facility_Plot_Latitude (N)]
Facility Plot Point Longitude   [Facility_Plot_Longitude (N)]

TABLE 5.82   Facility Owner Data Example

Facility_Number	Facility_Name	Facility_Plot_Point	Facility_Plot_Altitude	Facility_Plot_Latitude	Facility_Plot_Longitude
DC0001	JMC	Reference	800	−0.140716667	37.56385
DC0002	Daily Federal	Reference	800	−0.140716667	37.56385
DC0003	Fairview	Reference	800	−0.140716667	37.56385

Facility Organization Location Code

[FACILITY_LOCATION_CODE]

The facility organization location code captures the code used by the organization to designate the geographical location grouping system, region, zone, and so on used by the organization for its facilities (Table 5.83). For example, some corporations parse the United States by Northeast, Southeast, and Midwest. Some corporations use the time zones. Some federal agencies use regions. This information is important for strategic planning and financial allocations. Each grouping of facilities typically has its own facility management department and, therefore, it is important to be able to identify those groups so that they can properly operate their equipment and facilities according to their procedures and policies.

TABLE 5.83   Facility Organization Location Code Data Example

Facility_GUID	Facility_Number	Facility_Name	Facility_Location_Code	Facility_Country
LKFDh3wie...	DC0001	JMC	NE Region	United States
KJB8D0itW...	DC0002	Daily Federal	NE Region	United States
lk6hfd9Ar...	DC0003	Fairview	NE Region	United States

Facility Address

The following data points are used to capture the address of the facility. These data fields are self-explanatory and are not discussed in this book. These fields were developed for the United States and can be modified for other countries.

The address of the complex and facilities are important for shipping, code and regulation compliance, taxes, and other uses.

The following data fields are related to the facility address:

Facility Country	[Facility_Country]
Facility Address	[Facility_Address]
Facility City	[Facility_City]
Facility State	[Facility_State]
Facility Zip	[Facility_ZipCode]

Facility Priority

[FACILITY_PRIORITY]

The facility priority field is used to capture the priority of the facility based on its function (Table 5.84). At the time of this writing, the only comprehensive facility priority system, I could find, was used by the U.S. Coast Guard. Facility priorities are a new concept in facility management, but the positive impact can be significant. The inability to differentiate between the worth of facilities in a portfolio causes ineffective utilization of resources when responding to work or assigning resources in a multiple-facility/complex environment. It is not uncommon to have personnel sent to a facility to perform work that has a low impact on the organization and then have to reroute those resources to a higher-priority facility. A mobile repair team/technician when given two similar work orders for different facilities needs to know which facility to respond to first. Rerouting personnel and funds inappropriately can create a significant impact on customer service and create a drain on finances and resources. For example, suppose that a corporation has funds to install a new boiler in one of their facilities. Not knowing the priority of the facilities, a corporation might install the boiler in a low-use facility that has a low impact on their business as opposed to a high-impact facility that could improve their productivity.

TABLE 5.84   Facility Priority Data Example

Facility_GUID	Facility_Number	Facility_Name	Facility_Owner	Facility_Priority
LKFDh3wie...	DC0001	JMC	ABC Corporation	BUSH
KJB8D0itW...	DC0002	Daily Federal	JKL Corporation	CUSH
lk6hfd9Ar...	DC0003	Fairview	ABC Corporation	HQ

Note: I do not recommend using numbers for priorities unless specifically defined because sooner than later all facilities become a level 1, and what does a level 1, 2, 3, or 4 even mean? What is an A76 priority versus a B42 priority? Numeric systems soon lose their meaning. Lettering systems on the other hand can always be cross-referenced to a numbering system, according to an organizations matrix of importance, thereby allowing them to be interpreted by computers. Again, a reference table should be developed and used to prevent human entry errors (Table 5.85).

TABLE 5.85 Facility Priorities Example

Facility Priorities		
Code	Definition	Organization Importance Matrix
BUS	Business	–
BUSH	High Business Impact/Mission Critical	1
BUSM	Medium Business Impact	2
BUSL	Minimum Business Impact	3
CUS	Customer Service	–
CUSH	VIP/High Customer Impact	1
CUSM	Medium Customer Impact	2
CUSL	Minimum Customer Impact	3
SEC	Security	1
HQ	Headquarters	2
ADM	Administration	3
GEN	General	4
NON	Nonessential	5

SPACE DATA FIELDS

This section covers the minimum space data fields needed to designate where a piece of equipment is located within the facility. Figure 5.14 shows the space tables and any recommended reference tables. The location of equipment is very important to all aspects of facility management from repair, preventive maintenance, and operation to finance and emergency response. This guide does not include all of the required data for spaces that is needed for facility management. This guide only deals with the space data needed in relation to equipment. For example: The square footage (SQFT) of the room is not included because it does not affect the equipment located within the room.

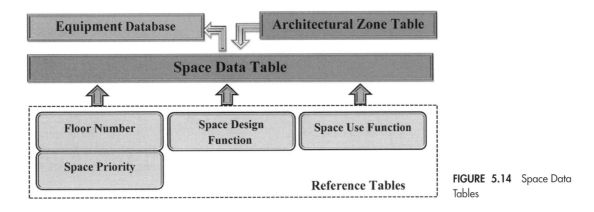

FIGURE 5.14 Space Data Tables

The SQFT of a space is very important to facility management, however. A facility management database should include all the information needed, of which equipment is but one subset.

When initially taking equipment inventories in a facility, the space data should be developed first so that it can be used in the equipment database fields when taking the equipment inventories.

Architectural Zone Data

Architectural zones are groups of spaces that make up a defined architectural structure of a facility. For example, a wing of a hospital might be made up of multiple patient rooms, closets, telecommunication rooms, and nursing stations. The wing is considered to be an architectural zone. A large facility might have a wing, concourse, section that encompasses multiple floors and spaces. To capture this grouping in a logical format a list of the descriptions that the floors and spaces can be tied to needs to exist. The architectural zone descriptions are typically assigned by the architect and engineer based on design of the facility. The spatial data are grouped in a separate table and linked to the space data because a zone can contain many spaces and replicating the data in the database would be time-consuming.

Architectural Zone GUID

[ARCHITECTURE_ZONE_GUID]

The Architectural Zone GUID is a defined space in the database for the unique identifier used to link all related zone data (Table 5.86). GUIDs are normally hidden from the end user and do not need to be user understandable. The Architectural Zone GUID would be linked to the associated spaces in the database.

TABLE 5.86   Architectural Zone GUID Data Example

Architectural_Zone_GUID	Audit_Short_Description
Ty3b0871W...	East Wing
K9eFwk10D...	Section A4
19tE0oP32...	E Ring
Typ3C0nCr...	Concourse
19tE0oP32...	Zone 4

Space_GUID	Architectural_Zone_GUID	Floor_Number	Blueprint_Room_Number
f9th35Dg1...	Ty3b0871W...	B1	109
Nnw2j08al...	K9eFwk10D...	2	
Y7hru8yhR...	19tE0oP32...	1	113

Architectural Zone Description

[ARCHITECTURE_ZONE_DESCRIPTION]

The architectural zone description data field is the text description for the zone (Table 5.87). The name can designated by the architect, engineer, or tenant. For example, Wing, Section, Train, or Ring.

TABLE 5.87 Architectural Zone Description Data Example

Architectural_Zone_GUID	Audit_Short_Description
Ty3b0871W...	East Wing
K9eFwk10D...	Section A4
19tE0oP32...	E Ring
Typ3C0nCr...	Concourse
19tE0oP32...	Zone 4

Space GUID

[SPACE_GUID]

The Space GUID is a defined space in the database for the unique identifier used to link all related location data (Table 5.88). GUIDs are normally hidden from the end user and do not need to be user understandable. The Space GUID would be linked to the associated equipment in the database.

TABLE 5.88 Space GUID Data Example

Space_GUID	Architectural_Zone_GUID	Floor_Number	Blueprint_Room_Number
f9th35Dg1...	Ty3b0871W...	B1	109
092Thuq23...	Ty3b0871W...	P1	P01
32Siqw87s...	Ty3b0871W...	1	101
Equipment Database			
Equipment_GUID	**Industry_Code_Description**	**Equipment_ID_Composite**	**Space_GUID**
o8ash05Rv...	Centrifugal Pump	ABC0000-P-189:AB	f9th35Dg1...
qrv35t47j...	Multiple Walled Vented Tank	ABC0000-TNK-02	092Thuq23...
POq8723F4...	Electrical Panel Board	ABC0000-XFMR-022-EPB-LP17	32Siqw87s...

Floor Number

[FLOOR_NUMBER]

The floor number is the number or letter designation used to describe the floor (Table 5.89). Try to stay away from using 1st, First, and the like because one person will enter 1ST, one will enter 1 ST, and another will enter first. Databases see these as different names, and it makes sorting the data and getting usable information more difficult. I recommend using industry standards. Example: ANSI/BOMI designation for the 1st floor is: 01. A reference table should be set up to be used for all facilities so that the user can only select the correct floor designation. This prevents human entry errors.

TABLE 5.89 Floor Number Data Example

Space_GUID	Floor_Number	Blueprint_Room_Number	Org_Room_Number
f9th35Dg1...	B1	109	B101
092Thuq23...	P1	P01	P1A
32Siqw87s...	1	101	101B
N37d075h2...	1	101	101C
Nnw2j08al...	2		220
Y7hru8yhR...	1	113	113A
I4h83pK09s...	1	113	113B
T41s1ssiL...	1	114	114
J0h3th357...	1	115	
O3htyuTer...	1	116	1034

Blueprint Room Number

[BLUEPRINT_ROOM_NUMBER]

The blueprint room number is the number or identification assigned to the space per the architect or engineer who designed the facility (Table 5.90). There are two room designation data fields; blueprint room number and organization room number. The reason that there are two data fields is that, once a facility is built, it is not uncommon for tenants to renumber or split up spaces. For example, an architect designs a large space and numbers the space 2100 on the blueprints. The tenant moves into the spaces and subdivides the space into an office, break room, and conference room and labels the rooms 2100A, 2100B, and 2100C, respectively. Because there is a difference between record documents and what is in the field, it is important to know what the original blueprint room number is in order to be able to understand the design of the space. This data field is used for the designation for the space that would be found on the record set of blueprints or in a building information model (BIM).

TABLE 5.90 Blueprint Room Number Data Example

Space_GUID	Floor_Number	Blueprint_Room_Number	Org_Room_Number
f9th35Dg1...	B1	109	B101
092Thuq23...	P1	P01	P1A

Space_GUID	Floor_Number	Blueprint_Room_Number	Org_Room_Number
32Siqw87s...	1	101	101B
N37d075h2...	1	101	101C
Nnw2j08al...	2		220
Y7hru8yhR...	1	113	113A
I4h83pK09s...	1	113	113B
T41s1ssiL...	1	114	114
J0h3th357...	1	115	
O3htyuTer...	1	116	1034

Organization Room Number

[ORG_ROOM_NUMBER]

The organization room number is the room or space identification number designated by the organization or corporation that is occupying the facility (Table 5.91). These numbers are typically different from the blueprint room numbers or a variation of them. For example, a space that has a blueprint room number 403 might be split up by an organization into four separate rooms: 403A, 403B, 403C, and Conference Room 4. Not capturing both the organization room number and the blueprint room number can lead to a lot of wasted manpower and resources being used to recreate the data. Buildings are designed to operate in a specific manner based upon the design of the building. When additional walls and rooms are added by the tenants the design characteristics can change for the facility. Having the ability to determine the intent of the equipment based on blueprint design as opposed to the actual space layout can be pivotal to the efficient operation of a facility. Another factor is the answering of service calls. If your organization calls a room a specific number and the tenant calls the room another number, there has to be a way to reconcile the differences. Besides, blueprint numbers rarely change, while tenant room numbers are in constant flux.

TABLE 5.91 Organization Room Number Data Example

Space_GUID	Floor_Number	Blueprint_Room_Number	Org_Room_Number
f9th35Dg1...	B1	109	B101
092Thuq23...	P1	P01	P1A
32Siqw87s...	1	101	101B
N37d075h2...	1	101	101C
Nnw2j08al...	2		220
Y7hru8yhR...	1	113	113A
I4h83pK09s...	1	113	113B
T41s1ssiL...	1	114	114
J0h3th357...	1	115	
O3htyuTer...	1	116	1034

Space Design Function

[SPACE_DESIGN_FUNCTION]

Determining the design function of the space is important in measuring the performance and operation of that space. Capturing what the actual design function of the space is will allow the owner and facility manager to examine how the space performs in relation to the facility and how similar spaces perform throughout the portfolio. This information is related to equipment in that a major part of determining how a space performs is also determining what equipment was installed to support the design function. For example, if I have two office spaces, can I determine what my projected operating costs would be for those types of space? What is the best design for those spaces? What are the average overtime costs for those spaces? The space design function data field is used to capture what the actual construction design function of the space was (Table 5.92). The space function types should be standardized for selection by the user as a reference table to prevent user errors (Table 5.93). It is recommended that you use OmniClass™ Table 13 Space by Function for this purpose (See Chapter 4, "Industry Standards").

TABLE 5.92   Space Design Function Data Example

Org_Room_Number	Space_Design_Code	Space_Design_Function
B101	13-59 00 00	Production, Fabrication, and Maintenance Spaces
P1A		
101B	13-55 29 21 11	Conference Room
101C	13-23 23 11	Building Manager Office
220	13-49 19 00	Data Center
113A	13-55 11 00	Office Spaces
113B	13-55 11 00	Office Spaces
114	13-55 11 00	Office Spaces
	13-55 11 00	Office Spaces
1034	13-23 19 31	Telecommunications Room

TABLE 5.93   Space Function Type Example

OmniClass™ Table 13 Spaces by Function	
Number	Title
13-59 00 00	Production, Fabrication, and Maintenance Spaces
13-55 29 21 11	Conference Room
13-23 23 11	Building Manager Office
13-49 19 00	Data Center
13-55 11 00	Office Spaces
13-55 11 00	Office Spaces
13-55 11 00	Office Spaces
13-55 11 00	Office Spaces
13-23 19 31	Telecommunications Room

OmniClass™ Table 13 is a product of Construction Specification Institute/Construction Specification Canada, Version OmniClass_13_2010-06-24

Space Design Code

[SPACE_DESIGN_CODE]

The Space design code is used to capture the code related to the design function type. In the Table 5.92 Space Design Function Data Example, the code is the OmniClass™ number related to the title, function, designated for the space.

Space Use Function

[SPACE_USE_FUNCTION]

The functional use of a space is as important in measuring the performance and operation of a space as the design function. It is not uncommon to find an office that has been converted to a conference room, computer data center, or kitchenette. Knowing the use of the space, combined with the design function of the space, gives owners and facility managers a better understanding of the operation and equipment usage within that space. The space use function data field is used to capture what the actual function of how the space is used (Table 5.94). The space use types should be standardized for selection by the user as a reference table to prevent user errors. It is recommended that you use the same table used for the design function of the Space, OmniClass™ Table 13 Spaces by Function for this purpose (See Chapter 4, "Industry Standards").

TABLE 5.94   Space Use Function Data Example

Org_Room_Number	Space_Use_Code	Space_Use_Function
B101	13-59 00 00	Production, Fabrication, and Maintenance Spaces
P1A		
101B	13-55 29 21 11	Conference Room
101C	13-23 23 11	Building Manager Office
220	13-49 19 00	Data Center
113A	13-55 11 00	Office Spaces
113B	13-55 11 00	Office Spaces
114	13-49 19 00	Data Center
	13-55 29 21 11	Conference Room
1034	13-23 19 31	Telecommunications Room

Space Use Code

[SPACE_USE_CODE]

The space use code is used to capture the code related to the use function type. In the Table 5.94 Space Use Function Data Example, the code is the OmniClass™ number related to the title, function, designated for the space.

Space Description

[SPACE_DESCRIPTION]

Space description data field is the database location for the text description of the space (Table 5.95). The name can be designated by the architect, engineer, or tenant; for example, Executive Board Room or WAN Server Room. Having a standard for naming rooms is important. Users entering information should avoid abbreviations and acronyms. A computer sees Room, rm, Mech, Mechancial, and so forth as different rooms/names when sorting the data.

TABLE 5.95 Space Description Data Example

Space_GUID	Floor_Number	Org_Room_Number	Space_Descirption	Space_ID_Composite
f9th35Dg1...	B1	B101	Mechanical Chiller Room	B1:109:B101
092Thuq23...	P1	P1A	East Parking Garage	P1:P01:P1A
32Siqw87s...	1	101B	Grand Conference	01:101:101B
N37d075h2...	1	101C	Manager's Office	01:101:101C
Nnw2j08al...	2	220	WAN 7-18 Room	02::220
Y7hru8yhR...	1	113A	Office	01:113:113A
I4h83pK09s...	1	113B	Office	01:113:113B
T41s1ssiL...	1	114	LAN Room 5	01:114:114
J0h3th357...	1		Conference Room	01:115:
O3htyuTer...	1	1034	Telecommunications Room	01:116:1034

Space Identification Composite

[SPACE_ID_COMPOSITE]

The space identification composite field is used to capture the label of the room (Table 5.96). A lot of organizations will predefine the labeling schema of a room. For example: Wing: Floor: Room Number: Description or WING A: 01:1218: Conference Room. If you look at most labeling systems, they are a composite of different data fields. Some of the data fields change more often than others.

For example, the organization room numbers change more often than blueprint room numbers. This is one of the main reasons that it is a poor practice to use these methods to create a UID for a database. Instead, you can combine the information from the different data fields and concatenate them into the space identification composite field. This then becomes the data field that is shown and used by the end users, as opposed to the GUID, to process work items such as service calls. While technically a composite field is not required, because a programmer can just only show those fields to an end user, this data field was included for simplicity of operation.

TABLE 5.96   Space Identification Composite Data Example

Space_GUID	Floor_Number	Org_Room_Number	Space_Descirption	Space_ID_Composite
f9th35Dg1...	B1	B101	Mechanical Chiller Room	B1:109:B101
092Thuq23...	P1	P1A	East Parking Garage	P1:P01:P1A
32Siqw87s...	1	101B	Grand Conference	01:101:101B
N37d075h2...	1	101C	Manager Office	01:101:101C
Nnw2j08al...	2	220	WAN 7-18 Room	02::220
Y7hru8yhR...	1	113A	Office	01:113:113A
I4h83pK09s...	1	113B	Office	01:113:113B
T41s1ssiL...	1	114	LAN Room 5	01:114:114
J0h3th357...	1		Conference Room	01:115:
O3htyuTer...	1	1034	Telecommunication Room	01:116:1034

Space Priority

[SPACE_PRIORITY]

The space priority field is used to classify the priority of the space based on its form or function (Table 5.97). The inability to differentiate between the priorities of work based on a location in a facility results in ineffective utilization of resources. At the time of this writing, a comprehensive space priority system could not be found. Prioritizing spaces is a relatively new concept in facility management. It is interesting to note that a lot of O&M contracts require a contract facility management teams to respond to emergency and urgent calls within a specific time period, but the spaces that would generate these calls are not prioritized. A technician when given two work orders of the same type for different spaces needs to know which to respond to first. Not knowing this can create a significant impact on customer service and a drain on funds and resources. Executive decisions need to be based on the impact that the space has on its productivity. The main door of an emergency room should have a higher response time than the back door of a loading dock. For example, the atrium to a corporate headquarters that has high public traffic will most likely have a higher work priority than an atrium to a furniture warehouse that has no public traffic. Both spaces are atriums, but one has a higher business impact on the corporation.

(continued)

[SPACE_PRIORITY] (continued)

TABLE 5.97   Space Priority Data Field

Space_GUID	Floor_Number	Org_Room_Number	Space_ID_Composite	Space_Priority
f9th35Dg1...	B1	B101	B1:109:B101	BUSM
092Thuq23...	P1	P1A	P1:P01:P1A	GEN
32Siqw87s...	1	101B	01:101:101B	NON
N37d075h2...	1	101C	01:101:101C	ADM
Nnw2j08al...	2	220	02::220	BUSH
Y7hru8yhR...	1	113A	01:113:113A	
I4h83pK09s...	1	113B	01:113:113B	
T41s1ssiL...	1	114	01:114:114	
J0h3th357...	1		01:115:	
O3htyuTer...	1	1034	01:116:1034	

Note: I do not recommend using numbers for priorities unless specifically defined because sooner than later all spaces become a level 1, and what is a level 1, 2, 3, or 4 even mean? What is an A76 versus a B42? The system soon loses its meaning. Lettering systems on the other hand can always be cross-referenced to a numbering system determined by what is important to the organization, then they can be interpreted by computers (Table 5.98).

TABLE 5.98   Space Priority Examples

Space Priorities		
Code	Definition	Organization Importance Matrix
BUS	Business	–
BUSH	High Business Impact/Mission Critical	1
BUSM	Medium Business Impact	2
BUSL	Minimum Business Impact	3
CUS	Customer Service	–
CUSH	VIP/High Customer Impact	1
CUSM	Medium Customer Impact	2
CUSL	Minimum Customer Impact	3
SEC	Security	1
HQ	Headquarters	2
ADM	Administration	3
GEN	General	4
NON	Nonessential	5

TENANT DATA FIELDS

Tenant information, while not as obvious, is very important to equipment data when related to the operation of an organization or corporation. Figure 5.15 shows the tenant table and any recommended reference tables. Large facilities can consist of multiple tenants that install their own equipment: air conditioners, heaters, refrigerators, microwaves, data centers, and the like. The equipment installed by tenants could be self-maintained, have maintenance contracted out, or be maintained by the facility management team. Tracking all of the plug loads and equipment according to which tenant owns what equipment, who maintains it, and the related resources can be very time intensive and costly. Chargebacks are developed by invoicing the correct tenant. Therefore, the equipment data should be tied to the tenant or owner.

FIGURE 5.15 Tenant Data Tables

Tenant GUID

[TENANT_GUID]

The Tenant GUID is a defined space in the database for the unique identifier used to link all related tenant data (Table 5.99). The tenant GUID is then linked to the equipment owned by the tenant in the equipment database.

TABLE 5.99 Tenant GUID Data Example

Tenant_GUID	Tenant_Name	Tenant_OrgName	Tenant_DeptName
4Fjgd7w21...	ABC Corporation	COMP	Legal
n2jP092gh...	Department of Energy	Nuclear Regulatory Commission	Budget Division
q05fEw29u...	Johnson Bank	Customer Accounts	Marketing Department
U734RnQck...	Town University	Administrations	Student Admissions

Equipment Database			
Equipment_GUID	Industry_Code_Description	Equipment_ID_Composite	Tenant_GUID
o8ash05Rv...	Centrifugal Pump	ABC0000-P-189:AB	4Fjgd7w21
A8FDy9w54...	Built-Up Indoor Air Handling Unit	ABC0000-AHU-050	4Fjgd7w21
fw565r713...	Single-Speed Three Phase AC Motor	ABC0000-MOT-978	4Fjgd7w21
qrv35t47j...	Multiple-Walled Vented Tank	ABC0000-TNK-02	4Fjgd7w21

Tenant Name

[TENANT_NAME]

The tenant name field is used to capture the official full name of the tenant, whether organization, person, or corporation (Table 5.100); for example, ABC Corporation or Department of Energy.

TABLE 5.100   Tenant Name Data Example

Tenant_GUID	Tenant_Name	Tenant_OrgName	Tenant_DeptName
4Fjgd7w21...	ABC Corporation	COMP	Legal
n2jP092gh...	Department of Energy	Nuclear Regulatory Commission	Budget Division
q05fEw29u...	Johnson Bank	Customer Accounts	Marketing Department
U734RnQck...	Town University	Administrations	Student Admissions

Tenant Organization Name

[TENANT_ORGNAME]

The tenant organization name field is used to capture the tenant's suborganizational name (Table 5.101). Large corporations and federal and state agencies have multiple departments or subagencies that use different financial streams to pay for different expenditures. Tying this information to the facility and its equipment can be vital to ensuring that the correct organizations are contacted or invoiced. For example, ABC Corporation might have a computer division ABC COMP or the Nuclear Regulatory Commission (NRC) under the Department of Energy.

TABLE 5.101   Tenant Organization Data Example

Tenant_GUID	Tenant_Name	Tenant_OrgName	Tenant_DeptName
4Fjgd7w21...	ABC Corporation	COMP	Legal
n2jP092gh...	Department of Energy	Nuclear Regulatory Commission	Budget Division
q05fEw29u...	Johnson Bank	Customer Accounts	Marketing Department
U734RnQck...	Town University	Administrations	Student Admissions

Tenant Department Name

[TENANT_DEPTNAME]

The tenant department name is used to capture the department name of the tenant (Table 5.102). Example: ABC COMP Legal Department or NRC Budget Division. The data capture of the department name is important for properly developing charges and scheduling resources.

TABLE 5.102   Tenant Department Data Example

Tenant_GUID	Tenant_Name	Tenant_OrgName	Tenant_DeptName
4Fjgd7w21...	ABC Corporation	COMP	Legal
n2jP092gh...	Department of Energy	Nuclear Regulatory Commission	Budget Division
q05fEw29u...	Johnson Bank	Customer Accounts	Marketing Department
U734RnQck...	Town University	Administrations	Student Admissions

Tenant Code

[TENANT_CODE(N)] (N denotes that multiple fields are possible.)

The tenant code field is used to capture any designated codes related to the tenant (Table 5.103). The purpose for this field is to have a common place in the database for financial and related codes. When a corporation or organization develops chargebacks, invoices, and other financial items, it typically has a budget code related to its client or use a provided customer code for these transactions. In a significant amount of these instances, the facility management is involved in developing the estimates or invoices and creating the paperwork. Having the data in an easy-to-find location, tied to the tenant and equipment, allows for a better utilization of resources. A good practice would be to tie the financial database codes directly to this field. For example: ABC07123 as the budget line code for ABC COMP Legal Department or PS12345 as the reimbursable work order accounting code related to NRC Budget Division. While only a single code is shown in the data example, it is possible to have multiple codes related to a tenant and equipment. If more than one code exists, then second, third, and further tenant code data fields would be added to the database. This code field is designed only for equipment-related tenant codes. For example, a chargeback is being used to charge a tenant that wants to run their office space additional hours after normal working hours. The chargeback is based on the electrical costs for running facility equipment those extra hours. Being able to link the equipment to the charge and thereby allow facility management to quickly determine what after-hours equipment is running is very important.

TABLE 5.103   Tenant Code Data Example

Tenant_GUID	Tenant_Name	Tenant_DeptName	Tenant_Code
4Fjgd7w21...	ABC Corporation	Legal	ABDC981756-98
n2jP092gh...	Department of Energy	Budget Division	D2-123561-9872
q05fEw29u...	Johnson Bank	Marketing Department	JB-17-1223339
U734RnQck...	Town University	Student Admissions	UT-001

JOB PLAN AND JOB TASK DATA FIELDS

Job tasks are any defined work that is required to be performed on equipment or the facility. Figure 5.16 shows the job plan and task tables and any recommended reference tables. The most common job task is preventive maintenance. A single job task should include all of the steps and tools that are required to be used to perform specific work on a piece of equipment. The purpose of including job task data fields in an equipment inventory book is that job tasks are one of the main reasons for developing an equipment inventory. The number of personnel or costs an organization has to allocate in their budget is directly related to the number of job tasks that have to be performed, which in turn is directly related to the amount of equipment in the facility. Therefore, it is important to understand the necessary job task data fields and their relationship to equipment. Job tasks should, and usually are, a separate data table in the database. Think of the job task database as a huge library of tasks. When work on a piece of equipment is required, the computer references the library and pulls out the related task for the technician. The computer then generates a work order for the work the technician is to perform. The beauty of this design is that if there is a lot of the same type of equipment that requires the same tasks, the task only has to be stored in the library once and then referenced for each similar piece of equipment.

Facility management normally places limitations on the job task function by limiting their discussion to just preventive maintenance and service calls.

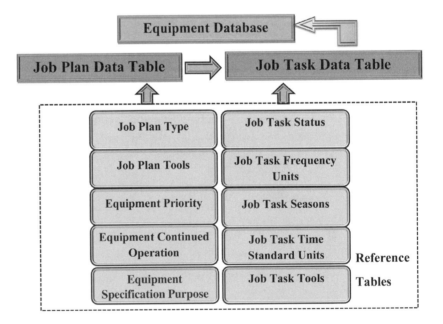

FIGURE 5.16 Job Plan and Task Data Tables.

A job task can realistically be split into two different types of tasks: scheduled and unscheduled. Preventive maintenance is just one form of a scheduled job task, while service calls are just one form of an unscheduled job task. Expanding job tasks to cover the multitude of other jobs performed within a facility can create an environment that significantly improves the overall performance of your facility. For example, environmental inspections are not normally included as part of the preventive maintenance job tasks. Instead, most inspections are captured and stored on a separate computer system away from the equipment associated with the inspections. Therefore, in order for an organization to match the environmental inspections to equipment within the field and develop trends and historical information the organization has to recreate data that already exists in their equipment database. Historical works of art should be inspected annually. Where are the data stored? Building operation plans and curtailment plans rely heavily on associated equipment. Shouldn't they be closely associated with the equipment database?

Job tasks are broken into two separate data tables: Job Plans and Job Tasks. Job plans are the actual written instructions, steps, or documents used to perform the scheduled equipment-related tasks. A job plan can be associated with multiple pieces of equipment. For example, a motor preventive maintenance job plan can be used to perform the maintenance on all of the motors in a facility. Multiple job plans can also be associated with a single piece of equipment. For example, a motor preventive maintenance job plan and a motor vibration analysis job plan can be assigned to each motor in the facility. A job task is the specific job item that is related to a particular piece of equipment. Basically, what are the line items of work that have to be performed on motor (ABC0000-MOT-001)? It is important to separate job plans from job tasks because facility management has to determine the number and costs of resources needed for a facility. One of the ways they accomplish this is to add all of the man-hours and costs required to perform the job plans in all of the separate job tasks. For example, a motor preventive maintenance job plan is linked to all of the 300 motors in a facility as job tasks. The man-hours needed to perform all of the tasks are added together to get the man-hours needed.

Job Plan GUID

[JOB_PLAN_GUID]

The Job Plan GUID is a defined space in the database for the unique identifier used to link all related job plan data (Table 5.104). The job plan GUID is then linked to the job task table in the database.

(continued)

[JOB_PLAN_GUID] (continued)

TABLE 5.104   Job Plan GUID Data Example

Job Plan GUID	Job_Plan_ID	Job_Plan_Title	Job Plan Description
Juk409d71...	FURN:01	Furnace Maintenance	Annual Furnace Maintenance
a09M56te1...	FURN:02	Furnace Check	Weekly Furnace Operational Checks
Yu11gh5gE...	VLV:01	Valve Maintenance	Annual Valve Torque and Packing Maintenance
Xjz678wL0...	VLV:02	Valve Maintenance	Biannual Operation Verification Valve Cycling
Zx09By29Hgi...	FX:01	Fire Extinguisher	Regulation Monthly Fire Extinguisher Checks

Job Task Database Tables			
Job_Task_GUID	Job Plan GUID	Job_Task_Seq_Number	Job_Task_ID_Composite
H7fjsgr09...	Juk409d71...	001	ABC0000-FURN:01-001
G7409873h...	Juk409d71...	002	ABC0000-FURN:01-002
P5et6ghr2...	Yu11gh5gE...	001	ABC0000-VLV:01-001

Job Plan Identification

[JOB_PLAN_ID]

Many organizations have a library they developed on their own of job plans for jobs that have to be performed. These job plans are normally based on some type of internal organization. For example, an organization might have developed a guide for performing the preventive maintenance on centrifugal pumps and called it P-1 and then created another guide on all of the maintenance on reciprocating pumps and called it P-2. While an organization should use manufacturer recommendations for maintenance, there is a simple reason why some organizations have developed their own library of job plans. Some facilities are hundreds of years old, and manufacturers' recommended maintenance does not exist for their equipment. Therefore, they have to develop their own. This data field is used to capture the numbering system for these types of internal guides (Table 5.105).

TABLE 5.105   Job Plan Identification Data Example

Job Plan GUID	Job_Plan_ID	Job_Plan_Title	Job Plan Description
Juk409d71...	FURN:01	Furnace Maintenance	Annual Furnace Maintenance
a09M56te1...	FURN:02	Furnace Check	Weekly Furnace Operational Checks
Yu11gh5gE...	VLV:01	Valve Maintenance	Annual Valve Torque and Packing Maintenance
Xjz678wL0...	VLV:02	Valve Maintenance	Biannual Operation Verification Valve Cycling
Zx09By29Hgi...	FX:01	Fire Extinguisher	Regulation Monthly Fire Extinguisher Checks
G3i8we902...	UST:01	Underground Storage Tank	Regulation Monthly Underground Storage Tank Checks
Ir67uY69e...	FM:01	Building Operation Plan	Requirement Annual Building Operation Plan
Q0okuW675...	FM:02	Curtailment Plan	Requirement Annual Curtailment Plan

Job Plan Title

[JOB_PLAN_TITLE]

The job plan name is used to capture the descriptive name of the job (Table 5.106). Job plan names are general in nature as related to equipment, because they typically cover a group of equipment types. For example the preventive maintenance for a squirrel cage motor is typically the same for a wide range of motors with various horsepower, voltage, and amperage. Therefore, there would only need to be one "Motor Preventive Maintenance" job plan. That job plan would then be applied to all of the related motors in the equipment database through the job tasks table. While equipment job plans are generic, the other types of scheduled job plans could be more specific. For example, "Curtailment Plan," "Building Operating Plan," "Environmental Oil Inspection," and so on.

TABLE 5.106   Job Plan Title Data Example

Job Plan GUID	Job_Plan_ID	Job_ Plan_Title	Job Plan Description
Juk409d71...	FURN:01	Furnace Maintenance	Annual Furnace Maintenance
a09M56te1...	FURN:02	Furnace Check	Weekly Furnace Operational Checks
Yu11gh5gE...	VLV:01	Valve Maintenance	Annual Valve Torque and Packing Maintenance
Xjz678wL0...	VLV:02	Valve Maintenance	Biannual Operation Verification Valve Cycling
Zx09By29Hgi...	FX:01	Fire Extinguisher	Regulation Monthly Fire Extinguisher Checks
G3i8we902...	UST:01	Underground Storage Tank	Regulation Monthly Underground Storage Tank Checks
Ir67uY69e...	FM:01	Building Operation Plan	Requirement Annual Building Operation Plan
Q0okuW675...	FM:02	Curtailment Plan	Requirement Annual Curtailment Plan

When developing an equipment database, realistically, only the scheduled job plans, names, and other data fields have to be defined. Unscheduled job plans are developed at the time of occurrence. For example: A call comes in to facility management from a tenant that air handler AHU-001 is broken and needs to be replaced. The team develops a project or job plan to replace that air handler.

Job Plan Description

[JOB_PLAN_DESCRIPTION]

The job plan description is a text field used to capture more information about the job plan (Table 5.107). For example, there might be two job plans with the title "Fire Extinguisher" and the job plan descriptions "Regulation Monthly Fire Extinguisher Checks" and "5 Year Hydro Test"; management has to distinguish between the two tasks.

(continued)

[JOB_PLAN_DESCRIPTION] (continued)

TABLE 5.107   Job Plan Description Data Example

Job Plan GUID	Job_Plan_ID	Job_Plan_Title	Job Plan Description
Juk409d71...	FURN:01	Furnace Maintenance	Annual Furnace Maintenance
a09M56te1...	FURN:02	Furnace Check	Weekly Furnace Operational Checks
Yu11gh5gE...	VLV:01	Valve Maintenance	Annual Valve Torque and Packing Maintenance
Xjz678wL0...	VLV:02	Valve Maintenance	Biannual Operation Verification Valve Cycling
Zx09By29Hgi...	FX:01	Fire Extinguisher	Regulation Monthly Fire Extinguisher Checks
G3i8we902...	UST:01	Underground Storage Tank	Regulation Monthly Underground Storage Tank Checks
Ir67uY69e...	FM:01	Building Operation Plan	Requirement Annual Building Operation Plan
Q0okuW675...	FM:02	Curtailment Plan	Requirement Annual Curtailment Plan

Job Plan Type

[JOB_PLAN_TYPE]

Job plans should be classified by the type of work and discipline that is performed (Table 5.108). Breaking job plans into different types allows the work to be organized into recognizable groups such as: predictive maintenance, preventive maintenance, fire life safety, environmental, historical preservation, and so forth. There is currently no industry standard for types of job tasks. It is recommended that you develop the job plan types in a separate reference table and then use that table as a drop-down menu for the database (Table 5.109). This makes the data uniform and prevents personnel from entering PM, Pm, pM, Prevent, which the database sees as different types.

TABLE 5.108   Job Plan Type Data Example

Job Plan GUID	Job_Plan_ID	Job_Plan_Title	Job_Plan_Type	Job Plan Document
Juk409d71...	FURN:01	Furnace Maintenance	PM	Furn.doc
a09M56te1...	FURN:02	Furnace Check	ETR	Furn.xls
Yu11gh5gE...	VLV:01	Valve Maintenance	PM	Valve.doc
Xjz678wL0...	VLV:02	Valve Maintenance	PM	Valve.xls
Zx09By29Hgi...	FX:01	Fire Extinguisher	ETR	Extinguisher.xls
G3i8we902...	UST:01	Underground Storage Tank	ENV	UST01.docx
Ir67uY69e...	FM:01	Building Operation Plan	FM	BOP_ABC0000.doc
Q0okuW675...	FM:02	Curtailment Plan	FM	CURT_ABC0000.doc

TABLE 5.109　Job Plan Type Example

Job Type	Abbrev	Description
Preventive Maintenance	PM	Scheduled job task
Predictive Maintenance	PDM	Scheduled job task
Equipment Tour	ETR	Scheduled job task
Environmental	ENV	Scheduled job task
Fire Life Safety	FLS	Scheduled job task
Equipment Tour	ETR	Scheduled job task
Historical Preservation	HPR	Scheduled job task
Measurement and Verification	MV	Scheduled job task
Facility Management	FM	Scheduled job task
Project	PRJ	Scheduled job task
Service Call	SC	Unscheduled
Repair	RP	Unscheduled

Job Plan Tool

[JOB_PLAN_TOOL(N)] (N denotes that multiple fields are possible.)

Job plans typically have a set of required or specialized tools needed to be used in order to complete the job plan. The job plan tools data field(s) is/are used to capture the generic or specialized tools need to complete the job plan (Table 5.110). For example, a technician who needed to calibrate a pressure gauge would need a second calibrated pressure gauge and a pressure source as a minimum in order to successfully complete the task. The tool names should be standardized for selection by the user as a reference table to prevent user and human errors (Table 5.111). It is recommended that you use OmniClass™ Table 35 Tools for this purpose (See Chapter 4, "Industry Standards").

TABLE 5.110　Job Plan Tool Data Example

Job Plan GUID	Job_Plan_ID	Job_Plan_Tool_Code	Job_Plan_Tool (1)	Job_Plan_Tool_Code	Job_Plan_Tool (N)
Juk409d71...	FURN:01	35-11 23 23 11 14	Thermography Equipment	35-51 11 21 31 21 11	Socket Wrenches
a09M56te1...	FURN:02	35-11 23 23 11 14	Thermography Equipment	35-51 11 21 31 21 11	Socket Wrenches
Yu11gh5gE...	VLV:01	35-51 11 21 31 21 14	Open-End Wrenches	35-51 11 21 31 21 74	Allen Wrenches
Xjz678wL0...	VLV:02	35-51 11 21 31 21 14	Open-End Wrenches	35-51 11 21 31 21 74	Allen Wrenches
Zx09By29Hgi...	FX:01				
G3i8we902...	UST:01	35-51 17 24 14 17	Ladders		
Ir67uY69e...	FM:01				
Q0okuW675...	FM:02				

(continued)

[JOB_PLAN_TOOL(N)] (N denotes that multiple fields are possible.) (*continued*)

TABLE 5.111   Standard Tool Reference Example

OmniClass™ Table 35 Tools	
Number	**Title**
35-11 23 23 11 11	Vibration Analysis Equipment
35-11 23 23 11 14	Thermography Equipment
35-11 23 23 11 21	Motor Testing Equipment
35-51 11 21 11 14	Hand-Held Drills
35-51 11 21 11 21	Bolt Cutters
35-51 11 21 11 24	Pipe Cutters
35-51 11 21 21 41	Pipe Benders
35-51 11 21 31 14	Hammers
35-51 11 21 31 17	Screwdrivers
35-51 11 21 31 21	Wrenches
35-51 11 21 31 21 11	Socket Wrenches
35-51 11 21 31 21 14	Open-End Wrenches
35-51 11 21 31 21 21	Crescent Wrenches
35-51 11 21 31 21 71	Pipe Wrenches
35-51 11 21 31 21 74	Allen Wrenches
35-51 17 24 14 17	Ladders

OmniClass™ Table 32 is a product of Construction Specification Institute/Construction Specification Canada, Version OmniClass_35_2006-03-28

It is important to note that OmniClass™ Table 35 was developed more with construction of buildings in mind than operation of facilities. The table is missing a lot of tools that would be useful to a facility manager or even a commissioning agent; for example, refrigeration gauges. However, this doesn't mean the table should not be used, but instead it should be developed to include all possible tools that could be useful to facility ownership and management. Because OmniClass™ is a suite of tables, improving the standard helps everyone in the industry and thereby improves the integration, resulting in lower costs for the organization in the long run. The table is well thought out, meets the industry's needs, and provides necessary integration with other tables in the standard (Table 5.110).

Job Plan Tool Code

[JOB_PLAN_TOOL_CODE(N)] (N denotes that multiple fields are possible.)

The job plan tool code is the data field used to capture the code related to the tools identified for the job plan tool field (Table 5.109).

Job Plan Document

[JOB_PLAN_DOCUMENT]

Job plan document data fields allow the user to download, attach, and develop the document that has the related steps and guidance for the performance of the job plan in the database (Table 5.112).

TABLE 5.112   Job Plan Document Data Example

Job Plan GUID	Job_Plan_ID	Job_ Plan_Title	Job Plan Document
Juk409d71...	FURN:01	Furnace Maintenance	Furn.DOC
a09M56te1...	FURN:02	Furnace Check	Furn.XLS
Yu11gh5gE...	VLV:01	Valve Maintenance	Valve.DOC
Xjz678wL0...	VLV:02	Valve Maintenance	Valve.XLS
Zx09By29Hgi...	FX:01	Fire Extinguisher	Extinguisher.XLS
G3i8we902...	UST:01	Underground Storage Tank	UST01.DOCX
Ir67uY69e...	FM:01	Building Operation Plan	BOP_ABC0000.DOC
Q0okuW675...	FM:02	Curtailment Plan	CURT_ABC0000.DOC

Job Task GUID

[JOB_TASK_GUID]

The Job Task GUID is a defined space in the database for the unique identifier used to link all of the related job task data (Table 5.113). The job task GUID is then linked to the equipment in the equipment database.

TABLE 5.113   Job Task GUID Data Example

Job_Task_GUID	Job Plan GUID	Job_Task_ID_Composite	Job_Task_Status
P5et6ghr2...	Yu11gh5gE...	ABC0000-VLV:01-001	Perform
L30jr98tw...	Yu11gh5gE...	ABC0000-VLV:01-002	Perform
0Rhu7e3gh...	Xjz678wL0...	ABC0000-VLV:02-001	Perform
78Fwi4rW2...	Zx09By29Hgi...	ABC0000-FX:01-001	Perform
k8Hjr9e0t...	Q0okuW675...	ABC0000-FM:02-001	Perform

Equipment Database			
Equipment_GUID	Equipment_ID_Composite	Job_Task_GUID (1)	Job_Task_GUID (N)
st7mnWq70...	ABC0000-GTV-14473	P5et6ghr2...	0Rhu7e3gh...
Xy398gnTy...	ABC0000-CHKV-02	L30jr98tw...	
Oju6rhYde...	ABC0000-FE-001	78Fwi4rW2...	k8Hjr9e0t...

Job Task Sequence Number

[JOB_TASK_SEQ_NUMBER]

The job task sequence number is used to capture the sequential number used for multiple occurrences of the same type of job tasks within an equipment database (Table 5.114). While one guide can be associated with multiple pieces of equipment, some databases will store each usage of the guide as a separate maintenance or task item in its job task library. For example, if there are four centrifugal pumps in a facility that require preventive maintenance according to performing guide P01 Annual Pump Maintenance, then a database would have job tasks P01-001, P01-002, P01-003, and P01-004 listed, the 001, 002, 003, and 004 being the sequential numbers of those job tasks. The databases separate the usage in this manner so that the maintenance programs can use a scheduling program for each of the separate tasks. Therefore, each pump can have its maintenance scheduled on different dates. Only the sequential number related to the job task should be captured in this data field.

TABLE 5.114   Job Task Sequence Number Data Example

Job_Task_GUID	Job Plan GUID	Job_Task_Seq_Number	Job_Task_ID_Composite
H7fjsgr09...	Juk409d71...	001	ABC0000-FURN:01-001
G7409873h...	Juk409d71...	002	ABC0000-FURN:01-002
P5et6ghr2...	Yu11gh5gE...	001	ABC0000-VLV:01-001
L30jr98tw...	Yu11gh5gE...	002	ABC0000-VLV:01-002
ORhu7e3gh...	Xjz678wL0...	001	ABC0000-VLV:02-001
78Fwi4rW2...	Zx09By29Hgi...	001	ABC0000-FX:01-001
k8Hjr9e0t...	Q0okuW675...	001	ABC0000-FM:02-001
G309Hy34s...	G3i8we902...	001	ABC0000-UST:01-001

Job Task Identification Composite

[JOB_TASK_ID_COMPOSITE]

Because multiple instances of a job task are captured in a database, a means to capture the related naming convention is required. For example, if you have two furnaces and each furnace requires maintenance job plan FURN:01, then in the database you would have FURN:01-001 and FURN:01-002. The job task identification composite data field is used to capture this data (Table 5.115). This will allow the facility management staff to sort all of their job tasks into a usable format. While programmers could only show those related fields to end users, such as equipment identification and space identification composites, this data field is included for the simplicity of use by facility staff. The field should be set up to be automatically filled by concatenating multiple predefined data fields (Table 5.116). Using predefined fields reduces the possibility of the human errors that would occur if the data were hand entered.

TABLE 5.115   Job Task Identification Composite Data Examples

Job_Task_GUID	Job Plan GUID	Job_Task_Seq_Number	Job_Task_ID_Composite
H7fjsgr09...	Juk409d71...	001	ABC0000-FURN:01-001
G7409873h...	Juk409d71...	002	ABC0000-FURN:01-002
P5et6ghr2...	Yu11gh5gE...	001	ABC0000-VLV:01-001
L30jr98tw...	Yu11gh5gE...	002	ABC0000-VLV:01-002
0Rhu7e3gh...	Xjz678wL0...	001	ABC0000-VLV:02-001
78Fwi4rW2...	Zx09By29Hgi...	001	ABC0000-FX:01-001
k8Hjr9e0t...	Q0okuW675...	001	ABC0000-FM:02-001
G309Hy34s...	G3i8we902...	001	ABC0000-UST:01-001

TABLE 5.116   Job Task Identification Composite Examples

Data Fields	Equipment Identification Composite
Job Task Name + Job Task Sequence Number	P01-001, VLV-002
Facility Number + Job Task Name + Job Task Sequence Number	ABC0000-P01-004
Equipment Acronym + Equipment Sequence+ Job Task Name + Job Task Sequence Number	FAN-098B-FilterChange-008

Job Task Status

[JOB_TASK_STATUS]

A premier equipment maintenance program allows the organization to determine if maintenance is to be performed or not. Reliability-centered maintenance (RCM) requires that deferred maintenance be documented. Therefore, there must be a place in the database that documents this decision. For example, suppose that an organization is planning, within one year, on a complete demolition and rebuild of one wing of its facility. Because of the preplanned demolition, there might not be a reason to continue to maintain some or most of the equipment within that wing. The job task status field is used to capture this designated status (Table 5.117). It is important for that organization to determine the job tasks they can defer. There are no industry standards for statuses of job tasks. It is recommended that a separate reference table be developed by an organization for the job task status (Table 5.118). The table would then be used as a drop-down menu for end users. Using a reference table reduces the chance of human errors during entry and thereby improves the parsing of data for reliable information.

TABLE 5.117   Job Task Status Data Example

Job_Task_GUID	Job_Task_Seq_Number	Job_Task_ID_Composite	Job_Task_Status
H7fjsgr09...	001	ABC0000-FURN:01-001	Perform
G7409873h...	002	ABC0000-FURN:01-002	Perform
P5et6ghr2...	001	ABC0000-VLV:01-001	Perform

(continued)

[JOB_TASK_STATUS] (continued)

Job_Task_GUID	Job_Task_Seq_Number	Job_Task_ID_Composite	Job_Task_Status
L30jr98tw...	002	ABC0000-VLV:01-002	Perform
ORhu7e3gh...	001	ABC0000-VLV:02-001	Perform
78Fwi4rW2...	001	ABC0000-FX:01-001	Perform
k8Hjr9e0t...	001	ABC0000-FM:02-001	Perform
G309Hy34s...	001	ABC0000-UST:01-001	Deferred

TABLE 5.118   Job Task Status Examples

Job Task Status	Description
Perform	Perform the job task.
Deferred	Job task has been differed or placed on hold.
Deleted	Job task, previously performed, is no longer necessary and has been deleted. Example: Environmental inspections on a fuel oil tank that has been removed. Task is no longer needed, but the organization has to maintain records for a specified number of years per regulations.

Job Task Status Related Cause

[JOB_TASK_STATUS_CAUSE]

When a job task is deferred or deleted, it is an excellent idea to document the reason or cause for the change in job status. For example, if equipment maintenance was deferred because of an upcoming renovation the organization could denote "Deferred Due to Pending Renovation." Another example is when a technician cannot gain access to a space to perform required maintenance; he or she could denote "Deferred, equipment inaccessible because of restricted access by XYZ organization." The notes placed in this field should be as descriptive as possible to ensure clarity of information (Table 5.119).

TABLE 5.119   Job Task Status Related Cause Data Example

Job_Task_GUID	Job_Task_ID_Composite	Job_Task_Status	Job_Task_Status_Cause
H7fjsgr09...	ABC0000-FURN:01-001	Perform	Normal Maintenance
G7409873h...	ABC0000-FURN:01-002	Perform	Normal Maintenance
P5et6ghr2...	ABC0000-VLV:01-001	Perform	Normal Maintenance
L30jr98tw...	ABC0000-VLV:01-002	Perform	Normal Maintenance
ORhu7e3gh...	ABC0000-VLV:02-001	Perform	Normal Maintenance
78Fwi4rW2...	ABC0000-FX:01-001	Perform	Normal Maintenance
k8Hjr9e0t...	ABC0000-FM:02-001	Perform	Operational Requirement
G309Hy34s...	ABC0000-UST:01-001	Deferred	Underground Storage Tank Removed

Job Task Performer

[JOB_TASK_PERFORMER]

One of the best things to know about any job task is which organization or company is responsible for performing the work. Note: This is not to be confused with which technician is tasked to perform the work, but refers to which organization, tenant, or corporation is responsible for the costs and resources related to that task. Countless man-hours and resources are spent in the industry recreating this information when something breaks or a regulation is violated. Maintenance is routinely missed because one organization believes that another is responsible for the work, while the other organization thinks the first one is responsible. There is no reason to have this lapse in coverage when the information can be easily captured and agreed upon at the onset. The job task performer allows the organization to capture the person or organization that is responsible for the performance of a job task (Table 5.120). For example, a tenant improvement includes the installation of an air conditioner for a data center. The air conditioner fails because no maintenance was performed on the unit. Was the tenant or the owner responsible for the maintenance? Therefore, who incurs the costs for the replacement? It is not a bad idea to get a signed letter of agreement from tenants and contractors that lists all of the equipment they are required to maintain.

TABLE 5.120 Job Task Performer Data Example

Job_Task_GUID	Job_Task_ID_Composite	Job_Task_Status	Job_Task_Performer
H7fjsgr09...	ABC0000-FURN:01-001	Perform	Maintenance Co
G7409873h...	ABC0000-FURN:01-002	Perform	Maintenance Co
P5et6ghr2...	ABC0000-VLV:01-001	Perform	Maintenance Co
L30jr98tw...	ABC0000-VLV:01-002	Perform	Maintenance Co
0Rhu7e3gh...	ABC0000-VLV:02-001	Perform	Maintenance Co
78Fwi4rW2...	ABC0000-FX:01-001	Perform	Fire Testers United
k8Hjr9e0t...	ABC0000-FM:02-001	Perform	ABC Corporation
G309Hy34s...	ABC0000-UST:01-001	Deferred	N/A

Job Task Frequency

[JOB_TASK_FREQUENCY]

Each job task has a reoccurring scheduled time period, the job task frequency, in which it has to be performed. This data field is used to capture the job task frequency so that facility management knows how often that task is required to be performed (Table 5.121). Frequency of performance is important information for scheduling, resource management, and planning. For example, if an organization wanted to know how much manpower it needed per year to perform all job tasks related to a facility, it would have to tally up all the manpower for each job task and then determine how often those tasks occur within that year. The only way to accomplish this is to capture the job task

(continued)

[JOB_TASK_FREQUENCY]

frequency. The frequency should be broken up into two data fields: job task frequency and job task frequency units. For example, if a job task is required to be performed once every two years, the job task frequency would be 2 and the job frequency unit would be year. The job task frequency should be a numeric number, and the job task frequency units should be a standard unit of measure for time. This allows the organization to parse the data easier than when the two fields are combined and thereby create meaningful schedules. Enter only the numerical value in the job task frequency field.

TABLE 5.121   Job Task Frequency Data Example

Job_Task_GUID	Job_Task_ID_Composite	Job_Task_Frequency	Job_Task_Frequency_Units
H7fjsgr09...	ABC0000-FURN:01-001	1	Year
G7409873h...	ABC0000-FURN:01-002	1	Year
P5et6ghr2...	ABC0000-VLV:01-001	1	Year
L30jr98tw...	ABC0000-VLV:01-002	1	Year
0Rhu7e3gh...	ABC0000-VLV:02-001	0.5	Year
78Fwi4rW2...	ABC0000-FX:01-001	1	Month
k8Hjr9e0t...	ABC0000-FM:02-001	1	Year
G309Hy34s...	ABC0000-UST:01-001	1	Month

Job Task Frequency Units

[JOB_TASK_FREQUENCY_UNITS]

The job task frequency unit is the standard unit of time measurement that is associated with the job task frequency (Table 5.122). For example: Week, Day, Month, or Year.

TABLE 5.122   Job Task Frequency Units Data Example

Job_Task_GUID	Job_Task_ID_Composite	Job_Task_Frequency	Job_Task_Frequency_Units
H7fjsgr09...	ABC0000-FURN:01-001	1	Year
G7409873h...	ABC0000-FURN:01-002	1	Year
P5et6ghr2...	ABC0000-VLV:01-001	1	Year
L30jr98tw...	ABC0000-VLV:01-002	1	Year
0Rhu7e3gh...	ABC0000-VLV:02-001	0.5	Year
78Fwi4rW2...	ABC0000-FX:01-001	1	Month
k8Hjr9e0t...	ABC0000-FM:02-001	1	Year
G309Hy34s...	ABC0000-UST:01-001	1	Month

Job Task Inspection Percentage

[JOB_TASK_INSP_PERCENT]

Most organizations have a percentage of their work that they require to be spot checked or quality inspected by an independent party. The purpose is to ensure that the job tasks are being performed properly and that their equipment is being maintained. This is especially important to an organization that contracts out their maintenance to a third party. Typically, an inspector gets a batch of all the completed job tasks and picks a random number to inspect. This method is time-consuming, ineffective, and not an accurate inspection of the facilities' equipment. Does the inspector typically inspect easy to access equipment? Is equipment of less significance inspected more often than equipment more critical to the operation of your organization? For example, a critical chiller requires an annual tube analysis. Shouldn't the chiller be inspected a higher percentage of time (while the chiller is disassembled) than an exhaust fan filter replacement is? An inspection percentage should be entered into this data field (Table 5.123). In the previous example, the chiller inspection should be 100%, while the exhaust fan inspection should be 10%. The percentage of inspections should be based on the resources of the organization and number of times that job task occurs. For example, if a facility has 300 air handlers and each air handler requires an annual filter replacement, then 10% inspections would result in 30 air handlers being inspected each year. Conversely, if a facility has two critical switchboards that are tested every two years, then the inspection for each should be set to 100%. You want to ensure that the maintenance has been performed on the switchboards, or it could be at least two years before you find the problem. Job tasks that are critical or infrequent should be set at a higher percentage.

TABLE 5.123 Job Task Inspection Percentage Data Example

Job_Task_GUID	Job_Task_ID_Composite	Job_Task_Insp_Percent	Job_Task_Season
H7fjsgr09...	ABC0000-FURN:01-001	100	Spring:Summer
G7409873h...	ABC0000-FURN:01-002	100	Spring:Summer
P5et6ghr2...	ABC0000-VLV:01-001	10	Any
L30jr98tw...	ABC0000-VLV:01-002	10	Any
0Rhu7e3gh...	ABC0000-VLV:02-001	10	Any
78Fwi4rW2...	ABC0000-FX:01-001	10	Any
k8Hjr9e0t...	ABC0000-FM:02-001	100	Spring
G309Hy34s...	ABC0000-UST:01-001	50	Any

The job task inspection frequency data field is used by an organization to designate a percentage of time that they require an independent inspection of that the job task to be performed.

Job Task Season

[JOB_TASK_SEASON]

Certain job tasks should only be done during certain seasons. You do not want to take out a chiller that supplies cooling to your building in the middle of summer. You do not want to take out a boiler for maintenance during the middle of winter. The job task season is used to define the season in which the job task is to be performed: summer, fall, winter, or spring. (Table 5.124). A reference table should be developed and used to prevent human entry errors (Table 5.125). Verbiage or a numerical code could be used or developed for the reference table, depending on the needs and flexibility of the database and related programs.

TABLE 5.124   Job Task Season Data Example

Job_Task_GUID	Job_Task_ID_Composite	Job_Task_Insp_Percent	Job_Task_Season
H7fjsgr09...	ABC0000-FURN:01-001	100	Spring:Summer
G7409873h...	ABC0000-FURN:01-002	100	Spring:Summer
P5et6ghr2...	ABC0000-VLV:01-001	10	Any
L30jr98tw...	ABC0000-VLV:01-002	10	Any
ORhu7e3gh...	ABC0000-VLV:02-001	10	Any
78Fwi4rW2...	ABC0000-FX:01-001	10	Any
k8Hjr9e0t...	ABC0000-FM:02-001	100	Spring
G309Hy34s...	ABC0000-UST:01-001	50	Any

TABLE 5.125   Seasons Example

Job Task Seasons	Numerical Code
Spring	1
Summer	2
Fall	3
Winter	4
Spring:Summer	5
Fall:Winter	6
Spring:Summer:Fall	7
...	8

Job Task Start Date

[JOB_TASK_START_DATE]

Each scheduled job task should have a start date in the database to indicate when the first instance of the job task should be started (Table 5.126). This information is important to future scheduling and for historical reference. For example, suppose that there are 48 air handlers in a facility that need annual maintenance. It does not make sense to have maintenance performed on all of the 48 air handlers in the same month, so instead the maintenance is spread out throughout the year in such a manner that maintenance is performed on only four air handlers each month. In order to accomplish this, the maintenance for the air handlers would have to be scheduled to start on different dates. It is recommended that you use the MM/DD/YYYY format for dates.

TABLE 5.126   Job Task Start Date Data Example

Job_Task_ID_Composite	Job_Task_Start_Date	Job_Task_Time_Standard	Job_Task_Time_Units
ABC0000-FURN:01-001	5/1/2005	48.00	Hour
ABC0000-FURN:01-002	8/1/2005	32.00	Hour
ABC0000-VLV:01-001	1/1/2006	1.00	Hour
ABC0000-VLV:01-002	4/1/2006	1.00	Hour
ABC0000-VLV:02-001	9/1/2005	15.00	Minute
ABC0000-FX:01-001	5/1/2005	8.00	Hour
ABC0000-FM:02-001	4/1/2006	5.00	Day
ABC0000-UST:01-001	5/1/2005	1.50	Hour

Job Task Time Standard

[JOB_TASK_TIME_STANDARD]

Each job task/job plan takes a specific amount of time to accomplish. This time standard can be acquired from averaging the time it takes to complete the task, a predesignated time standard, a labor estimation program, or the manufacturer's recommendation (Table 5.127). It is important to spend the time to populate the data because they are used as the basis of manpower needs and costs for your organization. For example, if your facility has 100 air handlers and each air handler requires a job task that takes 20 hours, your organization has to budget for 2,000 man-hours. Add in all the job tasks, with varying frequencies, on all the nondeferred equipment in a facility and you can quickly see how complex it is for facility and executive management to get an accurate representation of their needed resources. While the data field should be a numerical value based on the number of hours a task takes, realistically industry has estimated standard times using varying units: 2 hours, 4 days, 1 week, and so forth. Therefore, the job task time standard is actually made up of two data fields: job task time standard and job task time standard unit. The job task time standard should contain only a numerical value with a maximum of two decimal places (e.g., 1.50, 2.75, 12.15). The job task time standard unit data field should contain only the unit of time related to that job task time standard (e.g., minute, hour, day, week). The data can then be processed by a computer to easily determine the number of hours it takes to complete the job tasks in a facility.

(continued)

[JOB_TASK_TIME_STANDARD] (continued)

TABLE 5.127   Job Task Time Standard Data Example

Job_Task_ID_Composite	Job_Task_Start_Date	Job_Task_Time_Standard	Job_Task_Time_Units
ABC0000-FURN:01-001	5/1/2005	48.00	Hour
ABC0000-FURN:01-002	8/1/2005	32.00	Hour
ABC0000-VLV:01-001	1/1/2006	1.00	Hour
ABC0000-VLV:01-002	4/1/2006	1.00	Hour
ABC0000-VLV:02-001	9/1/2005	15.00	Minute
ABC0000-FX:01-001	5/1/2005	8.00	Hour
ABC0000-FM:02-001	4/1/2006	5.00	Day
ABC0000-UST:01-001	5/1/2005	1.50	Hour

Job Task Time Standard Units

[JOB_TASK_TIME_UNITS]

The job task standard units' data field is used to capture the units of measure associated to the job task time standard (Table 5.128).

TABLE 5.128   Job Task Time Standard Units Data Example

Job_Task_ID_Composite	Job_Task_Start_Date	Job_Task_Time_Standard	Job_Task_Time_Units
ABC0000-FURN:01-001	5/1/2005	48.00	Hour
ABC0000-FURN:01-002	8/1/2005	32.00	Hour
ABC0000-VLV:01-001	1/1/2006	1.00	Hour
ABC0000-VLV:01-002	4/1/2006	1.00	Hour
ABC0000-VLV:02-001	9/1/2005	15.00	Minute
ABC0000-FX:01-001	5/1/2005	8.00	Hour
ABC0000-FM:02-001	4/1/2006	5.00	Day
ABC0000-UST:01-001	5/1/2005	1.50	Hour

Job Task Tool

[JOB_TASK_TOOL(N)] (N denotes that multiple fields are possible.)

A job task may have a set of required or specialized tools needed to complete the job task in addition to those in the job plan. The job task tools data field(s) is(are) used to capture any additional tools need to complete that specific job task (Table 5.129). For example, a technician might need a ladder to get to a hard-to-reach valve. Knowing the additional tools needed saves the technician the time involved in having to return to the shop. The tool names should be standardized for selection by the user in the form of a reference table to prevent user errors (Table 5.130). It is recommended that you use OmniClass™ Table 35 Tools for this purpose (See Chapter 4, "Industry Standards").

TABLE 5.129 Job Task Tool Data Example

Job_Task_ID_Composite	Job_Task_Tool_Code (1)	Job_Task_Tool (1)	Job_Task_Tool_Code (N)	Job_Task_Tool (N)
ABC0000-FURN:01-001				
ABC0000-FURN:01-002				
ABC0000-VLV:01-001	35-51 11 21 31 17	Screwdrivers	35-51 17 24 14 17	Ladders
ABC0000-VLV:01-002				
ABC0000-VLV:02-001	35-51 11 21 31 21 21	Crescent Wrenches		
ABC0000-FX:01-001				
ABC0000-FM:02-001				
ABC0000-UST:01-001				

TABLE 5.130 Standard Tool Reference Example

OmniClass™ Table 35 Tools	
Number	Title
35-11 23 23 11 11	Vibration Analysis Equipment
35-11 23 23 11 14	Thermography Equipment
35-11 23 23 11 21	Motor Testing Equipment
35-51 11 21 11 14	Hand-Held Drills
35-51 11 21 11 21	Bolt Cutters
35-51 11 21 11 24	Pipe Cutters
35-51 11 21 21 41	Pipe Benders
35-51 11 21 31 14	Hammers
35-51 11 21 31 17	Screwdrivers
35-51 11 21 31 21	Wrenches
35-51 11 21 31 21 11	Socket Wrenches
35-51 11 21 31 21 14	Open-End Wrenches
35-51 11 21 31 21 21	Crescent Wrenches
35-51 11 21 31 21 71	Pipe Wrenches
35-51 11 21 31 21 74	Allen Wrenches
35-51 17 24 14 17	Ladders

OmniClass™ Table 32 is a product of Construction Specification Institute/Construction Specification Canada, Version OmniClass_35_2006-03-28

It is important to note that OmniClass™ Table 35 was developed primarily with the construction of buildings in mind rather than the operation of facilities. The table is missing a lot of tools that would be useful to a facility manager or even a commissioning agent—for example, refrigeration gauges. This doesn't mean that the table should not be used, but instead it should be developed to include all possible tools that could be useful to facility ownership and management. Because OmniClass™ is a suite of tables, improving the standard helps everyone in the industry and thereby improves integration, resulting in lower costs for the organization in the long run. The table is well thought out, meets the industry's needs, and provides necessary integration with other tables in the standard (Table 5.130).

Job Task Tool Code

[JOB_TASK_TOOL_CODE(N)] (N denotes that multiple fields are possible.)

The job task tool code is the data fields used to capture the code related to the tools identified for the job task tool field (Table 5.129).

CONDITION DATA FIELDS

It is important to capture and maintain what the condition of equipment is in a facility. Figure 5.17 shows the condition tables and any recommended reference tables. Equipment condition is important in making operational, financial, and executive decisions. For example, suppose that an air handler that supplies a critical data center is in poor condition and needs repairs. Facility management needs to know this information in order to properly address the situation and prevent an impact on the data center. The condition assessments data fields are used to capture information on the condition of equipment. The condition of the equipment can be captured during multiple types of surveys such as audits, inspections, operational tours, construction installation, and equipment commissioning. In the industry, there are actual surveys called condition assessments that are usually performed by an outside organization, to assess the condition of equipment within a facility. Typically, these assessments

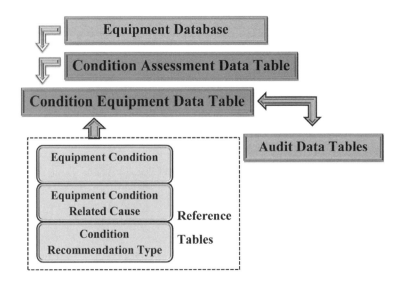

FIGURE 5.17 Condition Data Tables

are then delivered as a report in a document format that is not compatible with an organizations equipment database. Therefore, someone has to transpose the data, introducing human error, into a format that can be used and acted upon by the corporation. The performance of a quality inspection or condition assessment of equipment prior to installation is also a good practice. Equipment condition data are kept in a separate data table than the actual equipment data table to ensure that the history of the condition of the equipment is captured. You do not want to have the previous condition overwritten; instead, you want to be able to track the condition of that equipment over time.

Equipment condition data have been separated into two separate tables: Condition Assessment Data Table and Condition Equipment Data Table. The reason for the separate tables is because a condition assessment is typically done on multiple components within a facility and all of that information is compiled into a single document. Since a single document will be referencing numerous different components, the tables were separated so that the document, and its related information, only has to be captured once and then it can be linked to the various components. The condition of each piece of equipment needs to be captured individually. The condition equipment table allows the capture of this information.

Condition Assessment GUID

[CONDITION_GUID]

The Condition Assessment GUID is a defined space in the database for the unique identifier used to link all related condition assessment data (Table 5.131). This GUID is then linked to the condition equipment data.

TABLE 5.131 Condition Assessment GUID Data Example

Condition_GUID	Condition_Short_Description	Condition_Provider	Condition_Date
KJdir09f2...	Construction Condition Assessment of Facility ABC0000	KD Manufacturing	3/18/2000
9Hge67b56...	Condition Assessment Chill Water System 4-25-2005	Water Solutions INC	4/25/2005
0pPrg672q...	Condition Assessment Centrifugal Pumps 01-01-2010	John Doe	1/1/2010
Hjdgutr93...	Facility Construction Commissioning	KD Manufacturing	6/1/2000

Condition Equipment Database Table			
Cond_Equip_GUID	Condition_GUID	Equipment_GUID	Equipment_Condition
125Yu345w...	KJdir09f2...	o8ash05Rv...	Good
IO98YU76f...	9Hge67b56...	o8ash05Rv...	Poor
G0R3dskn5...	0pPrg672q...	o8ash05Rv...	Failure Possible

Condition Assessment Short Description

[CONDITION_SHORT_DESCRIPTION]

The purpose of the short description data field is to allow the organization to write a short description or title for the assessment (Table 5.132). The short description allows the company to easily sort and access the data in the database instead of having to open each document to find the information users are looking for. Condition assessments can be performed on a whole facility, a specific system, or new equipment. The short description should reflect the assessment performed. For example, Construction Condition Assessment of Facility ABC0000, Condition Assessment Fire Safety System 12-01-2000, Condition Assessment Boiler BLR-004.

TABLE 5.132 Condition Assessment Short Description Data Example

Condition_GUID	Condition_Short_Description	Condition_Provider	Condition_Date
KJdir09f2...	Construction Condition Assessment of Facility ABC0000	KD Manufacturing	3/18/2000
9Hge67b56...	Condition Assessment Chill Water System 4-25-2005	Water Solutions INC	4/25/2005
0pPrg672q...	Condition Assessment Centrifugal Pumps 01-01-2010	John Doe	1/1/2010
Hjdgutr93...	Facility Construction Commissioning	KD Manufacturing	6/1/2000

Condition Assessment Provider

[CONDITION_PROVIDER]

The condition assessment provider data field is used to capture the name of the company, person, or organization that performed the assessment (Table 5.133). Who provided the assessment is important for future referencing.

TABLE 5.133 Condition Assessment Provider Data Example

Condition_GUID	Condition_Short_Description	Condition_Provider	Condition_Date
KJdir09f2...	Construction Condition Assessment of Facility ABC0000	KD Manufacturing	3/18/2000
9Hge67b56...	Condition Assessment Chill Water System 4-25-2005	Water Solutions INC	4/25/2005
0pPrg672q...	Condition Assessment Centrifugal Pumps 01-01-2010	John Doe	1/1/2010
Hjdgutr93...	Facility Construction Commissioning	KD Manufacturing	6/1/2000

Condition Assessment Date

[CONDITION_DATE]

The condition assessment date is used to capture the date that the condition assessment was performed (Table 5.134). The data allow the organization to determine the chronological order of the assessments to properly schedule any additional assessments. For example, a facility management team requires an environmental inspection to determine the condition of all of the containment tanks at the facility every two years. In order to ensure that these inspections are performed every two years, the team needs to know when the last condition inspection was performed.

TABLE 5.134 Condition Assessment Date Data Example

Condition_GUID	Condition_Short_Description	Condition_Provider	Condition_Date
KJdir09f2...	Construction Condition Assessment of Facility ABC0000	KD Manufacturing	3/18/2000
9Hge67b56...	Condition Assessment Chill Water System 4-25-2005	Water Solutions INC	4/25/2005
0pPrg672q...	Condition Assessment Centrifugal Pumps 01-01-2010	John Doe	1/1/2010
Hjdgutr93...	Facility Construction Commissioning	KD Manufacturing	6/1/2000

Condition Assessment Document

[CONDITION_DOCUMENT]

The condition assessment document field is where the written documentation of the assessment would be stored in the database (Table 5.135). It is important to store the document for future reference.

TABLE 5.135 Condition Assessment Document Data Example

Condition_GUID	Condition_Provider	Condition_Date	Condition_Document
KJdir09f2...	KD Manufacturing	3/18/2000	Construction Initial Condition Assessment.PDF
9Hge67b56...	Water Solutions INC	4/25/2005	Chill Water Condition Assessment.DOC
0pPrg672q...	John Doe	1/1/2010	Centrifugal Pumps Condition Assessment.DOCX
Hjdgutr93...	KD Manufacturing	6/1/2000	ABC0000 Construction Commission.PDF

Condition Equipment GUID

[COND_EQUIP_GUID]

The Condition Equipment GUID is a defined space in the database for the unique identifier used to link all related equipment condition data (Table 5.136). The equipment GUID is then linked to the condition equipment table for each condition assessment. The equipment database is linked to the condition database, instead of placing all of this data in the equipment data table, to reduce the continued addition of fields into the equipment database.

(continued)

[COND_EQUIP_GUID] (continued)

TABLE 5.136   Condition Equipment GUID Data Example

Cond_Equip_GUID	Condition_GUID	Equipment_GUID
125Yu345w...	KJdir09f2...	o8ash05Rv...
IO98YU76f...	9Hge67b56...	o8ash05Rv...
G0R3dskn5...	0pPrg672q...	o8ash05Rv...

Equipment Database		
Equipment_GUID	Industry_Code_Description	Equipment_Operation_Description
o8ash05Rv...	Centrifugal Pump	Supply to Cooling Tower CT-03

Condition Database Table		
Condition_GUID	Condition_Short_Description	Condition_Provider
KJdir09f2...	Construction Condition Assessment of Facility ABC0000	KD Manufacturing

Equipment Condition

[EQUIPMENT_CONDITION]

The equipment condition data field is a predetermined field used to designate the condition of the equipment during installation, condition assessments, and audits (Table 5.137). A reference table should be developed for this field with predetermined entries to reduce human entry errors and allow management to parse the data in a more usable fashion (Table 5.138). The condition assessment observation data field, later on, would be used to enter more text information about the condition of the equipment. For example, suppose that a facility team wants to create a list of all the equipment in a database that is in poor condition. Unless the condition data were in a consistent predetermined format, the facility management team would have to manually sort the information. Manually sorting a database would be costly and defeats the purpose of having a database. There is no industry standard for equipment condition.

TABLE 5.137   Equipment Condition Data Example

Cond_Equip_GUID	Equipment_Condition	Condition_Cause	Equipment_Life_Used
125Yu345w...	Good	Newly Installed	10%
IO98YU76f...	Poor	Insufficient Maintenance	125%
G0R3dskn5...	Failure Possible	Component Exceeded Useful Life	150%
AdOh4Eqpt...	Failure Possible	Poor Maintenance	

TABLE 5.138   Equipment Condition Examples

Condition	Description
Unknown	Equipment has not been assessed or was inaccessible.
Inoperable	The equipment was found to be inoperable, broken, or failed.
Failure Possible	The equipment is in extremely poor condition and is expect to fail unless action is taken. Supporting utilities or environment could be a reason for possible failure.
Poor	The equipment has not been maintained and is in poor operating condition. Rust and/or damage are evident. Poor design or operating environment.
Fair	The equipment has had some maintenance performed on it and in decent condition. No major rust or damage.
Good	The equipment is well maintained and operable.
Excellent	The equipment is very well maintained and looks like it is in new condition.

Equipment Condition Related Cause

[CONDITION_CAUSE]

The equipment condition related cause field is used to further categorize the findings of the equipment condition based on a list of possible related causes (Table 5.139). A reference table should be developed for this field with predetermined entries to reduce human entry errors and allow management to parse the data in a more usable fashion. This categorization of related causes is used to predefine data for analysis (Table 5.140). There is no industry standard for equipment condition related cause.

TABLE 5.139   Equipment Condition Related Cause Data Example

Cond_Equip_GUID	Equipment_Condition	Condition_Cause	Equipment_Life_Used
125Yu345w...	Good	Newly Installed	10%
IO98YU76f...	Poor	Insufficient Maintenance	125%
GOR3dskn5...	Failure Possible	Component Exceeded Useful Life	150%
AdOh4Eqpt...	Failure Possible	Poor Maintenance	

TABLE 5.140   Equipment Condition Cause Examples

Condition Cause	Description
Component Exceeded Useful Life	Equipment is past its useful life and needs replacement.
Design or Production Problem	The equipment is not the correct component to meet installed design. Problem with the manufactured product meeting operational requirements. Equipment runs constantly or at maximum tolerances.
Does Not Meet Facility Requirements	The equipment is incorrectly sized or used, based on facility requirements for operation.
Insufficient Maintenance	The equipment has not been maintained.
Insufficient Environment	The equipment is not properly designed for the environment in which it was installed.
Insufficient Utility	The equipment is has poor electrical, water, or motive force supplied, which is causing the problems. Example: Pneumatic valve that is not functioning properly because supplied air pressure is too low.
No Issues	No Issues

Equipment Life Used

[EQUIPMENT_LIFE_USED]

Equipment life used is the percentage of the equipment expected life used up based on its actual condition (Table 5.141). A piece of equipment might have a higher used up life expectancy than what is normally projected because the equipment is in poor condition or is constantly run at maximum tolerances. There are calculations in the industry that can be used to determine when equipment is run above standards for extended periods of time. The calculations are used to determine premature aging of equipment. A percentage of life expectancy should be used for this data field. For example; 50% would equate to half of the life used, 100% would denote that the equipment is at the end of its life expectancy.

TABLE 5.141   Equipment Life Used Data Example

Cond_Equip_GUID	Equipment_Condition	Condition_Cause	Equipment_Life_Used
125Yu345w...	Good	Newly Installed	10%
IO98YU76f...	Poor	Insufficient Maintenance	125%
GOR3dskn5...	Failure Possible	Component Has Exceeded Useful Life	150%
AdOh4Eqpt...	Failure Possible	Poor Maintenance	

Equipment Life Remaining

[LIFE_REMAINING]

The equipment life remaining field is used to display the remaining life of equipment, based on its condition and its designed life expectancy (Table 5.142). While knowing the condition of equipment is important, the condition is used to determine what actions need to be taken by the facility staff. This field is a good indicator of what equipment needs to be assessed and scheduled for maintenance or replacement. For example, a pump that is getting close to its life expectancy would be included in the equipment that is slated for an upcoming condition assessment. There are many methods to determine the remaining life expectancy of equipment. The following is an example of just one method to create a metric for remaining life:

Life Expectancy − (Life Expectancy × Equipment Life Used)
(25 years − (25 years × 10%) = 22.5 years expected remaining
(25 years − (25 years × 125%) = −6.5 years expected remaining
(25 years − (25 years × 200%) = −25 years expected remaining

TABLE 5.142 Equipment Life Remaining Data Example

Cond_Equip_GUID	Condition_Cause	Equipment_Life_Used	Life_Remaining
125Yu345w...	Newly Installed	10%	22.50
IO98YU76f...	Insufficient Maintenance	125%	−6.50
G0R3dskn5...	Component Has Exceeded Useful Life	200%	−25.00
AdOh4Eqpt...	Poor Maintenance		

Condition Observation

[CONDITION_OBSERVATION]

The condition observation field is a text data field used to contain the detailed written notes about the condition of the equipment (Table 5.143); For example: Equipment was found in poor condition because of the wet environment in which it was installed. This is in violation of the manufacturer's recommendations for an installation environment.

TABLE 5.143 Condition Observation Data Example

Cond_Equip_GUID	Condition_Observation	Condition_Recom_Type
125Yu345w...	New pump	
IO98YU76f...	Poor maintenance, rust on casing, high vibration	Rebuild
G0R3dskn5...	Extremely bad condition. High vibration and extreme rust conditions	Replace
AdOh4Eqpt...		

Condition Recommendation Type

[CONDITION_RECOM_TYPE]

For each observation made on the condition of equipment there should be a corresponding recommendation to rectify any adverse findings. While a text data field relating to the condition recommendation is included in this book, there should be a means to sort the recommendations into some form of reasonable action types (Table 5.144) such as replace, repair, and so forth. Defining the different types of recommended actions allows the facility management staff to parse their data easily into actions that they can address (Table 5.145). For example, a facility management team wants to generate a list of all the equipment that is recommended for replacement. They could then take that list and prioritize their resources and funding. The types of recommendations should be developed into a reference table and then shown in the database as a drop-down menu. Developing defined types helps reduce human entry errors and improves the resultant data analysis. *(continued)*

[CONDITION_RECOM_TYPE] (*continued*)

TABLE 5.144 Condition Recommendation Type Data Example

Cond_Equip_GUID	Condition_Observation	Condition_Recom_Type
125Yu345w...	New pump	
IO98YU76f...	Poor maintenance, rust on casing, high vibration	Rebuild
G0R3dskn5...	Extremely bad condition. High vibration and extreme rust conditions	Replace
AdOh4Eqpt...		

TABLE 5.145 Condition Recommendation Type Examples

Recommendation Type	Description
Maintenance	Recommendation is for maintenance on equipment.
Repair	Recommendation is to repair on equipment.
Rebuild	Recommendation is to rebuild on equipment.
Replace	Recommendation is to replace equipment.

Condition Recommendation

[CONDITION_RECOMMENDATION]

The recommendation data field is used to capture the condition assessors' detailed recommendations based on their observation of the condition of the equipment (Table 5.146). For example: recommend replacement, recommend improved maintenance, recommend reduction in air filter replacement, and so on.

TABLE 5.146 Condition Recommendation Data Example

Cond_Equip_GUID	Condition_Recom_Type	Condition_Recommendation
125Yu345w...		None
IO98YU76f...	Rebuild	Rebuild pump or replace.
G0R3dskn5...	Replace	Replace as soon as possible; Imminent failure.
AdOh4Eqpt...		

COMMISSIONING DATA FIELDS

The purpose of the commissioning data fields is to allow facility management and the owners to capture the data obtained during the commissioning of equipment. Figure 5.18 shows the commissioning tables and any recommended reference tables. Commissioning is the setting up and testing of equipment to ensure

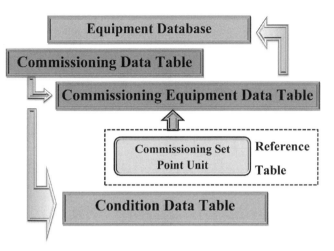

FIGURE 5.18 Commissioning Data Tables

that it runs at the optimal settings for the building. Knowing how the equipment was set up to operate at peak efficiency is important. Normally though, the data are supplied in a paper or form format that is not compatible with a database. The data are, therefore, not typically linked to the equipment. Facility management needs to know why the equipment was set up the way it was and what the designed operating parameters are. For example, suppose that a facility management team wants to know what the set points are for an air handling unit based on the last commissioning of the equipment. Typically, the team would have to find and then wade through a bunch of commissioning documents to find that information. Instead, the commissioning documents and their related data should be captured digitally and then linked directly to the equipment.

The commissioning data have been developed into a separate table because a facility will usually undergo commissioning multiple times. Each time a facility or system is commissioned, a new set of set points and information will be generated. The facility management team needs, at the same time, an accurate history of previous commissioning. For example, suppose that an organization contracts out the commissioning of its chilled water system. The contractor changes multiple set points in the chill water system so that they differ from those in the original design and construction commissioning documentation. In this instance, the facility management staff needs to know why the set points were changed, what the latest recommendation for the set points are, and why. The commissioning tables were also developed to reduce the replication of data in the equipment database. Commissioning usually involves multiple pieces of equipment, and it is more efficient to link commissioning documents to the multiple components in the equipment database than to link the document to each component in the database.

Commissioning data have been separated into two separate tables: Commissioning and Commissioning Equipment. The reason for two tables, as in condition assessment, is to separate the actual document from the equipment. Commissioning is normally performed on multiple pieces of equipment, and the purpose of the commissioning equipment data is to capture commissioning information of each individual piece of equipment.

During commissioning, it is normal practice to also determine the condition of the equipment. Instead of developing new data fields to document these conditions, the condition assessment database should be used.

Commissioning GUID

[COMMISSIONING_GUID]

The Commissioning GUID is a defined space in the database for the unique identifier used to link all related commissioning data (Table 5.147). This GUID is then linked to the commissioning equipment data.

TABLE 5.147   Commissioning GUID Data Example

Commissioning_GUID	Commission_Short_Description	Commission_Provider
Hjdgutr93...	Facility Construction Commissioning	KD Manufacturing
J2ew6bdur...	Fuel System Commissioning	KD Manufacturing
Ib6Ub9Lol...	HVAC Recommissioning	DG Engineering
IcDdp3pl3...	Furnace Recommissioning	Gas RUS Engineering

Commissioning Equipment Database Table		
Comm_Equip_GUID	Commissioning_GUID	Equipment_GUID
J89yh54uO...	Hjdgutr93...	o8ash05Rv...
Ght123YU3...	Hjdgutr93...	A8FDy9w54...
Uyt654olu...	Ib6Ub9Lol...	A8FDy9w54...

Commissioning Short Description

[COMMISSION_SHORT_DESCRIPTION]

The purpose of the short description data field is to allow the organization to write a short description or title of the document (Table 5.148). The short description will allow the company to easily sort and access the data in the database instead of having to open each document to find the commissioning information they are looking for. Commissioning can be performed on a whole facility, a specific system, or new equipment. For example, Construction Commission of Facility ABC0000, Commissioning Fire Safety System 12-01-2000, Commission Boiler BLR-004.

TABLE 5.148 Commissioning Short Description Data Example

Commissioning_GUID	Commission_Short_Description	Commission_Provider
Hjdgutr93...	Facility Construction Commissioning	KD Manufacturing
J2ew6bdur...	Fuel System Commissioning	KD Manufacturing
Ib6Ub9Lol...	HVAC Recommissioning	DG Engineering
IcDdp3pl3...	Furnace Recommissioning	Gas RUS Engineering

Commission Provider

[COMMISSION_PROVIDER]

The commission provider data field is used to capture the name of the company or organization that performed the commissioning (Table 5.149). This allows the organization to capture the data for future reference.

TABLE 5.149 Commission Provider Data Example

Commissioning_GUID	Commission_Short_Description	Commission_Provider	Commission_Date
Hjdgutr93...	Facility Construction Commissioning	KD Manufacturing	6/1/2000
J2ew6bdur...	Fuel System Commissioning	KD Manufacturing	8/1/2000
Ib6Ub9Lol...	HVAC Recommissioning	DG Engineering	12/28/2004
IcDdp3pl3...	Furnace Recommissioning	Gas RUS Engineering	5/5/2005

Commission Date

[COMMISSION_DATE]

The commission date is used to capture the date that the commissioning was performed (Table 5.150). This data allow the organization to determine the chronological order of commissioning to properly understand the progression of changes to set points in their facility.

TABLE 5.150 Commission Date Data Example

Commissioning_GUID	Commission_Short_Description	Commission_Provider	Commission_Date
Hjdgutr93...	Facility Construction Commissioning	KD Manufacturing	6/1/2000
J2ew6bdur...	Fuel System Commissioning	KD Manufacturing	8/1/2000
Ib6Ub9Lol...	HVAC Recommissioning	DG Engineering	12/28/2004
IcDdp3pl3...	Furnace Recommissioning	Gas RUS Engineering	5/5/2005

Commissioning Document

[COMMISSION_DOC]

The commission document data field is actually the place in the database that the organization would load the final commissioning document (Table 5.151). It is important to be able to capture the original document for future reference.

TABLE 5.151   Commissioning Document Data Example

Commissioning_GUID	Commission_Short_Description	Commission_Doc
Hjdgutr93...	Facility Construction Commissioning	ABC0000 Construction Commission.PDF
J2ew6bdur...	Fuel System Commissioning	ABC0000 Fuel Commission.PDF
Ib6Ub9Lol...	HVAC Recommissioning	ABC0000 HVAC 2004-12-28.DOCX
IcDdp3pl3...	Furnace Recommissioning	ABC0000 FURN Recomm.DOC

Commission Equipment GUID

[COMM_EQUIP_GUID]

The Commission Equipment GUID is a defined space in the database for the unique identifier used to link all related equipment commissioning data (Table 5.152). The equipment GUID is then linked to the commissioning equipment table for each commissioning. The equipment database is linked to the commissioning database to reduce the number of fields that need to be added to the equipment database.

TABLE 5.152   Commission Equipment GUID Data Example

Comm_Equip_GUID	Commissioning_GUID	Equipment_GUID
J89yh54uO...	Hjdgutr93...	o8ash05Rv...
Ght123YU3...	Hjdgutr93...	A8FDy9w54...
Uyt654olu...	Ib6Ub9Lol...	A8FDy9w54...

Equipment Database		
Equipment_GUID	Equipment_ID_Composite	Space_GUID
o8ash05Rv...	ABC0000-P-189:AB	f9th35Dg1...
A8FDy9w54...	ABC0000-AHU-050	N37d075h2...

Commissioning Data Table		
Commissioning_GUID	Commission_Provider	Commission_Date
Hjdgutr93...	KD Manufacturing	6/1/2000
Ib6Ub9Lol...	DG Engineering	12/28/2004

Commission Observation

[COMMISSION_OBSERVATION]

The commissioning observation data field is a text field used to capture in text form the detailed observations made during the commissioning of the equipment (Table 5.153). Commissioning observations should be limited to the problems that affect set points and commissioning information. Other observations should be captured as condition assessments. For example, suppose that a commissioning agent determines that the set points of a pressure detector have deviated and the pressure detector has to be recalibrated with new set points. The agent also notices that the pressure detector is old and in poor condition and should be replaced or rebuilt. The agent should comment about the set point changes and recalibration in the commissioning observations and record the poor condition and recommendation to replace the equipment in the condition assessment database. The reason why the information should be handled in this method is to ensure that when facility management queries condition assessment data for equipment that needs repair or replacement, the pressure detector will show up in the query.

TABLE 5.153   Commission Observation Data Example

Comm_Equip_GUID	Commission_Observation	Commission_Recommendation
J89yh54uO...	New equipment	N/A
Ght123YU3...	New equipment	N/A
Uyt654olu...	Set points drifted causing equipment to remain on longer periods of time. Found controller air leakage.	Tighten leaks and calibrate control system.
GoM1am1Dp...	New equipment	N/A
09Gh34Ftw...	New equipment	N/A
JkSK43Rk1...	Operating at a reduced rate because of designation as standby.	Alternate run time with other furnace.

Commission Recommendation

[COMMISSION_RECOMMENDATION]

For every commissioning observation that requires an action to be completed by the facility management staff, a recommendation should be included in the database (Table 5.154). Commission recommendation is a text-based data field included for this purpose.

TABLE 5.154   Commission Recommendation Data Example

Comm_Equip_GUID	Commission_Observation	Commission_Recommendation
J89yh54uO...	New equipment	N/A
Ght123YU3...	New equipment	N/A
Uyt654olu...	Set points drifted causing equipment to remain on longer periods of time. Found controller air leakage.	Tighten leaks and calibrate control system.
GoM1am1Dp...	New equipment	N/A
09Gh34Ftw...	New equipment	N/A
JkSK43Rk1...	Operating at a reduced rate due to designation as standby.	Alternate run time with other furnace.

Commissioning Set Points

The main purpose of commissioning equipment is to ensure that equipment is operating at its maximum efficiency to ensure that the facility is operating as designed. Equipment will be calibrated and set up to ensure that each component in a system is integrated with the other components in the system. For example, if you had multiple packaged air conditioning units supplying the heating and cooling to a warehouse and one of the unit's heating set points overlap the cooling set points for another unit, you now have a situation in which one unit is trying to cool the warehouse at the same time one unit is trying to heat the warehouse. These two units will never shut off, and their operation is counterproductive and costly. Part of equipment commissioning is to resolve or prevent these types of conflicts.

When the commissioning of a facility is complete, a document or report is handed over to the facility management staff describing what was done. The main data points that are important are the operational set points. Operational set points are the values that the equipment were calibrated to perform at. Over time, after commissioning, set points will drift or be changed by the facility staff. Having the original data from commissioning is important in understanding how the facility was designed or commissioned to operate.

For each piece of equipment there is the possibility of multiple different set points. For example, a pressure detector could be set at 5 psig for a low-pressure alarm and 50 psig for a high-pressure alarm. Each of the different set points should have its own data set in the database. Set points should not be confused with design or operating specifications (See "Equipment Specifications"). Specifications describe the design or operating parameters of a piece of equipment, whereas set points describe what values the equipment was calibrated to or set to maintain.

Commissioning Set Point Position

[SET POINT_POSITION(N)] (N denotes that multiple fields are possible.)

The set point position is used by the database to capture the action taken by the equipment when it reaches the defined set point value (Table 5.155). For example, an air handling unit turns on and starts to cool a space when temperature in the space reaches 74 degrees Fahrenheit. The position in this scenario would be "On."

TABLE 5.155 Commissioning Set Point Position Data Example

Comm_Equip_GUID	Set Point Position (1)	Set Point Unit (1)	Set Point Value (1)	Set Point Comment (1)	Set Point Position (N)
J89yh54uO...	On				
Ght123YU3...	On	Degree F	78	Maintain space temperatures	Off
Uyt654olu...	On	Degree F	82	Age causing higher set point to maintain space temperatures	Off
GoM1am1Dp...	Voltage	DC Voltage	2	Low-level alarm function	Voltage
09Gh34Ftw...	On	Degree F	45	Start on low outside air temperature	Off
JkSK43Rk1...	On	Degree F	45	Start on low outside air temperature	Off

Commissioning Set Point Unit

[SET POINT_UNIT(N)] (N denotes that multiple fields are possible.)

There are hundreds of different types of units of measure, such as psig, psia, inches of mercury, degrees Fahrenheit, and degrees Celsius, to which a set point can be calibrated. It is very important to know what the unit of measure was for the set point. This data field captures the unit of measure for the set point (Table 5.156). Using a reference table for units of measure is good practice to prevent human entry errors and allows proper sorting of the data. A better option is to use an industry standard. OmniClass™ Table 49, Properties from CSI/CSC, in draft format at the time of this writing, would be a very good substitute for having to develop an in-house reference table. Note: If you are going to use OmniClass™ Table 49 for this purpose, an additional data field that captures the OmniClass™ number is recommended. You would, therefore, have: Set point_Unit and Industry_Unit_Code. The OmniClass™ number would go into the unit code data field, and the description or unit of measure would go into the set point unit field.

TABLE 5.156 Commissioning Set Point Unit Data Example

Comm_Equip_GUID	Set Point Position (1)	Set Point Unit (1)	Set Point Value (1)	Set Point Comment (1)	Set Point Position (N)
J89yh54uO...	On				
Ght123YU3...	On	Degree F	78	Maintain space temperatures	Off
Uyt654olu...	On	Degree F	82	Age causing higher set point to maintain space temperatures	Off
GoM1am1Dp...	Voltage	DC Voltage	2	Low-level alarm function	Voltage
09Gh34Ftw...	On	Degree F	45	Start on low outside air temperature	Off
JkSK43Rk1...	On	Degree F	45	Start on low outside air temperature	Off

Commissioning Set Point Value

[SET POINT_VALUE(N)] (N denotes that multiple fields are possible.)

The purpose of the commissioning set point value is to capture the calibrated value of the set point (Table 5.157). Only a numeric value should be entered in this field.

TABLE 5.157 Commissioning Set Point Value Data Example

Comm_Equip_GUID	Set Point Value (1)	Set Point Comment (1)	Set Point Position (N)	Set Point Unit (N)	Set Point Value (N)
J89yh54uO...					
Ght123YU3...	78	Maintain space temperatures	Off	Degree F	62
Uyt654olu...	82	Age causing higher set point to maintain space temperatures	Off	Degree F	60
GoM1am1Dp...	2	Low-level alarm function	Voltage	DC Voltage	4
09Gh34Ftw...	45	Start on low outside air temperature	Off	Degree F	60
JkSK43Rk1...	45	Start on low outside air temperature	Off	Degree F	60

Commissioning Set Point Comment

[SET POINT_COMMENT(N)] (N denotes that multiple fields are possible.)

While it is important to capture the calibration set point of equipment, it is also important to understand the purpose of why that set point was chosen or any related comments. For example, suppose that three air handlers are set up to supply heat to a zone of spaces at different set points of 64, 60, and 56 degrees Fahrenheit, respectively. Unless facility management knew that the air handlers were set up to support each other in a cascading method to heat the spaces, they might change the set points of the equipment to all start at 64 degrees Fahrenheit. Changing the set points would defeat the purpose of the way they were commissioned to operate. Therefore, it is important to capture any comments related to the data (Table 5.158).

TABLE 5.158 Commissioning Set Point Comment Data Example

Comm_Equip_GUID	Set Point Position (1)	Set Point Unit (1)	Set Point Value (1)	Set Point Comment (1)	Set Point Position (N)
J89yh54uO...	On				
Ght123YU3...	On	Degree F	78	Maintain space temperatures	Off

Comm_Equip_GUID	Set Point Position (1)	Set Point Unit (1)	Set Point Value (1)	Set Point Comment (1)	Set Point Position (N)
Uyt654olu...	On	Degree F	82	Age causing higher set point to maintain space temperatures	Off
GoM1am1Dp...	Voltage	DC Voltage	2	Low-level Alarm Function	Voltage
09Gh34Ftw...	On	Degree F	45	Start on low outside air temperature	Off
JkSK43Rk1...	On	Degree F	45	Start on low outside air temperature	Off

AUDITS AND INSPECTION DATA FIELDS

While condition assessments are a more formal means to assess the condition of equipment, facility management teams will typically have an audit or inspection process internal to their organization that is used to check regulation compliance, level of maintenance, and even the condition of equipment. The audit and inspection data fields are used to allow facility management to capture the information about their quality control and inspection audits. The data fields also allow the team to organize and categorize their audits into a usable format based on the equipment. Figure 5.19 shows the audits table and any recommended reference tables. The term "inspection" is considered the same as the term "audit" in this application.

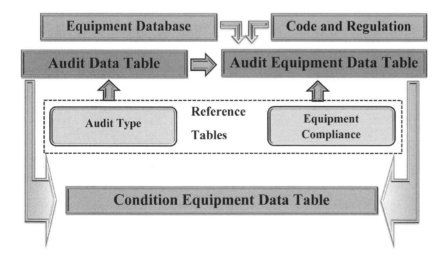

FIGURE 5.19 Audit and Inspection Data Tables

Audit data have been developed into a separate table because a facility will usually undergo multiple audits. Each time an audit is performed there will be a new set of information generated. The audit tables were developed to prevent having this large amount of data placed in the equipment database. The facility management team needs to have an accurate history of the audits for future reference. Audits and inspections usually involve multiple pieces of equipment, and it is more efficient to link audit documents to the multiple components in the equipment database than to link the document to each component in the database.

When performing audits of equipment, auditors will usually capture the condition of the related equipment. Instead of developing additional data fields to document these conditions, the condition assessment database should be used and linked to the audit table.

Audit GUID

[AUDIT_GUID]

The Audit GUID is a defined space in the database for the unique identifier used to link all related audit data (Table 5.159). This GUID is then linked to the audit equipment data.

TABLE 5.159 Audit GUID Data Example

Audit_GUID	Audit_Type	Audit_Provider	Audit_Date
HGkj0982s...	Environmental	ABC Environment Division	1/3/2004
Hyiusi89g...	Maintenance Compliance Audit	OM Services	4/15/2004
YH23GF3uh...	Fire Safety	Fire Marshal Bob	6/23/2004
J98khrdj1...	Operations and Maintenance	ABC FM Division	11/16/2004

Audit Equipment Table		
Audit_Equip_GUID	Audit_GUID	Equipment_GUID
Gt398gtT1...	J98khrdj1...	o8ash05Rv...
KJHs9847w...	HGkj0982s...	Nfk43lud3...
M0j9g0s8l...	Hyiusi89g...	Ohe33jG2x...

Audit Type

[AUDIT_TYPE]

The best practice when setting up a database is to have a way to categorize data so that it can be sorted and displayed for personnel. Therefore, the audit type data field is used to categorize the different types of audits that an organization performs (Table 5.160). It is recommended that you develop a reference table for this data field and then use it as a drop-down menu for personnel to select the type of audit. The reason for using a reference table is to reduce human input errors and improve the data collection capability of the organization. There is no industry standard for types of audits; therefore, I have included a sample of possible audit types (Table 5.161).

TABLE 5.160 Audit Type Data Example

Audit_GUID	Audit_Type	Audit_Provider	Audit_Date
HGkj0982s...	Environmental	ABC Environment Division	1/3/2004
Hyiusi89g...	Maintenance Compliance Audit	OM Services	4/15/2004
YH23GF3uh...	Fire Safety	Fire Marshal Bob	6/23/2004
97G6e905q...	Operations and Maintenance	Elevator Corp	9/17/2004
Ve7t6y54a...	Historical Preservation	Art Corp	10/1/2004
J98khrdj1...	Operations and Maintenance	ABC FM Division	11/16/2004

TABLE 5.161 Audits and Inspection Type Examples

Audit Type
Energy
Environmental
Maintenance
Operations and Maintenance
Building Operations
Fire Safety
OSHA
Historical Preservation

Audit Provider

[AUDIT_PROVIDER]

The audit provider field is used to capture the name of company or organization that performed the audit (Table 5.162). The reason for capturing this information is to allow the staff to have a point of contact for any questions or resolutions to the audit findings.

TABLE 5.162 Audit Provider Data Example

Audit_GUID	Audit_Type	Audit_Provider	Audit_Date
HGkj0982s...	Environmental	ABC Environment Division	1/3/2004
Hyiusi89g...	Maintenance Compliance Audit	OM Services	4/15/2004
YH23GF3uh...	Fire Safety	Fire Marshal Bob	6/23/2004
97G6e905q...	Operations and Maintenance	Elevator Corp	9/17/2004
Ve7t6y54a...	Historical Preservation	Art Corp	10/1/2004
J98khrdj1...	Operations and Maintenance	ABC FM Division	11/16/2004

Audit Date

[AUDIT_DATE]

The audit date data field is used to capture the date that the audit was completed (Table 5.163).

TABLE 5.163 Audit Date Data Example

Audit_GUID	Audit_Type	Audit_Provider	Audit_Date
HGkj0982s...	Environmental	ABC Environment Division	1/3/2004
Hyiusi89g...	Maintenance Compliance Audit	OM Services	4/15/2004
YH23GF3uh...	Fire Safety	Fire Marshal Bob	6/23/2004
97G6e905q...	Operations and Maintenance	Elevator Corp	9/17/2004
Ve7t6y54a...	Historical Preservation	Art Corp	10/1/2004
J98khrdj1...	Operations and Maintenance	ABC FM Division	11/16/2004

Audit Short Description

[AUDIT_SHORT_DESCRIPTION]

The purpose of the short description data field is to allow the organization to write a short description or title for the audit (Table 5.164). The short description will allow the company to easily sort and access the data in the database instead of having to open each document to determine what the audit was about.

TABLE 5.164 Audit Short Description Data Example

Audit_GUID	Audit_Type	Audit_Short_Description
HGkj0982s...	Environmental	Environmental Code Compliance Audit
Hyiusi89g...	Maintenance Compliance Audit	Elevator Safety Inspection
YH23GF3uh...	Fire Safety	Fire Safety Audit
97G6e905q...	Operations and Maintenance	Elevator Annual Audit
Ve7t6y54a...	Historical Preservation	Historical Preservation Maintenance Inspection
J98khrdj1...	Operations and Maintenance	FM Staff Annual Maintenance Inspection

Audit Document

[AUDIT_DOCUMENT]

The audit document field is the location in the database where the written documentation of the audit would be stored (Table 5.165). It is important to store the document for future reference.

TABLE 5.165 Audit Document Data Example

Audit_GUID	Audit_Short_Description	Audit_Doc
HGkj0982s...	Environmental Code Compliance Audit	ABC ENV Comp 2002.doc
Hyiusi89g...	Elevator Safety Inspection	Elevator INSP 2004 April.doc
YH23GF3uh...	Fire Safety Audit	Fire Safety Audit 2004.pdf
97G6e905q...	Elevator Annual Audit	Elevator Audit 2004.pdf
Ve7t6y54a...	Historical Preservation Maintenance Inspection	Historic Pres INSP 2004.doc
J98khrdj1...	FM Staff Annual Maintenance Inspection	Annual Maintenance Audit.xls

Audit Equipment GUID

[AUDIT_EQUIP_GUID]

The Audit GUID is a defined space in the database for the unique identifier used to link all related equipment audit data (Table 5.166). The equipment GUID is then linked to the audit equipment table for each audit. The equipment table is linked to the audit tables to reduce the need to add additional fields to the equipment database. Audits that have information relating to the condition of equipment would be linked to the condition assessment tables.

TABLE 5.166 Audit Equipment GUID Data Example

Audit_Equip_GUID	Audit_GUID	Equipment_GUID
Gt398gtT1...	J98khrdj1...	o8ash05Rv...
KJHs9847w...	HGkj0982s...	Nfk43lud3...
M0j9g0s8l...	Hyiusi89g...	Ohe33jG2x...

Equipment Database		
Equipment_GUID	Industry_Code_Number	Industry_Code_Description
o8ash05Rv...	23-27 17 13	Centrifugal Pump
Ohe33jG2x...	23-23 11 11 11 13	Traction Passenger Elevator
Nfk43lud3...	23-27 29 21 11 11	Aboveground Primary Tank Containment

Audit Data Table		
Audit_GUID	Audit_Type	Audit_Provider
HGkj0982s...	Environmental	ABC Environment Division
Hyiusi89g...	Maintenance Compliance Audit	OM Services
J98khrdj1...	Operations and Maintenance	ABC FM Division

Equipment Compliance

[EQUIPMENT_COMPLIANCE] (N denotes that multiple fields are possible.)

The equipment compliance data field is used by an auditor to denote whether equipment inspected complies with regulations or codes (Table 5.167). Numerous regulations can be associated with a single piece of equipment. For example, an elevator has to meet state and federal codes and fire life safety codes. This field is used to just denote whether or not the equipment is in compliance (yes or no) with the code or regulation. The actual regulation or code that is being audited should be entered into the next field, called the "compliance regulation data field."

TABLE 5.167   Equipment Compliance Data Example

Audit_Equip_GUID	Equipment_GUID	Equipment_Compliance (1)	Compliance_Regulation (1)	Equipment_Compliance (N)	Compliance_Regulation (N)
Gt398gtT1...	o8ash05Rv...				
KJHs9847w...	Nfk43lud3...	Yes	F3d3r4lcd...	Yes	1J0k32muc...
M0j9g0s8l...	Ohe33jG2x...	Yes	S4ywh4t2d...	Yes	iM4sghtq...
L10nRK3wl...	0Gdhew765...	Yes	T3eDuld33...		
T1G3rRBtr...	T3hg26J3Y...	N/A	N/A	N/A	N/A
S4v3Sh4rk...	Ohe33jG2x...	Yes	S4ywh4t2d...	Yes	iM4sghtq...
Gu1d3d3ds...	Nfk43lud3...	Yes	F3d3r4lcd...	Yes	1J0k32muc...
p3c13OC4k....	o8ash05Rv...	N/A	N/A	N/A	N/A

Compliance Regulation

[COMPLIANCE_REGULATION] (N denotes that multiple fields are possible.)

The compliance regulation data field is used to capture the regulation related to the equipment being audited (Table 5.168). The data fields that captures and organizes the different codes and regulations are covered later in this book (See Chapter 5, "Codes and Regulations"). Currently, there is no database that organizes and lists all of the codes and regulations associated with equipment types. Therefore, each organization would have to self-populate the data. When the data in the codes and regulation section are populated, each one would have its own GUID. The GUID from the related code or regulation that is being audited is the cross-reference data that should be placed in this data field.

TABLE 5.168 Compliance Regulation Data Example

Audit_Equip_GUID	Equipment_GUID	Equipment_Compliance (1)	Compliance_Regulation (1)	Equipment_Compliance (N)	Compliance_Regulation (N)
Gt398gtT1...	o8ash05Rv...				
KJHs9847w...	Nfk43lud3...	Yes	F3d3r4lcd...	Yes	1J0k32muc...
M0j9g0s8l...	Ohe33jG2x...	Yes	S4ywh4t2d...	Yes	iM4sghtq...
L10nRK3wl...	0Gdhew765...	Yes	T3eDuld33...		
T1G3rRBtr...	T3hg26J3Y...	N/A	N/A	N/A	N/A
S4v3Sh4rk...	Ohe33jG2x...	Yes	S4ywh4t2d...	Yes	iM4sghtq...
Gu1d3d3ds...	Nfk43lud3...	Yes	F3d3r4lcd...	Yes	1J0k32muc...
p3c13OC4k....	o8ash05Rv...	N/A	N/A	N/A	N/A

Codes and Regulations Database Tables					
Code_GUID	Code_Type	Code_Source	Code_Title (1)	Code_Designation(1)	Code_Title (2)
F3d3r4lcd...	Federal	EPA	Code of Federal Regulations	Title 40	Oil Pollution Prevention
1J0k32muc...	Federal	EPA	Code of Federal Regulations	Title 40	Oil Pollution Prevention
S4ywh4t2d...	Industry	ASME	Safety Code for Elevators and Escalators	A17.3	Cab Door Restriction System
iM4sghtq...	Industry	ASME	Safety Code for Elevators and Escalators	A17.3	In-Car Key Operated Stop Switch
T3eDuld33...	Industry	NFPA		80	Standard for Fire Doors and Other Opening Protectives

Audit Observation

[AUDIT_OBSERVATION]

The audit observation field is used to capture any detailed observation of the auditor about the equipment (Table 5.169). For example: "Equipment has not been inspected per NFPA requirements and, therefore, is in violation of fire codes."

TABLE 5.169 Audit Observation Data Example

Audit_Equip_GUID	Equipment_GUID	Audit_Observation
Gt398gtT1...	o8ash05Rv...	Equipment maintenance not being performed.
KJHs9847w...	Nfk43lud3...	Aboveground monitoring devices work and spill kit inventoried and in proper location.
M0j9g0s8l...	Ohe33jG2x...	Meets compliance; no actions needed.
L10nRK3wl...	0Gdhew765...	Operational and meets timing requirements.

(continued)

[AUDIT_OBSERVATION] (*continued*)

Audit_Equip_GUID	Equipment_GUID	Audit_Observation
T1G3rRBtr...	T3hg26J3Y...	Painting receives too much direct sunlight and frame shows signs of damage and aging.
S4v3Sh4rk...	Ohe33jG2x...	Elevator meets compliance, two bulbs in cab are burnt out.
Gu1d3d3ds...	Nfk43lud3...	Aboveground containment monitoring devices working. No liquid in containment berm.
p3c13OC4k....	o8ash05Rv...	Poor maintenance being performed on pump, overlubrication of motor.

Audit Recommendation

[AUDIT_RECOMMENDATION]

The audit recommendation data field is used to document any recommendations made by auditor (Table 5.170). It is important for the auditor to capture his or her recommendations needed to resolve any adverse audit finding. This provides the organization with a concrete list of actions that need to be performed. For example: "Have equipment pressure tested greater than 500 psig for 30 minutes per code."

TABLE 5.170 Audit Recommendation Data Example

Audit_Equip_GUID	Equipment_GUID	Audit_Recommendation	Audit_Resolution	Audit_Res_Date
Gt398gtT1...	o8ash05Rv...			
KJHs9847w...	Nfk43lud3...	None	None	
M0j9g0s8l...	Ohe33jG2x...	None	None	
L10nRK3wl...	0Gdhew765...	None	None	
T1G3rRBtr...	T3hg26J3Y...	Relocate painting to area with less direct sunlight and hire restorer to fix frame.	Restored frame and moved from direct sunlight	10/25/2004
S4v3Sh4rk...	Ohe33jG2x...	Replace bulbs in cab.	Bulbs replaced	9/17/2004
Gu1d3d3ds...	Nfk43lud3...	None	None	
p3c13OC4k....	o8ash05Rv...	Perform preventive mainte-nance and increase frequency of performance.	Motor and pump rebuilt	2/3/2005

Audit Resolution

[AUDIT_RESOLUTION]

The audit resolution field allows the organization to track its actions taken to resolve any adverse audit findings (Table 5.171). It is important to track and determine what corrective actions have been taken not only to meet compliance with regulations but also to ensure any ongoing equipment issues are addressed and documented. This provides a history of the equipment not only for the organization but also for future auditors. For example, suppose that facility staff is performing a maintenance inspection of HVAC equipment and find that a damper actuator is not operating properly. They review the equipment history and discover that a previous audit three months ago denoted the same problem and the resolution states that the actuator is ordered and scheduled to be replaced in six months. The auditors can then just reference the past audit about the damper instead of opening a new line item.

TABLE 5.171 Audit Resolution Data Example

Audit_Equip_GUID	Equipment_GUID	Audit_Recommendation	Audit_Resolution	Audit_Res_Date
Gt398gtT1...	o8ash05Rv...			
KJHs9847w...	Nfk43lud3...	None	None	
M0j9g0s8l...	Ohe33jG2x...	None	None	
L10nRK3wl...	0Gdhew765...	None	None	
T1G3rRBtr...	T3hg26J3Y...	Relocate painting to area with less direct sunlight and hire restorer to fix frame.	Restored frame and moved from direct sunlight	10/25/2004
S4v3Sh4rk...	Ohe33jG2x...	Replace bulbs in cab.	Bulbs replaced	9/17/2004
Gu1d3d3ds...	Nfk43lud3...	None	None	
p3c13OC4k....	o8ash05Rv...	Perform preventive maintenance and increase frequency of performance.	Motor and pump rebuilt	2/3/2005

Audit Resolution Date

[AUDIT_RES_DATE]

The Audit Resolution Date is used to enter the date that the audit finding was resolved (Table 5.172). It is important to note that only the date when the item's audit finding was actually resolved is entered into the database. Do not enter the date that someone put in a recommended resolution or comment. For example, suppose that the parts for a damper are ordered to fix a problem found during an audit, and someone puts in the date that the parts were ordered. The parts arrive but are never installed. The audit finding is never actually resolved because the staff already believes the issue is resolved because the resolution date field has a value in it.

(continued)

TABLE 5.172 Audit Resolution Date Data Example

Audit_Equip_GUID	Equipment_GUID	Audit_Recommendation	Audit_Resolution	Audit_Res_Date
Gt398gtT1...	o8ash05Rv...			
KJHs9847w...	Nfk43lud3...	None	None	
M0j9g0s8l...	Ohe33jG2x...	None	None	
L10nRK3wl...	0Gdhew765...	None	None	
T1G3rRBtr...	T3hg26J3Y...	Relocate painting to area with less direct sunlight and hire restorer to fix frame.	Restored frame and moved from direct sunlight	10/25/2004
S4v3Sh4rk...	Ohe33jG2x...	Replace bulbs in cab.	Bulbs replaced	9/17/2004
Gu1d3d3ds...	Nfk43lud3...	None	None	
p3c13OC4k....	o8ash05Rv...	Perform preventive maintenance and increase frequency of performance.	Motor and pump rebuilt	2/3/2005

WARRANTY DATA FIELDS

This section covers warranty data; it is important for a facility to be able to digitally capture the information related to equipment warranties. Figure 5.20 shows the warranty table and any recommended reference tables. The ability of a facility to quickly identify warranty information and recall data can be very vital in ensuring that an organization does not pay for repairs that are covered by the manufacturer's warranty. For example, suppose that 20 percent of the smoke detectors fail within six months of operation at a newly constructed facility. Who pays for the replacement of the equipment?

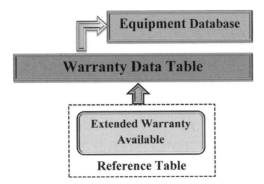

FIGURE 5.20 Warranty Data Tables

Warranty GUID

[WARRANTY_GUID]

The Warranty GUID is a defined space in the database for the unique identifier used to link all related equipment warranty data (Table 5.173). The warranty GUID is then linked to the equipment table for each warranty.

TABLE 5.173 Warranty GUID Data Example

Warranty_GUID	Warranty_Short_Description	Warranty_Number	Warranty_Provider_Name
wH00w3s1t...	KD Manufacturing Install Warranty	KD-2000-123456789	KD Manufacturing
n3vrCo1et...	Smoke Detector Warranty	Manufacturer	FireRUS Corporation
p4ym3d4t2...	Variable Frequency Drive Warranty	P2G0000100208	Energy System
Id0nW4n42...	Historic Rider Insurance	HSR-09-0023308	Bank of Money
C4sh0h34d...	Custodial Rider Insurance	JBC-009-0070-90	Just Be Clean Company

Equipment Database			
Equipment_GUID	Industry_Code_Description	Equipment_ID_Composite	Warranty_GUID
o8ash05Rv...	Centrifugal Pump	ABC0000-P-189:AB	wH00w3s1t...
Pv4ghT671...	Level Detector	ABC0000-LDET-22	wH00w3s1t...
T3hg26J3Y...	Fine Art Painting	ABC0000-FAPTG-02	Id0nW4n42...
Gj09Ht123...	Fine Art Sculpture	ABC0000-FASCLPTR-07	Id0nW4n42...

Warranty Short Description

[WARRANTY_SHORT_DESCRIPTION]

The warranty short description data field allows the user or provider to provide a short description of the warranty (Table 5.174). This short description is used by facility management and owners to improve their ability to sort and review their exist warranties. For example: "Warranty Jacob Air Handling Units Model 746, Warranty Smoke Detectors, Warranty Roof."

TABLE 5.174 Warranty Short Description Data Example

Warranty_GUID	Warranty_Short_Description	Warranty_Number	Warranty_Provider_Name
wH00w3s1t...	KD Manufacturing Install Warranty	KD-2000-123456789	KD Manufacturing
n3vrCo1et...	Smoke Detector Warranty	Manufacturer	FireRUS Corporation
p4ym3d4t2...	Variable Frequency Drive Warranty	P2G0000100208	Energy System
Id0nW4n42...	Historic Rider Insurance	HSR-09-0023308	Bank of Money
C4sh0h34d...	Custodial Rider Insurance	JBC-009-0070-90	Just Be Clean Company

Warranty Number

[WARRANTY_NUMBER]

The warranty number data field is used to capture the warranty number provided by the warranty provider for the policy (Table 5.175).

TABLE 5.175   Warranty Number Data Example

Warranty_GUID	Warranty_Short_Description	Warranty_Number	Warranty_Provider_Name
wH00w3s1t...	KD Manufacturing Install Warranty	KD-2000-123456789	KD Manufacturing
n3vrCo1et...	Smoke Detector Warranty	Manufacturer	FireRUS Corporation
p4ym3d4t2...	Variable Frequency Drive Warranty	P2G0000100208	Energy System
Id0nW4n42...	Historic Rider Insurance	HSR-09-0023308	Bank of Money
C4sh0h34d...	Custodial Rider Insurance	JBC-009-0070-90	Just Be Clean Company

Warranty Provider Name

[WARRANTY_PROVIDER_NAME]

The warranty provider name data field is used to capture the legal name of the company or entity that provides the warranty (Table 5.176). It is important to enter the name of the company or organization that is responsible for fulfilling the terms of the warranty.

TABLE 5.176   Warranty Provider Name Data Example

Warranty_GUID	Warranty_Short_Description	Warranty_Number	Warranty_Provider_Name
wH00w3s1t...	KD Manufacturing Install Warranty	KD-2000-123456789	KD Manufacturing
n3vrCo1et...	Smoke Detector Warranty	Manufacturer	FireRUS Corporation
p4ym3d4t2...	Variable Frequency Drive Warranty	P2G0000100208	Energy System
Id0nW4n42...	Historic Rider Insurance	HSR-09-0023308	Bank of Money
C4sh0h34d...	Custodial Rider Insurance	JBC-009-0070-90	Just Be Clean Company

Warranty Provider Contact Information

[WARRANTY_CONTACT]

The warranty provider contact information is used to capture the contact information of the warranty provider (Table 5.177). The address and main phone number for the company should be entered in this field. Do not enter personal sales or contact personnel contact information, since their position or information is likely to change within the warranty period. This field could be broken up into address, phone number, email, mobile phone, and so on.

TABLE 5.177 Warranty Provider Contact Data Example

Warranty_GUID	Warranty_Provider_Name	Warranty_Contact
wH00w3s1t...	KD Manufacturing	123 South Bend, One City, VA 12345 (800) 444-9999
n3vrCo1et...	FireRUS Corporation	Main Engine Lane, Small Town, MA 01010 (877) 888-8888
p4ym3d4t2...	Energy System	1812 New York Ave, Washington, DC 20400 (202) 344-1776
ld0nW4n42...	Bank of Money	Cayman Islands, 011-99-999-9999
C4sh0h34d...	Just Be Clean Company	123 Removal Lane, Exit Town, NJ 01234 (800) 800-8000

Warranty Installer Name

[WARRANTY_INSTALLER]

The warranty installer name is designed to capture the organization responsible for the installation of the equipment (Table 5.178). Part of warranty usage is ensuring that the component is installed correctly per manufacturer recommendations. Therefore, it is important to ensure that the warranty is valid or the responsible installer information is known. The organization should enter the legal name of the company that installed the equipment.

TABLE 5.178 Warranty Installer Data Example

Warranty_GUID	Warranty_Contact	Warranty_Installer
wH00w3s1t...	123 South Bend, VA 12345 (800) 444-9999	KD Manufacturer
n3vrCo1et...	Main Engine Lane, MA 344444 (877) 888-8888	KD Manufacturer
p4ym3d4t2...	1812 New York Ave, Washington DC 20400 (202) 344-1776	EnergyRUS
ld0nW4n42...	Cayman Islands, 011-99-999-9999	John Does
C4sh0h34d...	123 Removal Lane, Exit Town, NJ 01234 (800) 800-8000	N/A

Warranty Installer Contact Information

[WARRANTY_INSTALLER_CONTACT]

This data field captures and documents the contact information of the company legally responsible for the installation of the equipment (Table 5.179). The address and main phone number for the company should be entered in this field. Do not enter personal sales or marketing personnel information since their position or information is more likely to change. Practically speaking, this field could be broken up into address, phone number, email, mobile phone, and so forth.

(continued)

[WARRANTY_INSTALLER_CONTACT] (*continued*)

TABLE 5.179 Warranty Installer Contact Data Example

Warranty_GUID	Warranty_Installer	Warranty_Installer_Contact
wH00w3s1t...	KD Manufacturer	123 South Bend, Some City, VA 12345 (800) 444-9999
n3vrCo1et...	KD Manufacturer	123 South Bend, Some City, VA 12345 (800) 444-9999
p4ym3d4t2...	EnergyRUS	123 Clean Lane, Sustain, VA 12346 (877) 999-0009
Id0nW4n42...	John Does	18 Art Lane, New York, NY 98741 (800) 437-5678
C4sh0h34d...	N/A	N/A

Warranty Start Date

[WARRANTY_START_DATE]

Knowing the date that a warranty starts is very important to ensuring proper warranty management. The warranty start date is used to determine the end date of the warranty. This data field is used to capture the warranty start date (Table 5.180).

TABLE 5.180 Warranty Start Date Data Example

Warranty_GUID	Warranty_Installer_Contact	Warranty_Start_Date
wH00w3s1t...	123 South Bend, VA 12345 (800) 444-9999	2/1/2000
n3vrCo1et...	123 South Bend, VA 12345 (800) 444-9999	1/19/2000
p4ym3d4t2...	123 Clean Lane, Sustain, VA (877) 999-0009	4/5/2004
Id0nW4n42...	18 Art Lane, NY, NY 98741 (800) 437-5678	4/15/2001
C4sh0h34d...	N/A	6/1/2000

Warranty End Date

[WARRANTY_END_DATE]

Knowing the date that a warranty ends is very important to warranty management and facility management. A facility that can schedule condition assessments of equipment prior to the end of its warranty date can save possible funds by ensuring that the equipment is operating properly prior to the warranty running out. This data field is used to calculate or capture the end date of coverage for the warranty (Table 5.181).

TABLE 5.181   Warranty End Date Data Example

Warranty_GUID	Warranty_End_Date	Extended_Warranty_Available
wH00w3s1t...	3/1/2001	Yes: Not Purchased
n3vrCo1et...	1/19/2004	Yes: Purchased
p4ym3d4t2...	4/5/2007	Yes: Purchased
ld0nW4n42...	4/15/2004	Not Available
C4sh0h34d...	6/1/2005	Not Available

Extended Warranty Available

[EXTENDED_WARRANTY_AVAILABLE]

The extended warranty available data field is used to determine if an extended warranty is available and if it was purchased (Table 5.182). There are a significant number of times in which an extended warranty can be purchased that extends the manufacturer warranty. Knowing whether or not your organization purchased the extended warranty can save significant time and investigative resources.

TABLE 5.182   Extended Warranties Available Example

Warranty_GUID	Warranty_End_Date	Extended_Warranty_Available
wH00w3s1t...	3/1/2001	Yes: Not Purchased
n3vrCo1et...	1/19/2004	Yes: Purchased
p4ym3d4t2...	4/5/2007	Yes: Purchased
ld0nW4n42...	4/15/2004	Not Available
C4sh0h34d...	6/1/2005	Not Available

TABLE 5.183   Extended Warranties Available Reference

Extended Warranty
Yes: Purchased
Yes: Not Purchased
Not Available

Extended Warranty Number

[EXTENDED_WARRANTY_NUMBER]

The extended warranty number data field is used to capture the number provided by the warranty provider for the extended policy (Table 5.184).

(continued)

[EXTENDED_WARRANTY_NUMBER] (*continued*)

TABLE 5.184   Extended Warranty Number Data Example

Warranty_GUID	Extended_Warranty_Available	Extended_Warranty_Number
wH00w3s1t...	Yes: Not Purchased	
n3vrCo1et...	Yes: Purchased	BG-778-9007
p4ym3d4t2...	Yes: Purchased	P2G0000100208
ld0nW4n42...	Not Available	
C4sh0h34d...	Not Available	

Extended Warranty Provider Name

[EXTENDED_WARRANTY_PROVIDER]

The extended warranty provider name data field is used to capture the legal name of the warranty provider (Table 5.185).

TABLE 5.185   Extended Warranty Provider Name Data Example

Warranty_GUID	Extended_Warranty_Provider	Extended_Warranty_Contact
wH00w3s1t...		
n3vrCo1et...	Fire Co Warranties	Main Engine Lane, Small Town, MA 01010 (877) 888-8888
p4ym3d4t2...	Energy System	1812 New York Ave, Washington, DC 20400 (202) 344-1776
ld0nW4n42...		
C4sh0h34d...		

Extended Warranty Provider Contact Information

[EXTENDED_WARRANTY_CONTACT]

The extended warranty provider contact information is used to capture the contact information for the provider (Table 5.186). The address and main phone number for the company should be entered in this field. Do not enter sales or marketing personnel contact information, since their position or information is likely to change within the warranty period. This field could be broken up into address, phone number, email, mobile phone, and so on.

TABLE 5.186   Extended Warranty Provider Contact Data Example

Warranty_GUID	Extended_Warranty_Provider	Extended_Warranty_Contact
wH00w3s1t...		
n3vrCo1et...	Fire Co Warranties	Main Engine Lane, Small Town, MA 01010 (877) 888-8888
p4ym3d4t2...	Energy System	1812 New York Ave, Washington, DC 20400 (202) 344-1776
ld0nW4n42...		
C4sh0h34d...		

Extended Warranty Start Date

[EXTENDED_WARRANTY_START_DATE]

Knowing the date that an extended warranty starts is very important to ensuring proper warranty management. Does the warranty and extended warranty overlap? Is there a period between when the warranty ends and the extended warranty starts that there is no coverage? This data field is used to capture the extended warranty start date (Table 5.187).

TABLE 5.187   Extended Warranty Start Date Data Example

Warranty_GUID	Extended_Warranty_Contact	Extended_Warranty_Start_Date
wH00w3s1t...		
n3vrCo1et...	Main Engine Lane, Small Town, MA 01010 (877) 888-8888	1/19/2004
p4ym3d4t2...	1812 New York Ave, Washington, DC 20400 (202) 344-1776	4/5/2007
Id0nW4n42...		
C4sh0h34d...		

Extended Warranty End Date

[EXTENDED_WARRANTY_END_DATE]

Knowing the date that the extended warranty ends is very important to warranty management and facility management. This data field is used to calculate or capture the end date of coverage for the extended warranty (Table 5.188).

TABLE 5.188   Extended Warranty End Date Data Example

Warranty_GUID	Extended_Warranty_End_Date	Substantial_Completion_Date
wH00w3s1t...		3/1/2000
n3vrCo1et...	1/19/2008	3/1/2000
p4ym3d4t2...	4/5/2010	4/5/2004
Id0nW4n42...		
C4sh0h34d...		

Substantial Completion Date

[SUBSTANTIAL_COMPLETION_DATE]

Substantial completion date is a term used in new construction and major renovations to denote the date that an owner or organization accepts the substantial completion of a project or facility.

(continued)

[SUBSTANTIAL_COMPLETION_DATE] (*continued*)

In the United States, the federal governments, per the Federal Acquisition Regulations (FAR), requires contractors required to provide a 1-year contractor warranty that starts at the substantial completion date. Therefore, it is very important to capture the substantial completion date to determine warranty applicability (Table 5.189).

TABLE 5.189 Substantial Completion Date Data Example

Warranty_GUID	Extended_Warranty_End_Date	Substantial_Completion_Date
wH00w3s1t...		3/1/2000
n3vrCo1et...	1/19/2008	3/1/2000
p4ym3d4t2...	4/5/2010	4/5/2004
ld0nW4n42...		
C4sh0h34d...		

Warranty Document

[WARRANTY_DOCUMENT]

The warranty document field is where the written warranty document would be stored in the database (Table 5.190). It is important to store the document for future reference.

TABLE 5.190 Warranty Document Data Example

Warranty_GUID	Substantial_Completion_Date	Warranty_Document
wH00w3s1t...	3/1/2000	Construction Warranty 2000.pdf
n3vrCo1et...	3/1/2000	FireRUS Warranty Smoke DET. pdf
p4ym3d4t2...	4/5/2004	VFD Warranty 2004.doc
ld0nW4n42...		Art Rider Insurance.pdf
C4sh0h34d...		Custodial Insurance.pdf

Extended Warranty Document

[EXTENDED_WARRANTY_DOCUMENT]

The extended warranty document field is where the written warranty document would be stored in the database (Table 5.191). It is important to store the document for future reference.

TABLE 5.191   Extended Warranty Document Data Example

Warranty_GUID	Warranty_Document	Extended_Warranty_Document
wH00w3s1t...	Construction Warranty 2000.pdf	
n3vrCo1et...	FireRUS Warranty Smoke DET. pdf	Extended Smoke Det. Warranty.pdf
p4ym3d4t2...	VFD Warranty 2004.doc	Extended VFD Warranty.pdf
ld0nW4n42...	Art Rider Insurance.pdf	
C4sh0h34d...	Custodial Insurance.pdf	

CODE AND REGULATIONS DATA FIELDS

The code and regulation data fields are used to capture the codes and regulations to be enforced for equipment. Figure 5.21 shows the code and regulation table and any recommended reference tables. The codes and regulations are maintained in a separate database and, because a GUID is used, they can be linked to the equipment while reducing the repetition of data. for example, the ASME A17.2 standard is linked to elevators the NFPA standard is linked to each fire detector, the Energy Independence and Security Act of 2007 is linked to each advanced remote utility meter, or the ASHRAE standard is linked to a restroom exhaust fan ductwork. The data are vital to ensuring that facility managers have immediate access to all of the codes and regulations related to installed equipment. A significant amount of this information is predetermined during design construction to ensure that the facility meets federal, state, and local standards. This is the optimum point at which to capture this data. There is currently no single library of all the related codes and regulations, so an organization will have to self-populate most of it at this time. It should be noted that there are companies that pay to use a database compilation of codes and regulations. An organization would have to evaluate those databases and determine any fees associated with them.

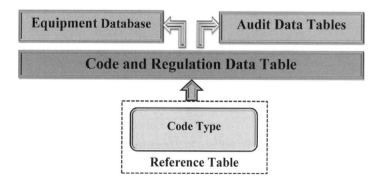

FIGURE 5.21 Code and Regulation Data Tables

Code GUID

[CODE_GUID]

The Code GUID is a defined space in the database for the unique identifier used to link all related codes and regulations data (Table 5.192). The Code GUID is then linked to the equipment table. The Code GUID is also used in the audit table for equipment compliance (See Chapter 5, "Audits and Inspection Data Fields: Equipment Compliance").

TABLE 5.192   Code GUID Data Example

Code_GUID	Code_Type	Code_Source	Code_Title (1)
F3d3r4lcd...	Federal	EPA	Code of Federal Regulations
1J0k32muc...	Federal	EPA	Code of Federal Regulations
S4ywh4t2d...	Industry	ASME	Safety Code for Elevators and Escalators
iM4sghtq...	Industry	ASME	Safety Code for Elevators and Escalators
wHoD4tS4i...	Industry	ASME	Safety Code for Elevators and Escalators
T3eDuld33...	Industry	NFPA	

Equipment Database			
Equipment_GUID	Equipment_ID_Composite	Code GUID (1)	Code GUID (2)
0Gdhew765...	ABC0000-FDMPR-07	T3eDuld33...	
Ohe33jG2x...	ABC0000-ELEV-15	S4ywh4t2d...	iM4sghtq...
Nfk43lud3...	ABC0000-ASTPCON-02	F3d3r4lcd...	1J0k32muc...

Audit Equipment Database		
Audit_Equip_GUID	Compliance_Regulation (1)	Compliance_Regulation (2)
KJHs9847w...	F3d3r4lcd...	1J0k32muc...
M0j9g0s8l...	S4ywh4t2d...	iM4sghtq...

Code Type

[CODE_TYPE]

Codes are typically based off of laws and regulations developed by state, federal, and industry entities. It is important for an organization to understand the type of code they are required to comply with (Table 5.193). For example, a state code in Virginia might not be required in the state of Maryland. Typing the codes also allows an organization to sort the required regulations into their separate types for analysis of data and compliance. The organization should develop a reference table for the type of codes and use this as a drop-down option for entries into this data field (Table 5.194). This reduces the chance for human entry errors and improves the ability to parse the data.

TABLE 5.193 Code Type Data Example

Code_GUID	Code_Type	Code_Source	Code_Title (1)
F3d3r4lcd...	Federal	EPA	Code of Federal Regulations
1J0k32muc...	Federal	EPA	Code of Federal Regulations
W3knOw3r3..	Federal	DOE	Energy Independence and Security Act of 2007
S4ywh4t2d...	Industry	ASME	Safety Code for Elevators and Escalators
iM4sghtq...	Industry	ASME	Safety Code for Elevators and Escalators
wHoD4tS4i...	Industry	ASME	Safety Code for Elevators and Escalators
T1m34tAgU...	Industry	ASME	Safety Code for Elevators and Escalators
T3eDuld33...	Industry	NFPA	
G3td0n1ta...	State	Virginia	Virginia Uniform Statewide Building Code
Tr1d3ntRu...	State	Virginia	Virginia Uniform Statewide Building Code
v3n3rShzl...	County	Tontario	Building Code

TABLE 5.194 Code Type Examples

Code Types
Federal
Industry
Military
State
County
Local

Code Source

[CODE_SOURCE]

The governing entity that is responsible for the development and issuance of the code or regulation should be captured in the code table (Table 5.195). This allows an organization to denote the responsible organization for the code so that, if there are inquiries, they have a source to contact. For example, if an organization wanted to know how to meet the 40 CFR, Part 112 Oil Pollution Prevention code developed by the Environmental Protection Agency, they could contact a specialist or the agency itself for clarification.

TABLE 5.195 Code Source Data Example

Code_GUID	Code_Type	Code_Source	Code_Title (1)
F3d3r4lcd...	Federal	EPA	Code of Federal Regulations
1J0k32muc...	Federal	EPA	Code of Federal Regulations

(continued)

[CODE_SOURCE] (continued)

Code_GUID	Code_Type	Code_Source	Code_Title (1)
W3knOw3r3..	Federal	DOE	Energy Independence and Security Act of 2007
S4ywh4t2d...	Industry	ASME	Safety Code for Elevators and Escalators
iM4sghtq...	Industry	ASME	Safety Code for Elevators and Escalators
wHoD4tS4i...	Industry	ASME	Safety Code for Elevators and Escalators
T1m34tAgU...	Industry	ASME	Safety Code for Elevators and Escalators
T3eDuld33...	Industry	NFPA	
G3td0n1ta...	State	Virginia	Virginia Uniform Statewide Building Code
Tr1d3ntRu...	State	Virginia	Virginia Uniform Statewide Building Code
v3n3rShzl...	County	Tontario	Building Code

Code Title

[CODE_TITLE(N)] (N denotes that multiple fields are possible.)

The title of the code is important to capture because some regulations contain multiple titles, sections, chapters, subsections, paragraphs, and so on and each has its own requirements and each could affect different equipment. For example, the Code of Federal Regulations (CFR) has numerous titles, title 40 CFR is Protection of Environment, 34 CFR is Education, and 10 CFR is Energy. Under title 40, Part 112 is "Oil Pollution Prevention," and under Part 112 are multiple subsections such as 112.8, which deals with spill prevention, and 112.20, which deals with facility response plans. Understanding the titles is important to being able to drill down into the code or regulation and determine the equipment compliance requirements (Table 5.196).

TABLE 5.196   Code Title Data Example

Code_GUID	Code_Source	Code_Title (1)	Code_Designation(1)
F3d3r4lcd...	EPA	Code of Federal Regulations	Title 40
1J0k32muc...	EPA	Code of Federal Regulations	Title 40
W3knOw3r3..	DOE	Energy Independence and Security Act of 2007	Public Law110 - 140

Code_GUID	Code_Title (2)	Code_Designation(2)
F3d3r4lcd...	Oil Pollution Prevention	Part 112
1J0k32muc...	Oil Pollution Prevention	Part 112
W3knOw3r3..	High-Performance Commercial Buildings	Section 421

Code_GUID	Code_Title (N)	Code_Designation(3)
F3d3r4lcd...	Spill Prevention, Control, and Countermeasure Plan requirements for onshore facilities (excluding production facilities).	§112.8
1J0k32muc...	Facility Response Plans	§112.20
W3knOw3r3..		

Code Designation

[CODE_DESIGNATION(N)] (N denotes that multiple fields are possible.)

Each code or regulation title is associated with a designation for the title, chapter, section, subsection, page, paragraph, and so on. For example, Sidewalks and Driveways maintenance is part of the Virginia Maintenance Code Part III, Section 302, and Subsection 302.3. The code designations are important to properly understanding and complying with regulations (Table 5.197).

TABLE 5.197 Code Designation Data Example

Code_GUID	Code_Source	Code_Title (1)	Code_Designation (1)
F3d3r4lcd...	EPA	Code of Federal Regulations	Title 40
1J0k32muc...	EPA	Code of Federal Regulations	Title 40
W3knOw3r3..	DOE	Energy Independence and Security Act of 2007	Public Law110 - 140

Code_GUID	Code_Title (2)	Code_Designation (2)
F3d3r4lcd...	Oil Pollution Prevention	Part 112
1J0k32muc...	Oil Pollution Prevention	Part 112
W3knOw3r3..	High-Performance Commercial Buildings	Section 421

Code_GUID	Code_Title (N)	Code_Designation (N)
F3d3r4lcd...	Spill Prevention, Control, and Countermeasure Plan Requirements for Onshore Facilities (Excluding Production Facilities).	§112.8
1J0k32muc...	Facility Response Plans	§112.20
W3knOw3r3..		

Code Comments

[CODE_COMMENTS]

The code comments allow the organization to input a description of the code and the basic requirements (Table 5.198). The vast majority of the time these comments can be pulled directly from the code itself.

TABLE 5.198 Code Comments Data Example

Code_GUID	Code_Comments	Code_Enforcement
F3d3r4lcd...	Spill prevention kits required, manual valves, and containment	Environmental Protection Agency
1J0k32muc...	Facility response plan required	Environmental Protection Agency
W3knOw3r3..		Department of Energy
S4ywh4t2d...	Door restriction requirements	State Inspector

(continued)

[CODE_COMMENTS] (continued)

Code_GUID	Code_Comments	Code_Enforcement
iM4sghtq...	Location, markings	State Inspector
wHoD4tS4i...	Operation, location, testing	State Inspector
T1m34tAgU...	Repair and replacement	State Inspector
T3eDuld33...	Operational at all times	State Fire Marshal
G3td0n1ta...	Exterior property and premise maintained in clean, safe, and sanitary condition	County
Tr1d3ntRu...	Kept in proper state of repair and maintained free of hazardous conditions	County
v3n3rShzl...	Snow clearance shall be only manual or salt application. No nonbiodegradeable chemicals that can get into watershed shall be used.	County

Code Enforcement

[CODE_ENFORCEMENT]

Every required code has a state, local, industry, or government organization or agency that is responsible for enforcing, interpreting, and governing the regulation. The enforcement data field is use to capture the name of the responsible agency or organization (Table 5.199). For example: Environmental Protection Agency, Virginia State Certified Inspector, or NFPA Certified Inspector.

TABLE 5.199 Code Enforcement Data Example

Code_GUID	Code_Comments	Code_Enforcement
F3d3r4lcd...	Spill prevention kits required, manual valves, and containment	Environmental Protection Agency
1J0k32muc...	Facility response plan required	Environmental Protection Agency
W3knOw3r3...		Department of Energy
S4ywh4t2d...	Door restriction requirements	State Inspector
iM4sghtq...	Location, markings	State Inspector
wHoD4tS4i...	Operation, location, testing	State Inspector
T1m34tAgU...	Repair and replacement	State Inspector
T3eDuld33...	Operational at all times	State Fire Marshal
G3td0n1ta...	Exterior property and premise maintained in clean, safe, and sanitary condition	County
Tr1d3ntRu...	Kept in proper state of repair and maintained free of hazardous conditions	County
v3n3rShzl...	Snow clearance shall be only manual or salt application. No nonbio-degradeable chemicals that can get into watershed shall be used.	County

Code Document

[CODE_DOCUMENT]

The code document field is used to download a copy of the actual code or regulation to the database (Table 5.200). Having direct access to the code helps the owner and the facility management team to understand it and ensure that they are compliant. Downloading the document ensures that valuable time and effort is not wasted by having staff continually research and find the documents when situations arrive. If Internet Web links are used to capture the document, the organization has to periodically review the links to ensure that the sites or documents have not been removed or replaced.

TABLE 5.200 Code Document Data Example

Code_GUID	Code_Enforcement	Code_Document
F3d3r4lcd...	Environmental Protection Agency	CFR.PDF
1J0k32muc...	Environmental Protection Agency	CFR.PDF
W3knOw3r3...	Department of Energy	EISA.PDF
S4ywh4t2d...	State Inspector	ASME 17 2004.PDF
iM4sghtq...	State Inspector	ASME 17 2004.PDF
wHoD4tS4i...	State Inspector	ASME 17 2004.PDF
T1m34tAgU...	State Inspector	ASME 17 2004.PDF
T3eDuld33...	State Fire Marshal	NFPA 8- 2001.PDF
G3td0n1ta...	County	VA USBC.PDF
Tr1d3ntRu...	County	VA USBC.PDF
v3n3rShzl...	County	VA Tont BC.PDF

OPERATION DOCUMENTS DATA FIELDS

There are numerous documents related to equipment such as technical manuals, wiring diagrams, operational manuals, and the like. Figure 5.22 shows the operation document table and any recommended reference tables. Therefore, there must be a way in which to store these documents in a logical manner so that they can then be linked to the equipment itself. A separate data table and document storage system should be used to store the vast number of documents that a facility should have access to. The documents can then be linked within the database to the associated equipment. It should be noted that, when similar equipment uses the same manuals, only one manual should be loaded into the database and then linked to each piece of related equipment.

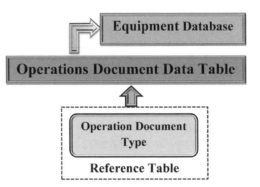

FIGURE 5.22 Operations
Documents Data Tables

Operation Document GUID

[OPS_DOC_GUID]

The Operations Document GUID is a defined space in the database for the unique identifier used to link all related document data (Table 5.201). The document GUID is then linked to the equipment table.

TABLE 5.201   Operation Document GUID Data Example

Operation_Document_GUID	Operation_Doc_Type	Operation_Document_Short_Description
Kayrg9873...	Operator Startup Procedure	GASCO Series IV Furnaces
J89yu67ty...	Maintenance Guide	GASCO Series IV Furnaces
St4r4tR3k...	Training Documents	Startup of Chill Water System
ump3ri31...	Operator Startup Procedure	ElectricCo Series 3400
S3m1cOLOn...	Emergency Operations	ElectricCo Series 3400
2B4iT1S3c...	Spare Parts List	ElectricCo Series 3400

Equipment Database		
Equipment_GUID	Equipment_ID_Composite	Ops_Doc_GUID (1)
o8ash05Rv...	ABC0000-P-189:AB	St4r4tR3k...
fw565r713...	ABC0000-MOT-978	F1n4liyS3...
1789gt435...	ABC0000-GENENG-01	ump3ri31...
Gt76YH887...	ABC0000-FURN-01	Kayrg9873...

Operations Document Type

[OPERATIONS_DOC_TYPE]

Because there are thousands of documents that are related to equipment, it makes sense to categorize the documents according to their type of information (Table 5.202). This allows personnel to retrieve the documents faster according to the information they need. It is recommended that a reference table be developed and then used as a drop-down menu for personnel using this data field (Table 5.203). Using prescribed data for the field reduces human input errors and improves the sorting of the documents.

TABLE 5.202 Operations Document Data Example

Operation_Document_GUID	Operation_Doc_Type	Operation_Document_Short_Description
Kayrg9873...	Operator Startup Procedure	GASCO Series IV Furnaces
J89yu67ty...	Maintenance Guide	GASCO Series IV Furnaces
KdW4nt2kn...	Wiring Control Diagrams	GASCO Series IV Furnaces
St4r4tR3k...	Training Documents	Startup of Chill Water System
ump3ri31...	Operator Startup Procedure	ElectricCo Series 3400
S3m1cOL0n...	Emergency Operations	ElectricCo Series 3400
2B4iT1S3c...	Spare Parts List	ElectricCo Series 3400
b33riSg00...	Material Safety Data Sheet	ElectricCo Series 3400
F1n4liyS3...	Troubleshooting Guide	Generic Motor Guide to Troubleshooting

TABLE 5.203 Operation Document Type Examples

Operation Document Types
Normal Operation
Operator Prestart Procedure
Operator Startup Procedure
Operator Shutdown Procedure
Operator Post Shutdown Procedure
Emergency Operations
Maintenance Guide
Wiring Control Diagrams
Removal and replacement instructions
Cleaning Requirements
Lubrication Data Guide
Spare Parts List
Special Tools List
Troubleshooting Guide
Product Cut Sheet
Certificates
Training Documents
Training Video
Environmental Conditions Technical Sheet
Hazardous Material Data Sheet
Material Safety Data Sheet
Safety Precautions

Operation Document Short Description

[OPERATION_DOCUMENT_SHORT_DESCRIPTION]

The purpose of the short description data field is to allow the organization to write a short description of the document (Table 5.204). Operation documents can be related to a whole facility, a specific system, or individual equipment: For example, Trane Air Handling Unit Model ABC, Refrigerant R-22, Cutler Hammer Chiller Model CH1234, or Carrier Air Conditioner 1234. When combined with the operation document type, the short description provides information for cataloging the document (for example, Wiring Control Diagram: Trane Air Handling Unit Model ABC; Material Data Sheet: Refrigerant R-22; or Training Documents: Cutler Hammer Chiller Model CH1234).

TABLE 5.204   Operation Document Short Description Data Example

Operation_Document_GUID	Operation_Doc_Type	Operation_Document_Short_Description
Kayrg9873...	Operator Startup Procedure	GASCO Series IV Furnaces
J89yu67ty...	Maintenance Guide	GASCO Series IV Furnaces
KdW4nt2kn...	Wiring Control Diagrams	GASCO Series IV Furnaces
St4r4tR3k...	Training Documents	Startup of Chill Water System
ump3ri31...	Operator Startup Procedure	ElectricCo Series 3400
S3m1cOLOn...	Emergency Operations	ElectricCo Series 3400
2B4iT1S3c...	Spare Parts List	ElectricCo Series 3400
b33riSg00...	Material Safety Data Sheet	ElectricCo Series 3400
F1n4liyS3...	Troubleshooting Guide	Generic Motor Guide to Troubleshooting

Operation Document

[OPERATION_DOCUMENT]

The operation document field is the placeholder that allows a document to be downloaded into the database (Table 5.205).

TABLE 5.205   Operations Document Data Example

Operation_Document_GUID	Operation_Document_Short_Description	Operation_Document
Kayrg9873...	GASCO Series IV Furnaces	FURNSeriesIVPSO.pdf
J89yu67ty...	GASCO Series IV Furnaces	FURNSeriesIVMaint.pdf
KdW4nt2kn...	GASCO Series IV Furnaces	FURNSeriesIVWire.pdf
St4r4tR3k...	Startup of Chill Water System	Chillwater Training.doc
ump3ri31...	ElectricCo Series 3400	Series3400OSP.pdf
S3m1cOLOn...	ElectricCo Series 3400	Series3400EOP.pdf

Operation_Document_GUID	Operation_Document_Short_Description	Operation_Document
2B4iT1S3c...	ElectricCo Series 3400	Series3400PL.pdf
b33riSg00...	ElectricCo Series 3400	Series3400 MSDS.pdf
F1n4liyS3...	Generic Motor Guide to Troubleshooting	Motor 1234.pdf

Operation Video

[OPERATION_VIDEO]

The operations video data field is the placeholder that allows a video to be downloaded into the database (Table 5.206).

TABLE 5.206 Operation Video Data Example

Operation_Document_GUID	Operation_Document	Operation_Video
Kayrg9873...	FURNSeriesIVPSO.pdf	FURNSeriesIVPSO.mpeg
J89yu67ty...	FURNSeriesIVMaint.pdf	
KdW4nt2kn...	FURNSeriesIVWire.pdf	
St4r4tR3k...	Chillwater Training.doc	
ump3ri31...	Series3400OSP.pdf	Series3400OSP.wmv
S3m1cOLOn...	Series3400EOP.pdf	
2B4iT1S3c...	Series3400PL.pdf	
b33riSg00...	Series3400 MSDS.pdf	
F1n4liyS3...	Motor 1234.pdf	Motor 1234.wmv

RESOURCES

OmniClass™, CSI/CSC website: www.omniclass.org

CHAPTER 6

Equipment Identification and Tags

For a discussion of equipment identification, labeling, and tagging, it is important to understand the way the terms are used in this book. Equipment identification is the convention used by an organization that uniquely identifies equipment in a manner that allows the facility staff to properly identify the different equipment in the field. Identification is the shorthand abbreviated identification that is used on blueprints, equipment tags, lockout-tagouts, clearances, and the like. ABC0000-AHU-001 would be an example of an equipment identification that tells technicians that they are looking at an air handling unit (AHU) with a sequential number 001 in building ABC0000. Labeling and tagging are the physical design, means, and methods of attaching the equipment identification to equipment. Equipment labels and tags are an attached material used to physically mark that equipment.

EQUIPMENT IDENTIFICATION

It is very important to properly identify equipment, to ensure continuity of operations during normal and emergency operations. This is especially important when a technician is unable to connect to the organization's computer-based inventory systems. Some equipment identification camps propose using only bar codes or radio frequency identifications (RFID) to identify the equipment, explaining that the technician has the ability to scan and access the database for the information. Realistically, bar codes and RFIDs should be incorporated in the tags, but when there is an emergency and technicians have to shut off equipment in the field, they need to be able to verify that they are working in the right building and on the correct equipment. Technicians will not always have access to the database, they may have forgotten their handheld equipment, or the bar code or RFID may not be working because of the environment in which it was installed. A technician might not have the time to scan every valve in a valve gallery to find the right one to operate. Therefore, equipment should always be tagged with its proper equipment identification. For example, suppose a technician has to isolate a fuel oil leak and must close ABC0000-VLV-004 in a valve gallery of 20 valves. The technician needs to be able to physically verify that he or she is closing VLV-004, not valve VLV-001, VLV-002, or VLV-003, and the technician has to perform this function quickly (Figure 6.1).

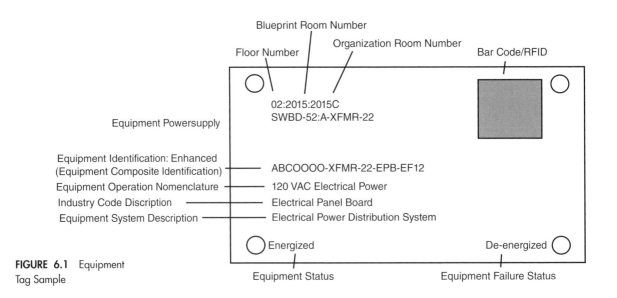

FIGURE 6.1 Equipment Tag Sample

There are numerous ways to develop an equipment identification schema. The recommended way is to make the schema as short as possible, for tagging and clearance reasons, while retaining enough information to assist the person in the field. Additional information that is beneficial to the operator can be included on tags without having to be included in the equipment identification (Figure 6.1). For example, ABC0000-AHU-001, which denotes an air handling unit with a sequence number of 001 in building ABC0000, is short but sufficient for the operator to properly identify the equipment. The identifier XYC0000-ABC0000-B102:11234-ZONE A-HVAC-AHU-001—which denotes air handling unit 001 of the HVAC system for Zone-A, in organization space number 11234, with blueprint room number B102, in building ABC0000 of campus XYC0000—is excessive. The technician knows that the building is part of the campus, knows that the air handling unit is part of the HVAC system, and probably has a good idea of where that air handling unit is located. Otherwise, the organization should start looking to hire a new technician. Now these fields can, and some should, be included on the equipment tag for that equipment, but they should not be part of the equipment identification. This guide recommends using two equipment identification schemas: a standard and an enhanced version.

Equipment Identification Standard Schema

The equipment identification shown in this guide is a composite of three equipment database fields. The database fields are: facility number, equipment acronym, and equipment sequence number (Table 6.1). This is the recommended minimum information for a component. All equipment should be identified by this method, with the exception of electrical distribution components that require enhanced identification. The facility number is included in the identification schema because in the industry there are instances in which a very large facility might have more than one facility number. Multiple facility numbers for a large building are typically due to financial accounting. A large building might be built in phases or at different times because of budgetary constraints. Because a large facility could have multiple facility numbers, it is very important to include the facility number in the equipment identification schema.

TABLE 6.1 Equipment Identification Standards

Facility Number + Equipment Acronym + Equipment Sequence Number
ABC0000-AHU-001
ABC0000-VLV-8743
ABC0000-P-52:A

Equipment Identification Enhanced Standard Schema

The enhanced equipment identification standard uses the same data fields as the standard identification but also includes two data fields from the related equipment assembly (parent) (Table 6.2). The equipment acronym and equipment sequence number of the parent assembly are included in the enhanced equipment identification. For example, circuit breaker (CB) number 01 on electrical breaker panel (EPB) number LP17 for facility number ABC0000 would be identified as ABC0000-EPB-LP17-CB-01. Electrical panel LP17 is the parent or equipment assembly data field related to that circuit breaker 01. Notice that the parent identification is the middle data in the schema, while the actual component is the final portion of the data. The reason for having an enhanced identification standard is to have a method of identification that incorporates the way the industry identifies and installs equipment. The installation of electrical circuit breakers is a prime example of industry standards. Every circuit breaker panel installed has its installed circuit breakers numbered starting with 1. For a large facility that has hundreds of electrical panel boards, there are literally hundreds of circuit breakers with the equipment sequence number 01. Although the equipment database can handle this effectively because it uses a GUID to identify each equipment record separately, a sort or printout of the circuit breakers would be overly complex for facility management (Table 6.3). When viewing a sort, the facility team would get all circuit breakers numbered 01 grouped

TABLE 6.2   Enhanced Equipment Identification Standards

Facility Number + Equipment Assembly (Parent) Equipment Acronym + Equipment Assembly (Parent) Equipment Sequence Number + Equipment Acronym + Equipment Sequence Number
ABC0000-EPB-18-CB-01
ABC0000-FDR-3-NTWKPROTDEV-18
ABC0000-SWBD-52:A-ACB-22

TABLE 6.3   Circuit Breaker Sort without a Parent

Equipment Identification Composite	Equipment Operation Nomenclature
ABC0000-CB-01	Supply Handling Unit AHU-001
ABC0000-CB-01	Supply Pump P-19B
ABC0000-CB-01	Spare
ABC0000-CB-02	Supply Transformer XFMR-AB7
ABC0000-CB-02	Supply EPB-LP18
ABC0000-CB-02	Spare

TABLE 6.4 Circuit Breaker Sort with the Parent Examples

Equipment Identification Composite	Equipment Operation Nomenclature
ABC0000-EPB-LP17-CB-01	Supply Handling Unit AHU-001
ABC0000-EPB-LP17-CB-02	Supply Transformer XFMR-AB7
ABC0000-EPB-LP18-CB-01	Supply Pump P-19B
ABC0000-EPB-LP18-CB-02	Spare
ABC0000-EPB-LP19-CB-01	Spare
ABC0000-EPB-LP19-CB-02	Supply EPB-LP18

together, with no concept of which electrical panel the breaker was associated with. The equipment assembly data included in an enhanced system regroups circuit breakers into their respective panel boards (Table 6.4).

Including the equipment assembly information in the equipment identification solves this problem and has the additional benefit of allowing personnel in the field to directly troubleshoot electrical problems.

Using an enhanced identification system for the electrical system provides substantial benefits for emergency response and troubleshooting.

Example: A technician has lost power to air handling unit 10 (AHU-010) (Figure 6.2). Dispatch radioed the technician that AHU-010 is powered from ABC0000-EPB-EF12-CB-01. Because of the identification schema, the

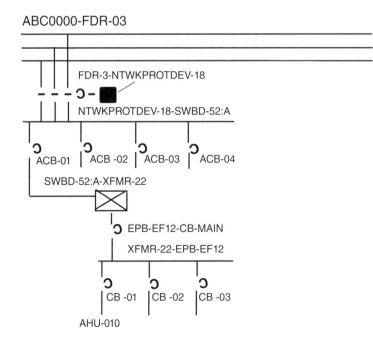

FIGURE 6.2 Electrical Distribution Example.

technician understands that circuit breaker (CB-01) is on electrical panel EPB-EF12. When the technician arrives at the panel, he or she finds that breakers CB-01 and CB-Main are closed. Because the electrical panel is also labeled with its parent ABC0000-XFMR-22-EPB-EF12, the technician knows to check transformer XFMR-22. Having arrived at transformer XFMR-22, the technician notes that it does not have electrical power. Because the transformer is labeled ABC0000-SWBD-52:A-XFMR-22, the technician now knows to go to switchboard SWBD-52:A. Upon arriving at the switchboard, the technician observes that air circuit breaker ACB-01 is trip-free. This example shows that the technician could literally follow an electrical fault all the way back to the electrical feeder without consulting a computer. Conversely, if this same facility lost a feeder, all of the electrical components affected by the fault could be determined.

EQUIPMENT LABEL AND TAG

The equipment tag section deals with the design of the tag, the data to include, and how the tag is installed. Each organization should decide what information it requires on the tags and then determine the design of the tag. There is no standard that could be uniformly applied across facility management and construction projects at this time. Obviously, the more information that is included, the more expensive the tags are. However, the more data included on a tag, the more efficient and effective your facility staff can be in the operation of the building. The more information a technician has, the less human error is likely to occur. A reduction in human error saves money for a corporation. Figures 6.3 and 6.4 are examples of a balanced amount of information on equipment tags.

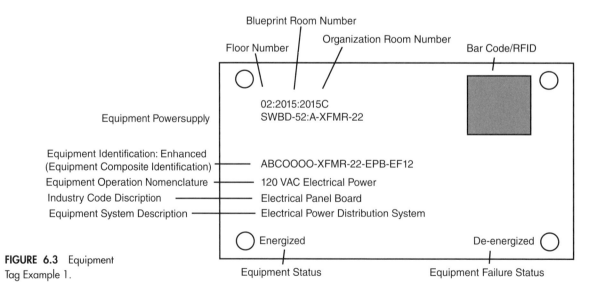

FIGURE 6.3 Equipment Tag Example 1.

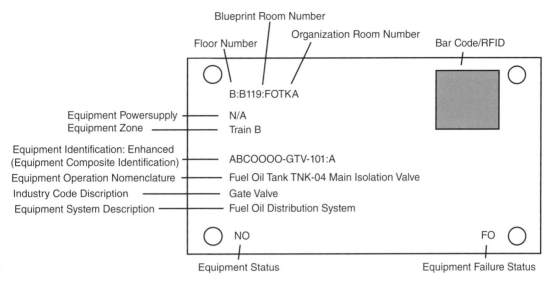

FIGURE 6.4 Equipment Tag Example 2.

Because equipment information has been stored in defined data fields in a uniform manner, an organization just needs to decide what data fields they want to include on their equipment tags (See Chapter 5, "Equipment Data Points"). Once the data required to be on the equipment tags are decided, then the design and layout of the tag can be determined.

The following is a list of recommended data fields to include on the tag:

- Equipment composite identification (equipment identification schema)
- Equipment operation nomenclature
- Industry code description
- Equipment system
- Space composite identification (location)
- Equipment power supply
- Equipment zone
- Equipment status
- Equipment failure status
- Equipment barcode/RFID

The cost of replacing all of the tags in an existing facility can be prohibitive for any organization that tries to accomplish the task all at once, in a large facility. The best way to accomplish the task is to ensure that contracts and procedures for new construction, renovations, or projects include the new equipment data formats, equipment identification, and equipment tag design, and that the equipment is properly tagged at these times. The organization can also order the tags and then have them installed on the equipment as staff performs preventive maintenance, tours, or service calls. The concept that the equipment has to be labeled right this second often leads to resistance from management, because of the cost. Stainless-steel laser-etched tags with all of the recommended information could cost up to $2.00 each. A large facility could have 50,000 components that need to be tagged. The cost could be about $100,000, not counting the labor and materials needed to install the tags. Realistically, if the facility is operating correctly already, the equipment can be labeled over a longer period of time to reduce the cost impact. The equipment tags, by themselves, do not have to be expensive. Tags can range in material from laser-etched stainless steel to paper in a plastic sleeve holder. The environment in which the equipment tag has to be hung should be the determining factor for the material used.

There are some good equipment-tagging practices and principles that should be included in operational guidance or contracts:

- Personnel are responsible for identifying lost, incorrectly labeled, un-readable, or damaged tags, and for notifying the proper personnel for replacement tags.
- Tags should be placed on or near the component being identified, in a manner that clearly associates the tag with the respective component.
- Tags should be permanently attached to the component in a way that will not interfere with the normal operation or testing of the component (e.g., attached to the yoke of the valve, not to a removable part of the valve such as the hand wheel).
- Valves operated by reach rods or chains, or other remotely operated components, should have an additional tag installed at the operating device.
- Tags for chain operators should be attached to a small piece of tubing (PVC) through which the chain passes, to ensure that the label always remains at the bottom of the chain loop.
- Tags that cover a group of equipment, for example fire detectors 01–50 located in a single room, should be placed in an area that conforms to the following.
  - Tags should be close to an opening in the room.
  - There should be easy access to the tag.
  - The location should be conspicuous and easy to find.
  - The tag should be placed in a position in which it will not be covered.

- The tag should be placed in an area that reduces the chance of tampering.
- The tag should be placed in a common location.
- Tags should be readable from the normal operating location or position (i.e., an operator should not have to manipulate the tag to read it; the label should be facing out).
- If a new tag cannot be immediately provided, a temporary label should be installed until a new tag can be procured.
- The tag should be made of a material that can withstand the environment in which it is installed.

Capturing all of the equipment information in a database but not properly planning to tag the equipment to improve your organization's efficiency can be very counterproductive.

CHAPTER 7

Inventorying Equipment

Once you have established an understanding of what information is involved in a comprehensive equipment inventory, you can begin the process of capturing the information your company needs to succeed. The equipment inventory of a large facility takes considerable planning. You do not just send people out to start inventorying equipment. Does the organization even need to take an equipment inventory? What is the current level and quality of equipment for your organization?

ANALYZING EQUIPMENT INVENTORY

The first thing any organization should accomplish is an analysis of the extent and quality of its existing equipment inventories. Recently I was asked to develop an estimate for the operational contract cost for a two-million-square-foot facility. One of the main elements in estimating operation costs is to tabulate the annual preventive maintenance man-hours. The preventive maintenance man-hours are based on the type of equipment and equipment counts of the facility. Once the man-hours are determined, using the labor costs for the geographical location, the equipment operational costs can be determined. I was given a list of 1,200 pieces of equipment for the facility! Yes, 1,200 pieces of equipment for a two-million-square-foot facility. To better illustrate the problem: A facility of that size should have a minimum of approximately 25,000 pieces of equipment that have to be maintained. In any discussion of cost-estimating operation and maintenance (O&M) contracts, there is a contingency of experts who believe that O&M contracts should be based on the type of facility and a cost per square foot. In itself, this is not a bad idea. The problem is that the majority of current O&M contracts are based on extremely poor equipment inventory levels. How is it possible to accurately determine existing cost per square foot when the majority of the contracts in use are incorrectly estimated? The core data the estimates are based on are incorrect. Only if all of the equipment inventories are fixed and standardized to the same format will it be possible to accurately determine what a feasible cost per square foot should be in the industry. A two-million-square-foot facility with an O&M contract based on 1,200 pieces of equipment is going to skew the data significantly and thereby affect all of the facilities in a portfolio. The other information necessary to effectively determine a cost per square foot is the actual types of equipment in the facility. A chiller requires a lot more maintenance than a ball valve.

Evaluate the Inventory

The following steps should be taken to evaluate a facility:

- Gather the existing equipment inventory for the facility.
- What discipline levels are represented: mechanical, electrical, plumbing, civil, architectural, food services, horticultural, historical preservation, fire life safety, vertical and horizontal transportation, environmental, etc.? Most facilities have based their operation on only mechanical, HVAC, and plumbing inventories. This is shortsighted (see Chapter 2, "Financial and Resource Impact of Equipment Inventories on Facilities").
- What is the type of equipment inventory? Determine whether the inventory is a partial list, preventive maintenance, component-level, or complete inventory. The equipment level impacts the company's exposure to risk and its ability to benefit from the inventory. (See Chapter 3, "Equipment Inventory Types and Systems.")
- What is the quality of the inventory?
- Are the data consistent with industry standards? This impacts the interoperability of the information. (See Chapter 4, "Industry Standards.")

- Were reference tables or common conventions used, or was the information hand-entered? Hand-entered data typically have a number of spelling and usage problems. To a computer, "Room" is different from "Rm."
- What is the equipment count, and does it make sense?
- Determine the company's level of exposure. The poorer the equipment quality, the more exposure to a company.
- Determine the course of action.

Once the quality of the equipment inventories has been determined, the decision has to be made whether or not to reinventory the facility. The benefits of ensuring that you have an accurate and comprehensive inventory are covered in Chapter 2.

INVENTORY PLANNING

There are some initial steps and decisions that should be made before an inventory of a facility is performed:

- What method should be employed to inventory the facility?
- What level of expenditure should be planned?
- What data points need to be captured?
- Which standards should be used?
- What reference tables need to be developed?

Method of Capturing Inventories

There are multiple ways in which to gather equipment inventories and their related information. The two main methods are (1) having in-house resources walk the facility and capture the information, and (2) having the work outsourced. The two main ways to outsource equipment inventory are (1) having a third-party contractor perform the inventory, and (2) making the inventory a deliverable, as part of a facility management operations and maintenance contract. There are distinct advantages to both methods.

Using in-house resources to gather equipment inventories ensures that, especially in companies with a large portfolio, the equipment information is captured in a consistent manner. Even if the physical capturing of inventories is outsourced, it is still important to have in-house personnel manage the project, review the data, and ensure that data are consistent and meets contractual requirements. It also improves the operational awareness of the facility manager.

Since an understanding of equipment inventories is critical to understanding the operation of facilities, making the equipment inventory process a part of the training of future facility managers is very beneficial to any organization. You cannot beat hands-on experience. Once an inventory is captured, knowledgeable personnel in the organization and the facility management staff will have to maintain the inventory over the life of the facility. Because in large organizations, especially those with a large number of properties, many internal organizations are impacted by equipment data such as project management, construction, budget, facility management, and the like, having experts in-house who can help integrate this information between disciplines is very important.

Outsourcing is a common method of capturing inventories. When deciding to outsource, there are a number of things that have to be taken into account: the contract, the different types of contractors, contractor training, and review processes. The first item that has to be tackled is ensuring that the contract and contract language are consistent. The development of a boilerplate for contracts is highly recommended to ensure that data are captured consistently across the portfolio. The second item to determine is whether to use a third-party contractor who specializes in equipment or whether to use existing operation and maintenance (O&M) contracts. There is an obvious advantage to using third-party experts: This would make it easier to ensure that all equipment inventories are performed the same way. Using current O&M contractors can be beneficial because they should be familiar with the facility already. The disadvantage is that if you have a lot of facilities using different O&M contractors, then they all have to be trained to capture equipment information the same way. Otherwise, the data will be suspect. Of course, if you are already using an O&M contractor to operate your facility, the question that begs to be asked is: Why haven't they performed and delivered an accurate inventory already? Contractors and in-house personnel need to be trained to ensure that everyone is using and understands the same concepts. Finally, each process should have a review and evaluation period, with predefined milestones, to ensure that the equipment inventory is being captured and processed correctly and in a timely manner.

Centralized versus Decentralized

No matter whether a company uses in-house resources or contracts out the work, a discussion should be held on whether the inventory should be managed and performed as a centralized or decentralized process. A centralized process is one in which a specialized team or department oversees and/or performs all of the tasks related to an inventory. A decentralized process (the more common of the two) is one in which each facility and its management are responsible for their equipment information.

Because it is very important to capture accurate equipment information in a consistent manner, in order to reap the benefits of the inventory, centralized inventory processes have distinct advantages over decentralized. The main advantages of a centralized system are the consistency of the data, the use of dedicated specialized experts, and the consistent methods used to capture and review that information. Let's face it—facility managers already have a lot on their plates. Speaking from experience, it is easier to train one team of people with the proper experience than to train every facility manager and O&M contractor. Reviewing equipment lists for errors and compatibility is an exhausting process for anyone. The more experience personnel have in performing these tasks, the more efficient and accurate your equipment inventory will be. For example: Say a contractor delivers a list of equipment for a facility that includes five air handling units. Did the contractor include and associate the motors with the air handling units? Are the correct job tasks for preventive maintenance included? Did the contractor include the cooling towers, fire extinguishers, chillers, emergency generators, and so on? These are questions that experience teaches one to ask.

Level of Expenditure

The next decision that has to be made is the equipment level that a company wants to achieve. Previous chapters discussed the types of equipment inventories and the benefits of having a component-level or complete inventory. The reality is that a company might not have the resources to capture inventories at these levels, even with the numerous benefits and the fast payback in energy savings. Therefore, it is important to predetermine the level of equipment inventory a company wants to achieve.

First, decide what type of inventory the company wants to accomplish: preventive maintenance, component-level, or complete. Second, it is important to determine which disciplines a company wants to capture. As a minimum, the electrical, mechanical, plumbing, fire life safety, vertical and horizontal transportation, architectural, and environmental should be considered. The levels and disciplines can be mixed and matched to meet the resources available to the company: component-level mechanical, complete-level electrical, preventive maintenance level environmental, and so forth.

Finally, some of these costs can be deferred by ensuring that the information is properly captured in construction projects. The company's level of exposure should be considered before deferring large portions of equipment inventories. Remember, the poorer the inventory, the more long-term cost and risks the company has to assume. It is always better to do it right the first time and reap the benefits.

Determine Data Points

There are multiple ways to capture the data; Excel, database software, or a program developed in-house. At some point in the future, there should be commercial off-the-shelf software that can be utilized. An organization needs to ensure not only that any purchased software has the needed data points but also that the data are captured in the correct format. A major step in capturing any inventory is to determine which data fields a company wants to capture. Appendix 1, "Equipment Data Usage and Cross-Reference Worksheet," is included in this book to help facilitate this discussion.

The schedule of capturing these data points should also be determined. A company might decide to capture only a basic set of information and then set up future construction and projects requirements to capture any additional information they want. In this manner, the complete set of data can be captured over time.

Once the data fields are determined, determine who is responsible for collecting the information. Ensure that construction projects requirements and contracts include the data points and specify who is responsible for collecting the information. Some of the information can be captured by the architect/ engineer (for example, equipment GUID, industry code, industry description, equipment sequence number, design parameters, etc.) and some by the construction manager (for example, equipment install date, condition of equipment, commissioning data, operation documents, etc.). It is very important to be clear about who is responsible for the data at certain phases of design and construction. The data collection methods should be mapped out and should include points at which the data captured will be verified by the organization.

Standard Determination

Standards were covered in Chapter 4, "Industry Standards." Once the determination of which data points to use is made, the industry standards used to support those specific data points need to be determined. Then the data field names for those standards should be cross-referenced to the suggested database field names in this book.

A cross reference can also be developed from any existing equipment database to the new data fields and industry standards. Cross-referencing the data field names will allow your information technology team to import and cross-reference current data into the company's new equipment database structure.

Reference Tables

Developing and using reference tables is highly recommended. The use of reference tables allows personnel to enter the exact same information into the database in the exact same manner, and helps to eliminate human error. Repopulating the reference tables prior to taking equipment inventories also prevents the company from having to revisit that information at a later date and enter any missing data.

The following is a list of recommended reference tables:

Equipment Data Table

- Equipment Type: Industry Code Number: Industry Code Description: Equipment Acronym (NCS/ASME) (OmniClass ™ Table 23)
- Equipment System Code: Equipment System Description (OmniClass™ Table 23)
- Equipment Priority
- Equipment COOP (Yes/No)
- Equipment Curtailment
- Equipment Normal Operational Status (Yes/No)
- Equipment After-Hours Operational Status (Yes/No)
- Equipment Status
- Equipment Failure Status
- Equipment Purchased Condition
- Equipment Specification Purpose
- Equipment Specification Unit (OmniClass ™ Table 49)
- Equipment Tag Condition
- Equipment Security Level

Facility Data Table

- Facility Designation
- Facility Design Function/Code (OmniClass™ Table 11)
- Facility Use Function/Code (OmniClass™ Table 11)
- Facility Organization Location Code
- Facility Priority

Space Data Table

- Floor Number (ANSI/BOMA)
- Space Design Function/Code (OmniClass™ Table 13)
- Space Use Function/Code (OmniClass™ Table 13)
- Space Priority

Job Plan and Task Data Table

- Job Plan Type
- Job Plan Tools/Code (OmniClass™ Table 35)
- Job Task Status
- Job Task Status Related Cause
- Job Task Frequency Unit
- Job Task Season
- Job Task Time Standard Unit
- Job Task Tools/Code (OmniClass™ Table 35)

Condition Data Table

- Equipment Condition
- Equipment Condition Related Cause
- Condition Recommendation Type

Commissioning Data Table

- Commissioning Set Point Unit (Industry)

Audit and Inspection Data Table

- Audit Type
- Equipment Compliance (Yes/No)

Warranty Data Table

- Extended Warranty Available

Code and Regulations Data Table

- Code Type

Operations Documents Data Table

- Operation Document Type

EQUIPMENT INVENTORIES

There are two main ways to capture an equipment inventory: during new construction/projects and in an existing facility. The most accurate equipment inventory will be during new construction because an existing facility will not be able to open up walls and hard-to-access areas to find all of the equipment.

New Construction Inventories

As previously mentioned, when building a new facility it is important to know what data you need and who is responsible for that data. Once this is established, the contracts and responsibilities can be properly assigned and then verified during the whole process. For example, the architect might be responsible for architectural and equipment zones, space blueprint numbers, design specifications, and so forth. The construction management team might be responsible for installed equipment information such as make, model, and serial number. The commissioning agent would be responsible for commissioning data, and the facility management team for data such as tenant information and space organization room numbers. It is always a good practice to include experts in facility management in these discussions.

The following items should be considered:

- Map out responsibility for data points.
- Determine and decide equipment verification points.
- Verify proper contract language (there are good examples on the Web related to BIM).

Existing Facility Inventories

There is a specific order in which to perform an equipment inventory for existing facilities that streamlines the process and reduces the amount of time spent revisiting the same data. In initial equipment inventories there are certain sections of the data that are only there for future use, such as audit and commissioning data. While this data can be important, the data are not normally captured during an initial inventory of an existing facility.

Determine how intrusive the equipment inventory process will be, given the related costs. Should the equipment above the ceiling be inventoried? Does the audit need to be performed at night or on weekends?

The following tables should be performed prior to sending teams out to capture the equipment information:

- Complex Table
- Facility Table
- Space Table

- Tenant Table
- Job Task Table

It is easier to walk the facility and define the campus, facility, and space locations that will be associated with the equipment first than it is to update the space data while capturing the equipment data. If you do not take the location information first, then that information will have to be updated at a later date. A large facility can have over tens of thousands of pieces of equipment, and this can become an updating nightmare, if updating is done at all.

Next, or at the same time as the location data, update the job plan data for any existing preventive maintenance procedures or guidance. This gives the personnel capturing the equipment information the means to assign the job plans to the correct equipment as they take the inventory. Remember that the job plan data are different from the job task data. When a job plan is assigned to a piece of equipment, it is done by creating a job task that is assigned to the equipment.

When you are ready to start taking the equipment inventory, it is vital to have a plan and ensure that the team is trained, that team members understand the order in which to capture the information, and that they have a plan of attack related to the design of the facility. The order in which the different disciplines are taken can be important. It is important to have personnel who can properly identify, and have an understanding of, the equipment types whose information they are capturing. The team has to be capable of telling the difference between a screw chiller and a rotary chiller; otherwise, the company risks getting inaccurate data.

The most efficient way to start an inventory is to have the team capture as much information as possible from the blueprints before it travels out in the field to verify the information.

If the inventory team is large, and the blueprints for the facility are poor or nonexistent, it is also more efficient to use self-developed equipment asset numbers to initially identify the equipment. (See Chapter 5, "Equipment Data Points," Equipment Organization Asset Number section.) You can create asset numbers (Facility number + Sequential number starting at 000001) on paper self-adhesive labels printed by a laser printer, so team members can affix the labels to the equipment as they capture information. Each team member can be given a numerical range of asset labels. For example, John would be given asset labels ABC0001-000001 to ABC0001-000300, Christine would be given asset labels ABC0001-000301 to ABC0001-000600, and so forth. Team members would not enter the equipment sequence number into the database as they inventoried the equipment, but would instead enter the equipment organization asset number from one of their labels as they affixed it to the equipment they were inventorying. This method allows multiple people to inventory the building at the same time without adding conflicting equipment sequence numbers. When the database is completed, the equipment sequence numbers can be added to the equipment to prevent the duplication of numbers. The equipment tags would then be ordered and placed on the proper equipment with the matching equipment organization asset number. Otherwise, John might enter equipment sequence number 001 for the first ball valve he encounters, while at the same time Christine does the same thing. Then there would be two ball valves in the facility with equipment sequence number 001. This would create duplicate equipment identifications in the database and affect all later metrics.

It is highly recommended that the electrical distribution equipment be inventoried first. The electrical equipment data are used to populate the electrical power supply for most of the other disciplines: mechanical, civil, fire and life safety, and so on, so there is a data dependency. The added advantage is that the electrical distribution system is made up of a much simpler and straightforward design and has fewer types of equipment. Therefore, the electrical distribution system becomes an easier discipline in which to train personnel and have them learn the inventory process. Most people have some concept of the electrical breaker panels in their homes, but few understand or have a chiller plant.

The order in which the equipment information is taken is important. The parent equipment of any equipment assembly has to be captured first. Capturing the parent first allows the subassembly, or child, to be assigned to the parent (see Chapter 5, "Equipment Data Point," Equipment Assembly section). For example, for an air handling unit, you would capture the air handling unit information first and then the motors, dampers, coils, and so on, for that unit. For electrical components, the parent is considered the major piece of equipment supplying power to that component. For example, in a situation in which a feeder supplies power to a network protector, the feeder information would be captured first. You would then work from the feeder through the electrical distribution system down to the electrical panels and breakers.

The fire alarm and control system is very similar to the electrical distribution. You have a main fire alarm control panel that is connected to secondary panels and/or fire, smoke, and heat detectors. Therefore, personnel taking inventories on this system should start with the main fire control panel and work out to the detectors.

Once the electrical distribution system is completed and stored in the database for reference, then start taking the equipment related to the other disciplines.

The final step to any equipment inventory is for the organization to review the information. The following steps should be used as a guideline to verify the data:

- Is all of the required information filled out?
- Are there any duplicate equipment or space entries? Having two AHU-001s or two spaces numbered 01:112 affects the use of the data.
- Does the information make sense?
- Are the counts right? Are there 10 floors in a 9-floor building? Are there really only four emergency lights in a large facility?
- Is there missing equipment? Do you have water-cooled chillers but no cooling towers? Are there really no restroom exhaust fans or fire extinguishers?
- Does the size of the equipment specifications make sense? Does the facility really have 100 extremely large air handling units rated at 75,000 CFM? Is the roof of an 800,000-square-foot facility only 1,000 square feet?
- Is the equipment paired up with the correct job task? Why is an emergency generator load test job task paired up to a main entrance revolving door?
- Are there misspelled words or data entry problems that can be rectified or fixed?

When the review and inventory have been completed it is very important to capture what lessons have been learned.

There are many ways to take an equipment inventory, and there is always room for improvement. Developing a list of these improvements and applying them to the next project can significantly improve the process and save valuable costs and resources. The important thing to remember is that in this world of ever-increasing competition, where everyone is striving to increase efficiency while reducing the use of dwindling resources, any improvement to any process, no matter how small, improves this world for everyone.

Equipment Data Usage and Cross-Reference Worksheet

Equipment Data Table Fields	Guide Data Field Name	Organization/Industry Data Field Name	Use Yes/No
Equipment Zones			
Equipment Zone GUID	EQUIPMENT_ZONE_GUID		
Equipment Zone Description	EQUIPMENT_ZONE_DESCRIPTION		
Equipment Data			
Equipment GUID	EQUIPMENT_GUID		
Industry Code Description	INDUSTRY_CODE_DESCRIPTION		
Industry Code Number	INDUSTRY_CODE_NUMBER		
Equipment Operation Description	EQUIPMENT_OPERATION_DESCRIPTION		
Equipment Acronym	EQUIPMENT_ACRONYM		
Equipment Sequence Number	EQUIPMENT_SEQUENCE		
Equipment Identification Composite	EQUIPMENT_ID_COMPOSITE		
Equipment Space	SPACE_GUID		

Equipment Data Table Fields	Guide Data Field Name	Organization/Industry Data Field Name	Use Yes/No
Equipment Plot Point (N)	EQUIPMENT_PLOT_POINT(N)		
	EQUIPMENT_PLOT_ALTITUDE(N)		
	EQUIPMENT_PLOT_LATITUDE(N)		
	EQUIPMENT_PLOT_LONGITUDE(N)		
Equipment Location Description	EQUIPMENT_LOCATION_DESCRIPTION		
Previous Equipment Identification	PREVIOUS_EQUIPMENT_ID		
Previous Equipment GUID	PREVIOUS_EQUIPMENT_GUID		
Equipment Organization Asset Number	EQUIPMENT_ORG_ASSET_NUMBER		
Equipment Power Supply	EQUIPMENT_POWER_SUPPLY		
Equipment System Description	EQUIPMENT_SYSTEM_DESCRIPTION		
Equipment System Code	EQUIPMENT_SYSTEM_CODE		
Equipment Assembly	EQUIPMENT_ASSEMBLY		
Equipment Control (N)	EQUIPMENT_CONTROL(N)		
Equipment Alarm (N)	EQUIPMENT_ALARM(N)		
Equipment Indication (N)	EQUIPMENT_INDICATION(N)		
Equipment Failure Impact (N)	EQUIPMENT_FAILURE_IMPACT(N)		
Equipment Space Relationship	EQUIPMENT_SPACE_REL		
Equipment Priority	EQUIPMENT_PRIORITY		
Equipment Continued Operation	EQUIPMENT_COOP		
Equipment Owner	EQUIPMENT_OWNER		
Equipment Curtailment	EQUIPMENT_CURTAILMENT		
Equipment Operation Schedule	EQUIPMENT_OPERATION_SCHEDULE		
Equipment Normal Operations Status	EQUIPMENT_NORM_OP		
Equipment After-Hours Operation Status	EQUIPMENT_AFTER_OP		
Equipment Status	EQUIPMENT_STATUS		
Equipment Failure Status	EQUIPMENT_FAILURE		
Equipment Tag Condition	EQUIPMENT_TAG		
Equipment Security Level	EQUIPMENT_SECURITY_LEVEL		
Equipment Manufacturer	EQUIPMENT_MANUFACTURER		
Equipment Model Name	EQUIPMENT_MODEL_NAME		
Equipment Model Number	EQUIPMENT_MODEL_NUMBER		
Equipment Serial Number	EQUIPMENT_SERIAL_NUMBER		
Equipment Manufactured Date	EQUIPMENT_MANF_DATE		
Equipment Manufacturer Shelf Life	EQUIPMENT_SHELFLIFE		

Equipment Data Table Fields	Guide Data Field Name	Organization/Industry Data Field Name	Use Yes/No
Equipment Installed Date	INSTALLED_DATE		
Equipment Life Expectancy	LIFE_EXPECTANCY		
Equipment Age	EQUIPMENT_AGE		
Equipment Operation Age	EQUIPMENT_OPS_AGE		
Equipment Purchased Condition	PURCHASED_CONDITION		
Equipment Installation Cost	EQUIPMENT_INSTALLATION_COST		
Equipment Specification Purpose (N)	SPEC_PURPOSE (N)		
Equipment Specification Unit (N)	SPEC_UNIT (N)		
Equipment Specification Value (N)	SPEC_VALUE(N)		
Complex Data Fields			
Complex GUID	COMPLEX_GUID		
Complex Number	COMPLEX_NUMBER		
Complex Name	COMPLEX_NAME		
Site Plot Point (N)	SITE_PLOT_POINT(N)		
	SITE_PLOT_ALTITUDE(N)		
	SITE_PLOT_LATITUDE(N)		
	SITE_PLOT_LONGITUDE(N)		
Complex Address			
Complex Address Line 1	COMPLEX_ADDRESS1		
Complex Address Line 2	COMPLEX_ADDRESS2		
Complex Address City	COMPLEX_CITY		
Complex Address State	COMPLEX_STATE		
Complex Address Zip Code	COMPLEX_ZIPCODE		
Complex Address Country	COMPLEX_COUNTRY		
Facility Data Fields			
Facility GUID	FACILITY_GUID		
Facility Number	FACILITY_NUMBER		
Facility Name	FACILITY_NAME		
Facility Alias Name (N)	FACILITY_ALIAS(N)		
Facility Owner	FACILITY_OWNER(N)		
Facility Designation	FACILITY_DESIGNATION		
Facility Design Code	FACILITY_DESIGN_CODE		
Facility Design Function	FACILITY_DESIGN_FUNCTION		
Facility Use Code	FACILITY_USE_CODE		
Facility Use Function	FACILITY_USE_FUNCTION		
Facility Plot Point (N)	FACILITY_PLOT_POINT(N)		

Equipment Data Table Fields	Guide Data Field Name	Organization/Industry Data Field Name	Use Yes/No
	FACILITY_PLOT_ALTITUDE(N)		
	FACILITY_PLOT_LATITUDE(N)		
	FACILITY_PLOT_LONGITUDE(N)		
Facility Organization Location Code	FACILITY_LOCATION_CODE		
Facility Address:			
Facility Address Line 1	FACILITY_ADDRESS1		
Facility Address Line 2	FACILITY_ADDRESS2		
Facility Address City	FACILITY_CITY		
Facility Address State	FACILITY_STATE		
Facility Address Zip Code	FACILITY_ZIPCODE		
Facility Address Country	FACILITY_COUNTRY		
Facility Priority	FACILITY_PRIORITY		
Space Data Fields			
Architectural Zone Data			
Architectural Zone GUID	ARCHITECTURE_ZONE_GUID		
Architectural Zone Description	ARCHITECTURE_ZONE_DESCRIPTION		
Space Data			
Space GUID	SPACE_GUID		
Floor Number	FLOOR_NUMBER		
Blueprint Room Number	BLUEPRINT_ROOM_NUMBER		
Organization Room Number	ORG_ROOM_NUMBER		
Space Design Code	SPACE_DESIGN_CODE		
Space Design Function	SPACE_DESIGN_FUNCTION		
Space Use Code	SPACE_USE_CODE		
Space Use Function	SPACE_USE_FUNCTION		
Space Description	SPACE_DESCRIPTION		
Space Identification Composite	SPACE_ID_COMPOSITE		
Space Priority	SPACE_PRIORITY		
Tenant Data Fields			
Tenant GUID	TENANT_GUID		
Tenant Name	TENANT_NAME		
Tenant Organization Name	TENANT_ORGNAME		
Tenant Department Name	TENANT_DEPTNAME		
Tenant Code (N)	TENANT_CODE(N)		
Job Plan and Job Task Data Fields			
Job Plan GUID	JOB_PLAN_GUID		

Equipment Data Table Fields	Guide Data Field Name	Organization/Industry Data Field Name	Use Yes/No
Job Plan Identification	JOB_PLAN_ID		
Job Plan Title	JOB_PLAN_TITLE		
Job Plan Description	JOB_PLAN_DESCRIPTION		
Job Plan Type	JOB_PLAN_TYPE		
Job Plan Tool Code N	JOB_PLAN_TOOL_CODE		
Job Plan Tool N	JOB_PLAN_TOOL		
Job Plan Document	JOB_PLAN_DOCUMENT		
Job Task GUID	JOB_TASK_GUID		
Job Task Sequence Number	JOB_TASK_SEQ_NUMBER		
Job Task Identification Composite	JOB_TASK_ID_COMPOSITE		
Job Task Status	JOB_TASK_STATUS		
Job Task Status Related Cause	JOB_TASK_STATUS_CAUSE		
Job Task Performer	JOB_TASK_PERFORMER		
Job Task Frequency	JOB_TASK_FREQUENCY		
Job Task Frequency Units	JOB_TASK_FREQUENCY_UNITS		
Job Task Inspection Percentage	JOB_TASK_INSP_PERCENT		
Job Task Season	JOB_TASK_SEASON		
Job Task Start Date	JOB_TASK_START_DATE		
Job Task Time Standard	JOB_TASK_TIME_STANDARD		
Job Task Time Standard Units	JOB_TASK_TIME_UNITS		
Job Task Tool CodeN	JOB_TASK_TOOL_CODE		
Job Task Tool N	JOB_TASK_TOOL		
Condition Data Fields			
Condition GUID	CONDITION_GUID		
Condition Assessment Short Description	CONDITION_SHORT_DESCRIPTION		
Condition Assessment Provider	CONDITION_PROVIDER		
Condition Assessment Date	CONDITION_DATE		
Condition Assessment Document	CONDITION_DOCUMENT		
Condition Equipment GUID	COND_EQUIP_GUID		
Equipment Condition	EQUIPMENT_CONDITION		
Equipment Condition Related Cause	CONDITION_CAUSE		
Equipment Life Used	EQUIPMENT_LIFE_USED		
Equipment Life Remaining	LIFE_REMAINING		
Condition Observation	CONDITION_OBSERVATION		
Condition Recommendation Type	CONDITION_RECOM_TYPE		

Equipment Data Table Fields	Guide Data Field Name	Organization/Industry Data Field Name	Use Yes/No
Condition Recommendation	CONDITION_RECOMMENDATION		
Commissioning Data Fields			
Commissioning GUID	COMMISSIONING_GUID		
Commissioning Short Description	COMMISSION_SHORT_DESCRIPTION		
Commission Provider	COMMISSION_PROVIDER		
Commission Date	COMMISSION_DATE		
Commissioning Document	COMMISSION_DOC		
Commission Equipment GUID	COMM_EQUIP_GUID		
Commission Observation	COMMISSION_OBSERVATION		
Commission Recommendation	COMMISSION_RECOMMENDATION		
Commissioning Set Point Position (N)	SET POINT_POSITION(N)		
Commissioning Set Point Unit (N)	SET POINT_UNIT(N)		
Commissioning Set Point Value (N)	SET POINT_VALUE(N)		
Commissioning Set Point Comment (N)	SET POINT_COMMENT(N)		
Audits and Inspection Data Fields			
Audit GUID	AUDIT_GUID		
Audit Type	AUDIT_TYPE		
Audit Provider	AUDIT_PROVIDER		
Audit Date	AUDIT_DATE		
Audit Short Description	AUDIT_SHORT_DESCRIPTION		
Audit Document	AUDIT_DOCUMENT		
Audit Equipment GUID	AUDIT_EQUIP_GUID		
Equipment Compliance (N)	EQUIPMENT_COMPLIANCE		
Compliance Regulation (N)	COMPLIANCE_REGULATION		
Audit Observation	AUDIT_OBSERVATION		
Audit Recommendation	AUDIT_RECOMMENDATION		
Audit Resolution	AUDIT_RESOLUTION		
Audit Resolution Date	AUDIT_RES_DATE		
Warranty			
Warranty GUID	WARRANTY_GUID		
Warranty Short Description	WARRANTY_SHORT_DESCRIPTION		
Warranty Number	WARRANTY_NUMBER		
Warranty Provider Name	WARRANTY_PROVIDER_NAME		
Warranty Provider Contact Information	WARRANTY_CONTACT		
Warranty Installer Name	WARRANTY_INSTALLER		

Equipment Data Table Fields	Guide Data Field Name	Organization/Industry Data Field Name	Use Yes/No
Warranty Installer Contact Information	WARRANTY_INSTALLER_CONTACT		
Warranty Start Date	WARRANTY_START_DATE		
Warranty End Date	WARRANTY_END_DATE		
Extended Warranty Available	EXTENDED_WARRANTY_AVAILABLE		
Extended Warranty Number	EXTENDED_WARRANTY_NUMBER		
Extended Warranty Provider Name	EXTENDED_WARRANTY_PROVIDER		
Extended Warranty Provider Contact Information	EXTENDED_WARRANTY_CONTACT		
Extended Warranty Start Date	EXTENDED_WARRANTY_START_DATE		
Extended Warranty End Date	EXTENDED_WARRANTY_END_DATE		
Substantial Completion Date	SUBSTANTIAL_COMPLETION_DATE		
Warranty Document	WARRANTY_DOCUMENT		
Extended Warranty Document	EXTENDED_WARRANTY_DOCUMENT		
Code and Regulations			
Code GUID	CODE_GUID		
Code Type	CODE_TYPE		
Code Source	CODE_SOURCE		
Code Title (N)	CODE_TITLE(N)		
Code Designation (N)	CODE_DESIGNATION(N)		
Code Comments	CODE_COMMENTS		
Code Enforcement	CODE_ENFORCEMENT		
Code Document	CODE_DOCUMENT		
Operation Documents			
Operation Document GUID	OPS_DOC_GUID		
Operation Document Type	OPERATION_DOC_TYPE		
Operation Document Short Description	OPERATION_DOCUMENT_SHORT_DESCRIPTION		
Operation Document	OPERATION_DOCUMENT		
Operation Video	OPERATION_VIDEO		

Process Flow Maps

The process flow maps included in this guide are developed for each process relating to a specific set of data. They are basic in nature; the concept is to give the reader and programmers a basic outline of the way the data are captured and interrelated. More complex diagrams can be created, using these as a template. For example, instead of yes/no decision points, a programmer could use skip/continue/Main Menu decision points. The entry into the data set could also be programmed to allow users to select whether they want to add an equipment zone or add a piece of equipment.

Editing and sorting functions have not been included in the process flow maps. Each data set should have the capability of editing the data set and each field contained within.

When selecting data from a populated database, the program should only have to capture the GUID information. Since users will not understand the GUID, they can be shown multiple fields from the database to improve the selection process—and then the GUID can be captured or the data linked.

EQUIPMENT DATA PROCESS MAP

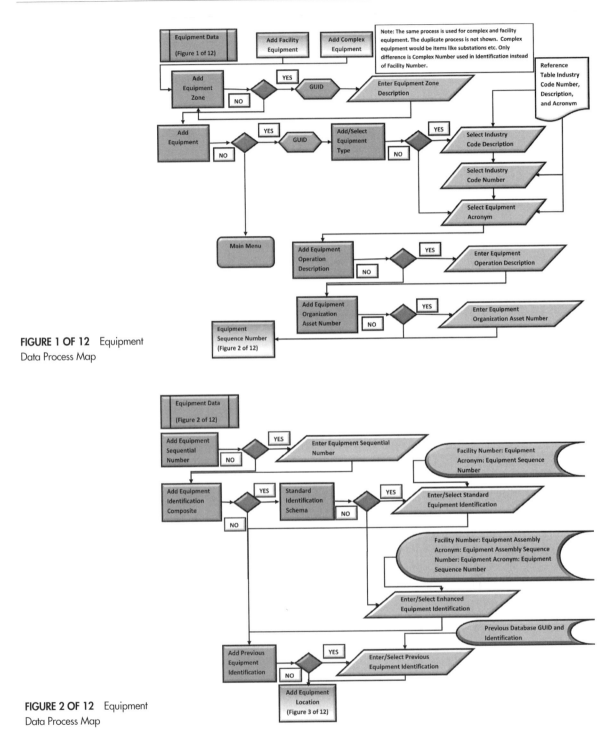

FIGURE 1 OF 12   Equipment Data Process Map

FIGURE 2 OF 12   Equipment Data Process Map

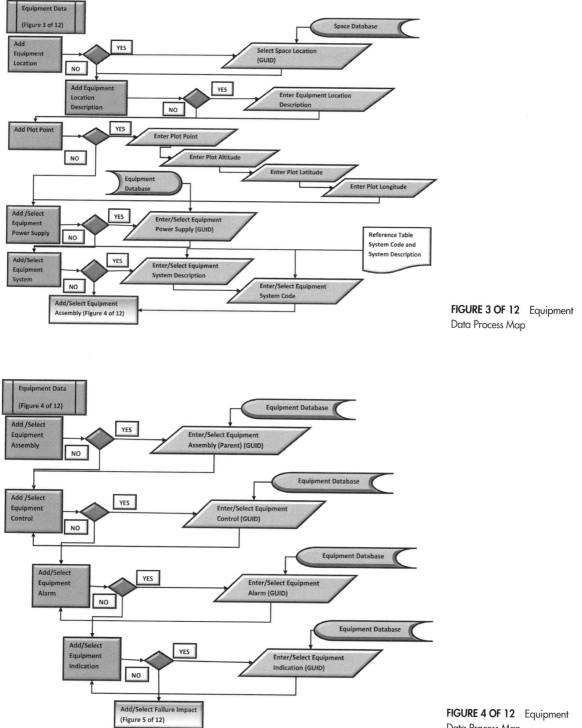

FIGURE 3 OF 12   Equipment Data Process Map

FIGURE 4 OF 12   Equipment Data Process Map

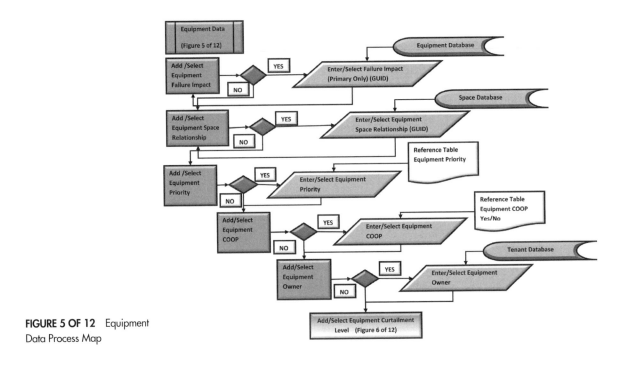

FIGURE 5 OF 12   Equipment
Data Process Map

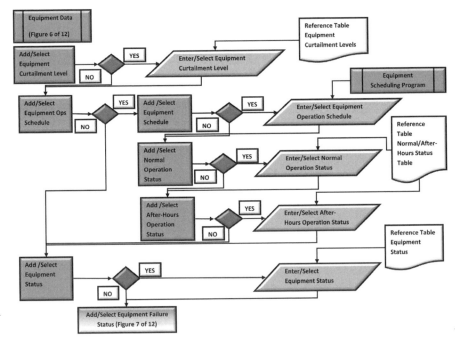

FIGURE 6 OF 12   Equipment
Data Process Map

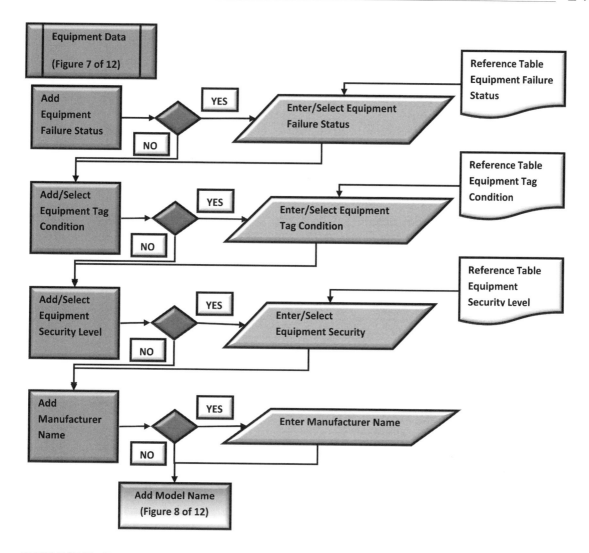

FIGURE 7 OF 12   Equipment Data Process Map

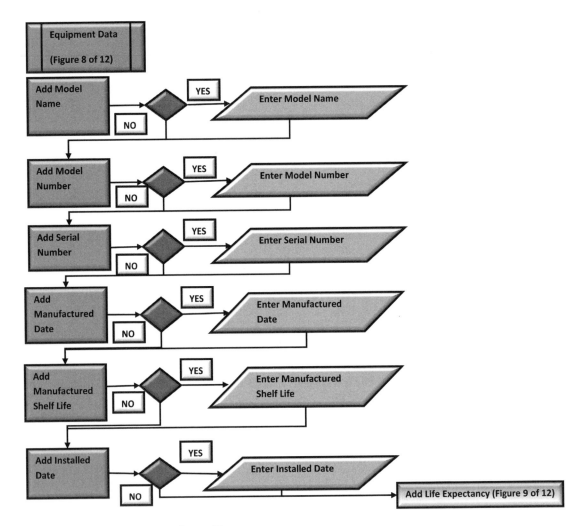

FIGURE 8 OF 12 Equipment Data Process Map

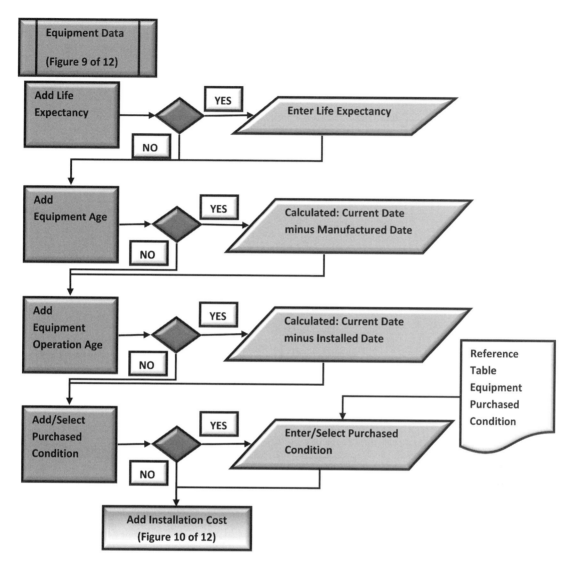

FIGURE 9 OF 12   Equipment Data Process Map

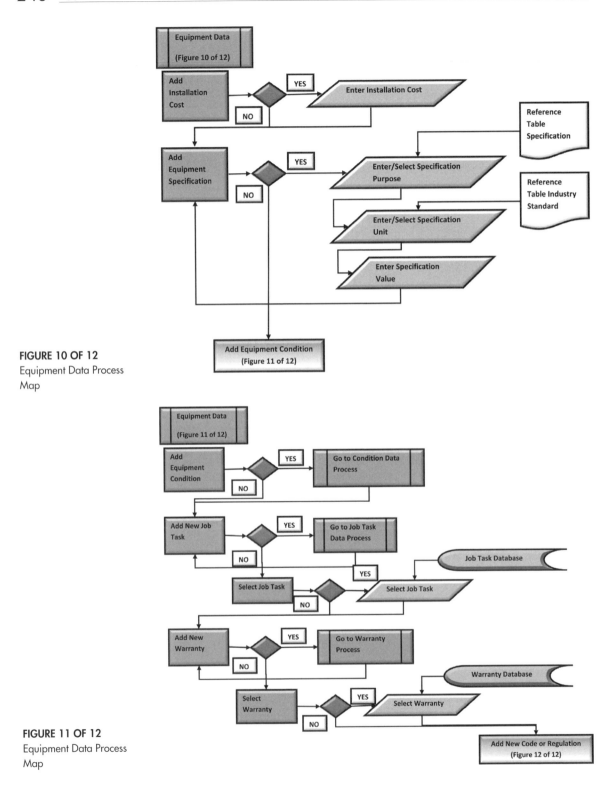

FIGURE 10 OF 12
Equipment Data Process
Map

FIGURE 11 OF 12
Equipment Data Process
Map

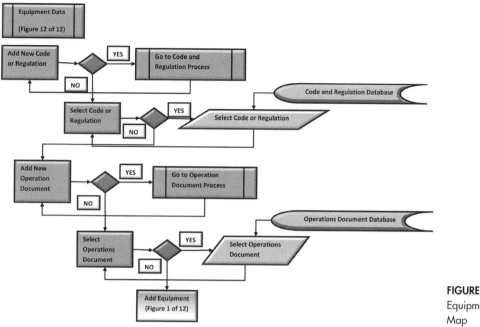

FIGURE 12 OF 12
Equipment Data Process
Map

COMPLEX DATA PROCESS MAP

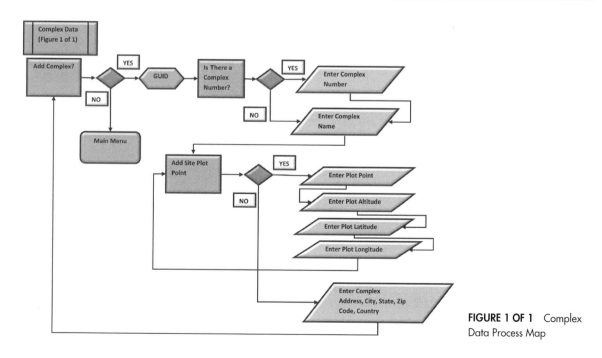

FIGURE 1 OF 1   Complex
Data Process Map

FACILITY DATA PROCESS MAP

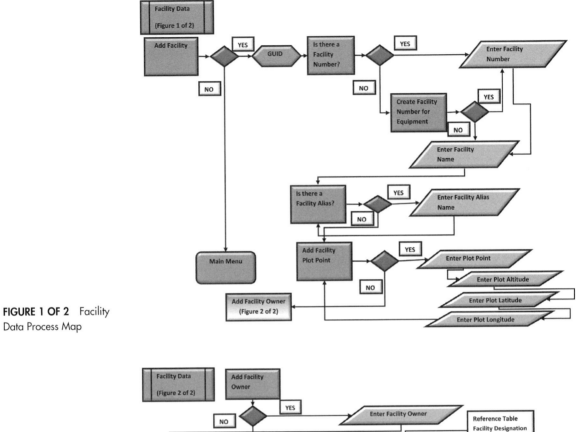

FIGURE 1 OF 2 Facility Data Process Map

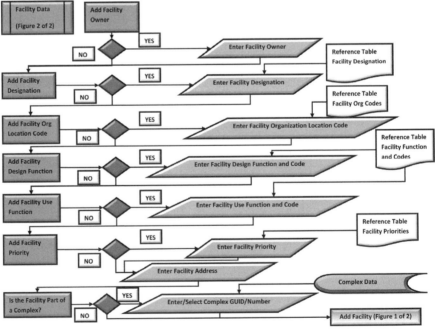

FIGURE 2 OF 2 Facility Data Process Map

SPACE DATA PROCESS MAP

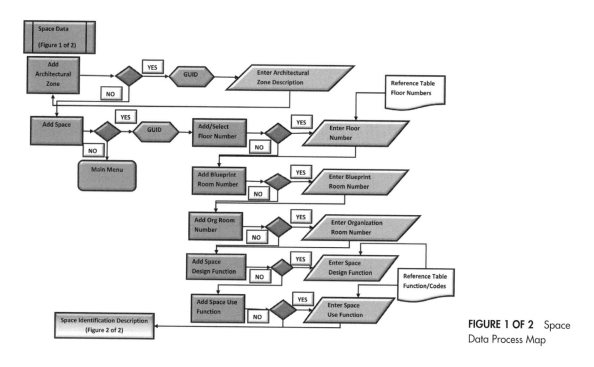

FIGURE 1 OF 2   Space Data Process Map

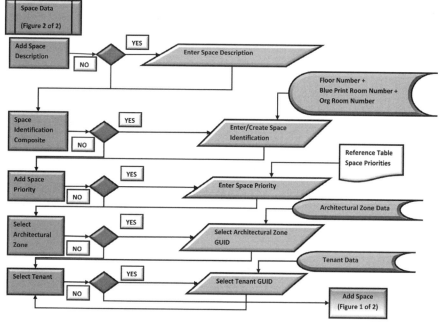

FIGURE 2 OF 2   Space Data Process Map

TENANT DATA PROCESS MAP

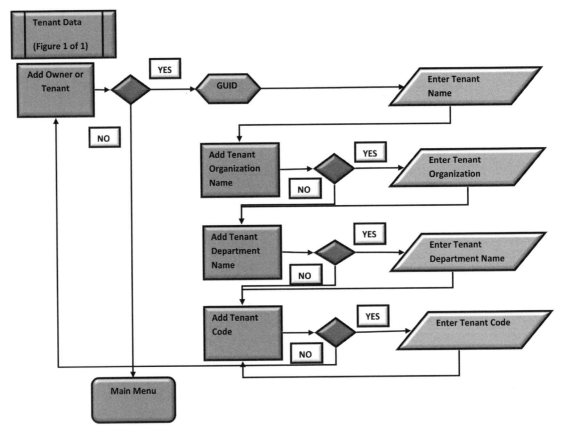

FIGURE 1 OF 1   Tenant Data Process Map

JOB PLAN AND TASK DATA PROCESS MAP

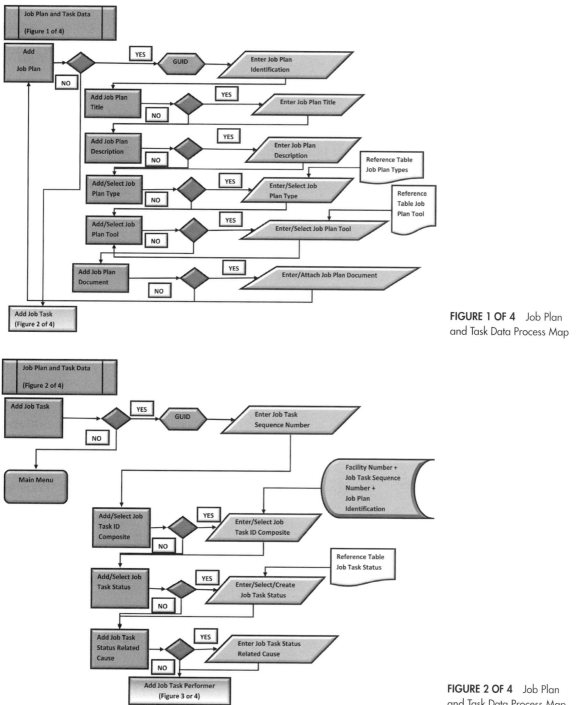

FIGURE 1 OF 4   Job Plan and Task Data Process Map

FIGURE 2 OF 4   Job Plan and Task Data Process Map

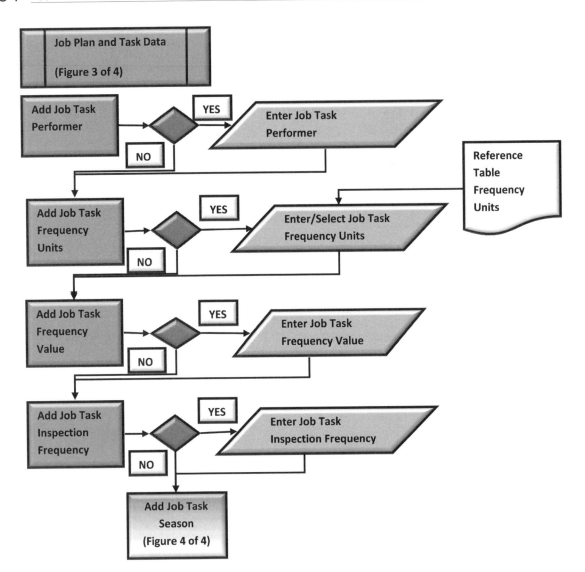

FIGURE 3 OF 4   Job Plan and Task Data Process Map

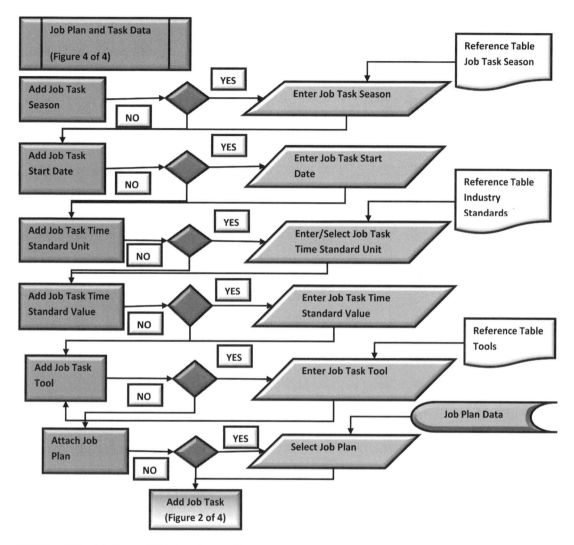

FIGURE 4 OF 4   Job Plan and Task Data Process Map

CONDITION DATA PROCESS MAP

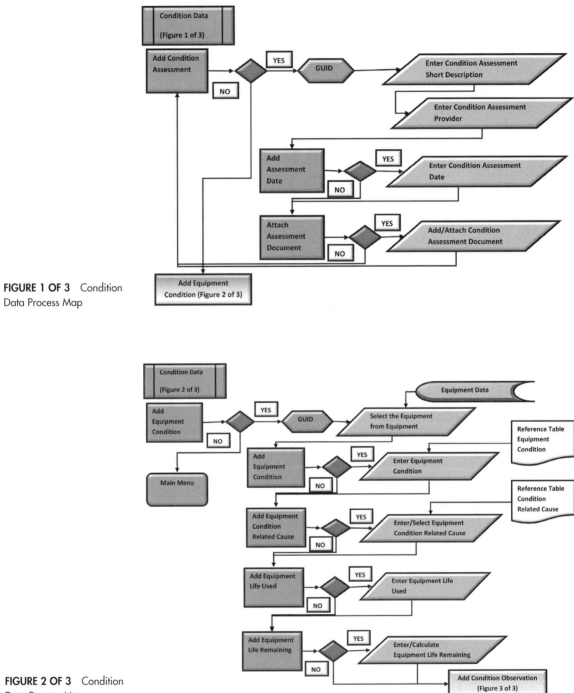

FIGURE 1 OF 3   Condition
Data Process Map

FIGURE 2 OF 3   Condition
Data Process Map

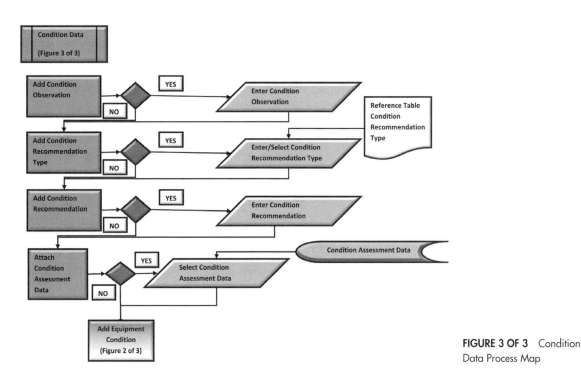

FIGURE 3 OF 3 Condition Data Process Map

COMMISSIONING DATA PROCESS MAP

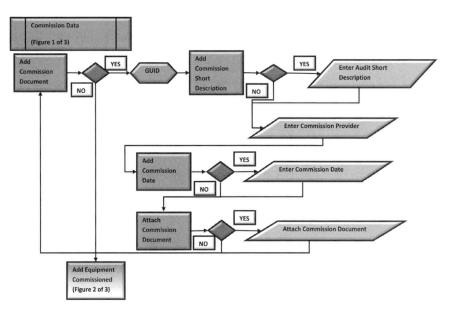

FIGURE 1 OF 3 Commissioning Data Process Map

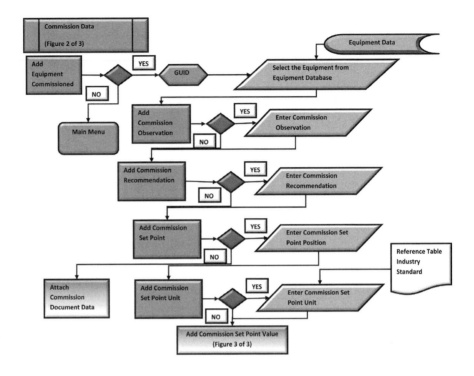

FIGURE 2 OF 3   Commissioning Data Process Map

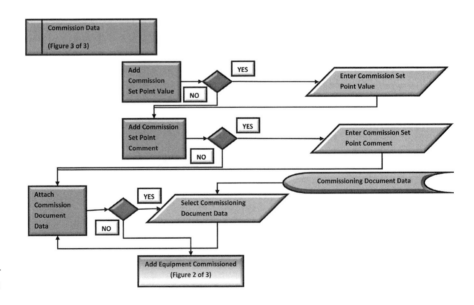

FIGURE 3 OF 3   Commissioning Data Process Map

AUDIT AND INSPECTION DATA PROCESS MAP

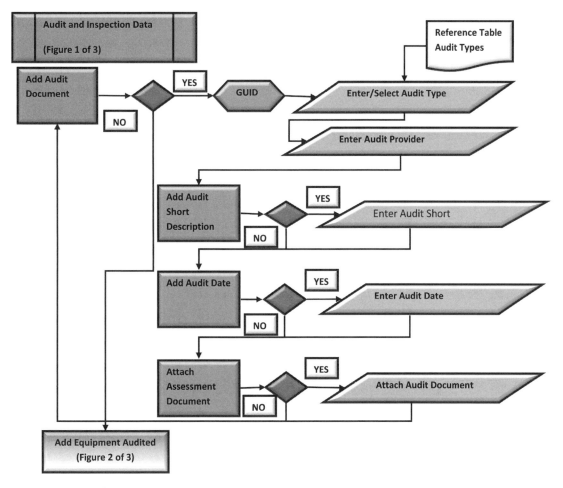

FIGURE 1 OF 3   Audit and Inspection Data Process Map

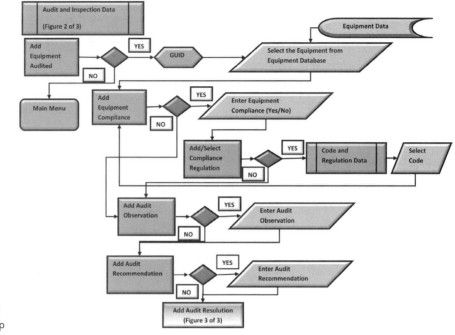

FIGURE 2 OF 3   Audit and
Inspection Data Process Map

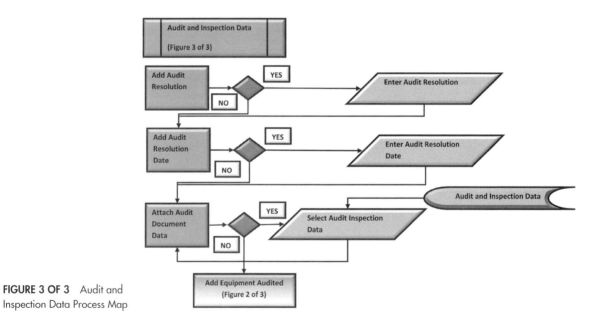

FIGURE 3 OF 3   Audit and
Inspection Data Process Map

WARRANTY DATA PROCESS MAP

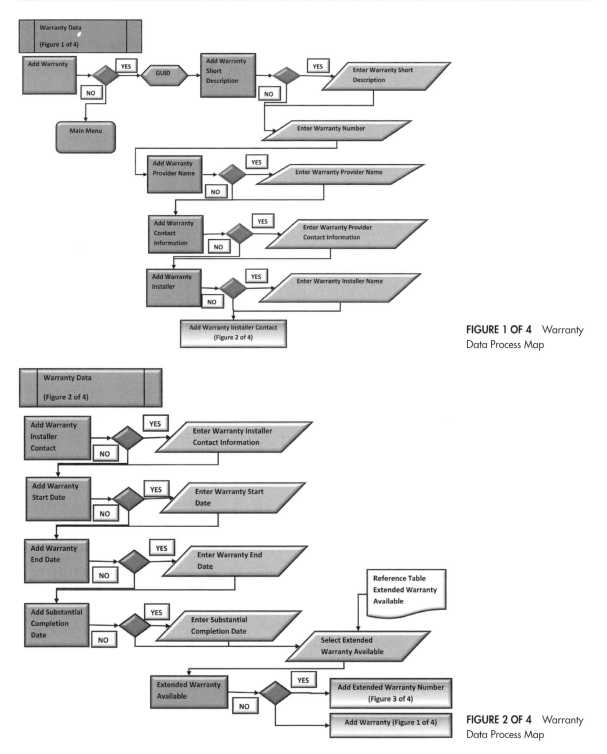

FIGURE 1 OF 4   Warranty Data Process Map

FIGURE 2 OF 4   Warranty Data Process Map

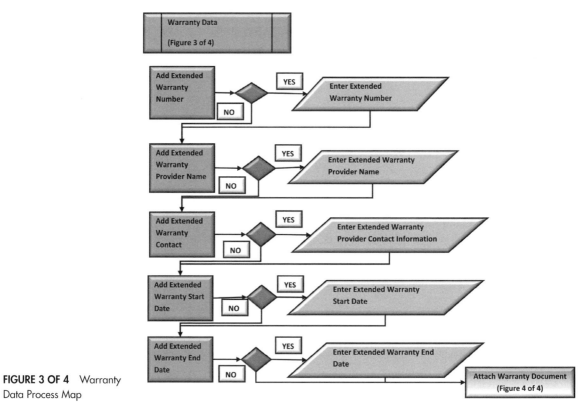

FIGURE 3 OF 4 Warranty
Data Process Map

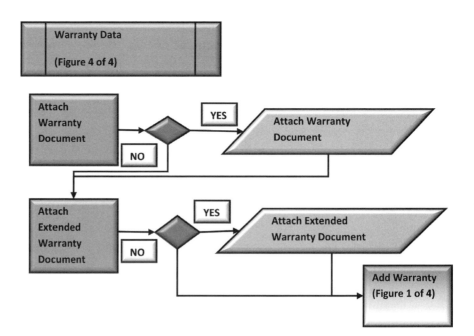

FIGURE 4 OF 4 Warranty
Data Process Map

CODE AND REGULATION DATA PROCESS MAP

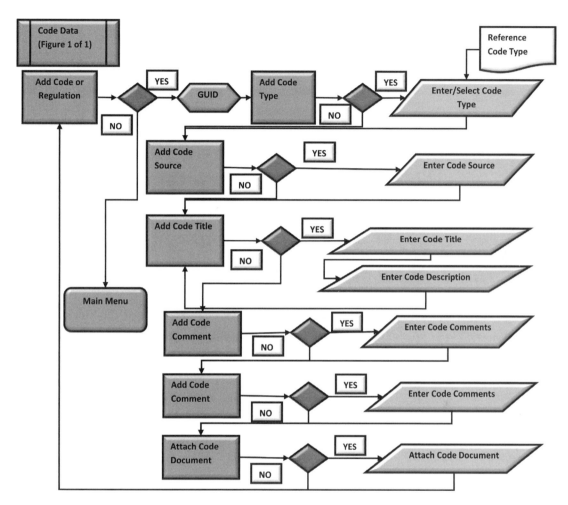

FIGURE 1 OF 1   Code and Regulation Data Process Map

OPERATION DOCUMENTS DATA PROCESS MAP

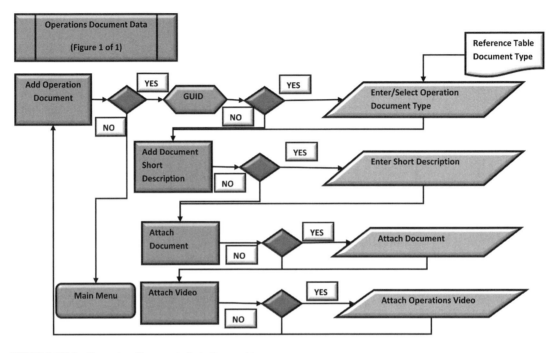

FIGURE 1 OF 1   Operations Documents Data Process Map

Index